To my father,
Whose boundless love became the soil where my confidence grew,
Whose quiet strength and unwavering integrity lit my path,
Whose passion for words became my own,
And whose spirit walks beside me, whispering wisdom and love.
This book is dedicated to you, Behzad Behzadi, my baba.

Praise for *The Unexpected CEO*

"This book reveals how the most underestimated among us can become the most transformative. *The Unexpected CEO* tells not only a story of survival and success, but a powerful case for human potential."

—Mrs. Cherie Blair

"Shirin's story is so inspiring. It reminds us that the people who overcome adversity are often capable of the most extraordinary things. She went from political exile and trauma to becoming a billion-dollar CEO—and never lost her deep empathy or her commitment to service. This memoir is a gift to anyone striving to live with courage and compassion."

—Lawrence R. Armstrong, Chairman, Ware Malcomb; Vice Chair, Orange County United Way; and *New York Times* Bestselling Author, *Layered Leadership*

"I met Shirin in the business world numerous years ago and selfishly kept her in my personal orbit ever since. Her strength of character in facing adversity, passion in helping others to achieve their visions, and commitment to chosen family are among the many attributes making her an inspiring role model in every aspect of her life. Often painfully real and always profoundly impactful, *The Unexpected CEO* is a deeply moving memoir highlighting the opportunity to be found in hardship and the ultimate reward in uplifting others. A must-read for personal and professional growth."

—Kath Carter, former Global Strategy and Transactions Partner—Markets, Business Development and Talent, EY

"Shirin's leadership journey—from bulletproof glass to the boardroom—shows that deeply empathic, values-driven leadership isn't just possible, it's profitable. Her focus on trust, culture, integrity, and people development isn't a detour from performance—it's the path to it. For current and aspiring leaders, Shirin challenges outdated models of power and sets a new, more humane standard—one that today's workforce demands and future generations will expect by default."

—Tal Goldhamer, former Partner, Chief Learning Officer, EY Americas

"Shirin's story is beyond inspirational. Having faced huge personal and business challenges, she shows us that by staying focused on the positive and on our goals, we can accomplish anything and achieve great success while retaining integrity, compassion and grace. Shirin, thank you for helping us all be better people."

—Susan B. Parks, President and CEO, Orange County United Way

"This book is more than inspiration—it's a guide to unlocking your own resilience. Readers will learn what it takes to face fear, reframe failure, and rise through purpose. Shirin Behzadi's story is fuel for anyone ready to rewrite their own."

—Betsy Schwartz, National Mental Health Leader and Advocate

The
Unexpected
CEO

The
Unexpected
CEO

MY JOURNEY FROM
GAS STATION CASHIER
TO BILLION-DOLLAR CEO

SHIRIN BEHZADI

Matt Holt Books
An Imprint of BenBella Books, Inc.
Dallas, TX

Matt Holt is an imprint of BenBella Books, Inc.
8080 N. Central Expressway
Suite 1700
Dallas, TX 75206
benbellabooks.com
Send feedback to feedback@benbellabooks.com

BenBella and *Matt Holt* are federally registered trademarks.

Printed in the United States of America
10 9 8 7 6 5 4 3 2 1

Library of Congress Control Number: 2025018940
ISBN 9781637747537 (hardcover)
ISBN 9781637747544 (electronic)

Editing by Lydia Choi
Copyediting by Shelby Harbour
Proofreading by Lisa Story and Jill Kramer
Text design and composition by PerfecType, Nashville, TN
Illustrations by Misa Art
Cover design by Paul McCarthy
Cover image © Shutterstock / Nenad Cvetkovic
Printed by Lake Book Manufacturing

Contents

PART THREE
Success

PART FOUR
Becoming a CEO and Making Empathic Change a Reality

Foreword

THERE ARE STORIES THAT INSPIRE YOU to leave your comfort zone, and then there are stories that will transform your life.

Shirin Behzadi's journey is one of those rare, remarkable stories. A story that dares you to dream bigger, rise higher, and believe that no starting point—no matter how humble or hard—can limit the destiny of someone who is fiercely committed to their calling.

From arriving in the United States as a teenager without her parents, with no money, no safety net, and no blueprint for success . . . to rising as the CEO of a billion-dollar company, Shirin's life answers one of the most profound questions in leadership: *Are leaders born, or are they made?*

Her story whispers *both*.

Born with an unshakable core of courage and character—nurtured by the loving example of her father, a community leader and entrepreneur—Shirin began shaping her destiny with her toy desk that she placed next to his. That quiet apprenticeship became the soil where her bold vision was planted. Even when the world around her said, "No," her father said, "Go."

She went. She dared. She did.

Along the way, she redefined what's possible—not just for herself, but for every young girl who has ever been told to stay silent . . . for every outsider who has felt unseen . . . and for every dreamer who's ever been laughed at for believing in more.

The Unexpected CEO is not just a book. It's a blueprint for resilience. A testimony of tenacity. A love letter to courage. And a beacon for all who know that the odds may be stacked—but they are never final.

Shirin is no longer just the girl behind a bulletproof shield at the gas station counter. She's now a global leader, philanthropist, board advisor, and powerhouse voice in boardrooms and beyond. But what makes her truly unforgettable is not just the billion-dollar success she built—it's the billion-watt light she carries, igniting hope and possibility in all who read her books or hear her speak.

As you turn these pages, prepare to be transformed. But more importantly—prepare to step into your greatness. Because if she could do it . . . so can you.

Let Shirin's story awaken the unexpected CEO inside of *you*.

—Les Brown
Author, speaker, global influencer

Words from the Family

SARA MADANI (daughter)

My mom is the most incredible mother I could have ever dreamed of: nurturing, supportive, unconditionally loving, wise, trustworthy—the list goes on.

But my mom is so much more than just a mother. She is a powerhouse: a businesswoman, leader, entrepreneur, public speaker, author, magazine cover girl, award recipient, and more.

Yet, when I think of her, one word comes to mind: *Mom.*

It's funny, but when I call her for life advice on a random Tuesday afternoon, when I come home crying after a tough day and fall into her arms, when I ask for her opinion on an outfit before an event, or when I just need her to show me the way, the successful entrepreneur and business mogul fade from my mind. In those moments, she's simply my mom—always there with a never-ending well of love and wisdom.

And that's intentional. It speaks volumes about the person she is and how she chooses to live her life—with an unwavering commitment to her morals and a clear vision of the impact she wants to have on the world and her loved ones. Throughout her many achievements, both personally and professionally, she leads with good intentions, always guided by what is right and who she wants to be. She has no ego, nor does she define herself solely by her accomplishments. Instead, she uses her success and resilience to be a present mother, a global citizen, and a reliable friend, daughter, and sister.

Everything my mom has done—whether it's rising from the ashes after a difficult period or closing a multimillion-dollar business deal—has been in pursuit of bringing good to the world and those around her, including me.

As you'll see in this book, my mom has faced unbelievable trials and tribulations. Yet she doesn't let those experiences make her bitter or angry. Instead, she uses them to become more resilient, more empathetic, and more present—always leading with her morals.

You'll also learn that my mom has achieved extraordinary professional and financial success in the face of it all. But it's important to remember as you read: my mom uses her self-made status not to boast but to inspire and connect with others, to bring opportunity to our family, and to be a beacon of representation for those who need it.

My mom's actions are always driven by her desire to bring positivity and light to the world. How she's managed to accomplish so much and still be so deeply rooted in her role as *mom* is a beautiful, selfless feat. I encourage you to turn these pages with trust in your heart, knowing you're reading the words of someone who is incredibly well intentioned, loving, and wise. Let her experiences guide you and inspire you to believe in yourself. I've had the privilege of having her wisdom my whole life, and I'm so grateful that through this book, you get to experience it too.

SAM MADANI (son)

When my mom agreed to write her book, I was ecstatic.

For years, everyone in her life has been asking her to publicly share her story. And for years, she repeatedly dismissed the idea with a laugh and a wave. She only began to entertain the idea once she realized her story might help others.

When she found out her story made the cover of *Forbes* in March 2019, I called my mom to congratulate her. Her response shocked me—she genuinely asked, "Is the article good?"

My jaw dropped to the floor. "You're on the cover of *Forbes* and you haven't read the article?!"

I then remembered who I was talking to—this is the same person who finds every opportunity to give credit rather than take credit, the person who wants to uplift everyone around her and help them succeed, the person who goes to the ends of the earth for those she loves without expecting so much as a thank-you.

After the *Forbes* article came out, strangers began sharing stories with my mom about how her story impacted their lives. That article clearly resonated with people; it helped them find the strength to get through their own adversity, empowered them to start companies, and so much more.

Over time, my mom began to realize that her story could help more people. I soon realized that the reason she kept refusing to write the book is because she thought people were asking her to tell her story for her own sake.

So once my mom became more open-minded about writing her book, my sister and I did research, reached out to our favorite authors, and put together a binder with step-by-step instructions on what it would take to write a book. We gave that to her as a gift, hoping to articulate how much good her book would do in the world. The pitch was successful—she agreed that very day to write this book!

While I've learned that it's impossible to overstate how talented my mom is, I was still floored when I read even the first draft of this book. Her words leapt off the page like they'd been waiting decades to be read. It's a story of overcoming adversity and developing superhuman resilience, a story of taking control of your life and staying true to your values even when you're put to the ultimate test.

It's a story of freedom.

I'm so proud of my mom for not shying away from the ugly details in her story. To call her challenges "hurdles" doesn't do them justice—they weren't bumps in the road; they were seismic shifts, and she navigated each one. I know for a fact it wasn't easy for her to relive those memories as she wrote this book. But like any other type of adversity in her life, she found the positives and did the hard work. She described her journey of becoming an author as a "cathartic experience" because it helped her process the traumas she's experienced.

When I started my company, the first person I pitched it to was my mom. I know she loves me and wants me to succeed, which is why she's always my toughest critic. She found fundamental flaws in my last hundred business ideas, but when I pitched her BOMANI, she told me to go for it. It was the most meaningful endorsement I could have asked for.

Since launching my company and asking my mom to be our first advisor, I've enjoyed the rewarding, eye-opening experience of being able to work with her and learn from her in a professional capacity. I believe one of my mom's greatest strengths—if not her greatest strength—is her ability to identify each person's unique talents and help them develop those talents.

Mentors, managers, and advisors often push you to be their version of what they think you should be; they mold you into their idea of success. Conversely, my mom pushes you to be you, to focus on what you're naturally good at and develop those talents. This rare approach has proven to be much more effective, and it's something I aim to emulate in my life as well.

So, as you turn the first page of this book, I hope you take your time and enjoy the journey. It's a page-turner, to say the least, and I believe that everyone who reads it will find something to take away. Remember—it's a happy story in the end!

PERZAN IRANI (husband)

From the earliest days of our relationship, I witnessed firsthand Shirin living by her powerful motto: "Doing well by doing good." It wasn't just something she said; it was the essence of how she moved through the world, whether interacting with waiters or boardroom executives—everyone received her genuine respect, care, and kindness. That was when I knew I was in the presence of someone truly extraordinary.

Reading Shirin's story in these pages, I found myself brought to tears numerous times, even though I knew many of the stories intimately. What moved me most was her unwavering perseverance, her ability to hold on to grace and compassion even in the toughest of circumstances, and her authentic desire to see others succeed. Shirin's journey, shaped by resilience and warmth, affirms my belief in the profound strength and potential for grace that lie at her core—and in each of us.

I watched closely as this book took shape, a passion project crafted in countless afternoons and late-night writing sessions in a corner of our family room. Often, the process surfaced tender emotional states—traumatic memories and difficult moments from her past—that Shirin courageously faced, gradually integrated, and ultimately transformed into sources of strength and inspiration. For Shirin, this meant finding the courage to deeply examine her journey, process it, and ultimately share her powerful experiences in these pages and through her remarkable speaking engagements.

A particular memory that stands out vividly is Shirin's first public speech at a Women's Survivorship Conference. Seeing the standing ovation she received, and witnessing the hope, courage, and newfound strength ignited in the audience's eyes, is a moment permanently etched into my memory. Her story, her presence, and her words have the power to transform lives, including mine.

What readers must understand is that Shirin's genuine concern for others is not a performance—it is fundamentally who she is. Her success as a CEO and as a person stems directly from her authenticity, tenacity, and profound warmth. The challenging path she traveled never hardened her; instead, it solidified her commitment to treating others with unwavering respect and dignity.

No one knows Shirin like I do, and I can honestly say she is exactly who she appears to be, at all times. There is no mask or facade. She is a true companion, partner, confidant, and inspiration.

As you turn these pages, my hope is that Shirin's absorbing story of courage, kindness, and unwavering integrity will awaken in you not only admiration but also the courage to embrace your own journey with renewed compassion and strength.

Introduction

Learning to Walk Again

As the fog of illness gradually lifted, I found myself with a heightened sense of awareness. I felt like I had awakened. I could see and feel things more clearly than ever before, experiencing a profound sense of enlightenment and inspiration.

TALKING WAS VERY HARD. My entire face had been broken—twice. My nose was filled with gauze that reached my skull, left in there to seal the hole where surgeons had gone through my nasal passage to remove a large brain tumor. I had a hard time remembering words and, most of the time, enunciating them. As others talked, I was mostly an observer. This experience changed my view altogether. It's incredible how much one can learn about others by listening and observing.

After the brain surgery, I needed to learn to walk again. I decided that after I mastered walking around the coffee table, I would try to make my way down the hallway. And then, maybe someday, I could walk up the stairs.

Every two weeks, it was back to St. John's Hospital in Santa Monica for cleaning and vacuuming my nose. A lineup of nurses and medical students stood and watched as Dr. Carrau inserted instruments up my nose and behind my skull. He would cut and clean, and the horrified look on the faces of the audience made me feel even more nauseous than I already felt.

After an entire month of having a fever, the doctors finally decided to take the gauze out of my skull. I didn't know that there was not one, but several pieces, of gauze packed inside, many of them the size of tangerines . . . and that they would have to be pulled out of my nostrils while I was awake—one by one! The pain was unreal. But once they were out, my fever broke at last.

The crisis began when I was hit one morning with devastating symptoms. I went to the hospital, where my tumor was eventually discovered. After consulting a few surgeons, I found a doctor I trusted who would remove the brain tumor through my septum.

I was still recovering from this long and challenging surgery when the doctors discovered I had lost most of the spinal fluid in my skull. I was in agony, with pain and fever, and I faced sudden death—that much loss of spinal fluid would normally halt one's breathing. As my doctors rushed me to emergency surgery, it became clear that there was little hope of survival. Miraculously, the leak was repaired, but because of this setback, I faced an even tougher recovery journey:

I had lost my balance and ability to walk. Regaining mobility and fitness played out over many years, as I will share later in this book.

As my doctor said as I began physical therapy, "You heal by moving."

The truth in those words would be revealed as time went on.

—————

Trauma is your history; it's not your destiny. Adversity is an opportunity to learn. Rumi says a wound is where the light comes through, and there's truth to that.

Once I had recovered, this book became inevitable. I wrote it because it was already written. It's almost as if I'm writing down the story that has long existed, but needed to be told.

I wrote to share the wisdom of what I've learned from that child, that young girl, that woman who lived through so much adversity and trauma and yet maintained her principles and optimism. I felt compelled to give her a voice because, though many tried to silence her along the way, she found her way to build an amazing life. I believe it's my duty, my obligation, to impart the principles and foundations of transforming adversity into success that I've learned through experience. I want to encourage others to find their way to the life they want to build, no matter where they are starting from or how many obstacles they face.

I wrote because I wanted leaders in our communities to see how allowing each person to blossom is the right thing to do—and it's good business too. The displaced, discounted, poor woman I once was went on to make hundreds of millions of dollars for those who put their trust in her. I wrote so that people can find pieces of themselves in the many challenges and obstacles I faced, and so that they, too, can grow through them.

This is a book about hope. A book to teach through storytelling that it's possible to find your way out and build what you want . . . and that there are some basic principles one can apply to accomplish this.

This is also a book about business success, from leadership to raising capital to communications to change management. I've learned that building and growing companies requires following principles similar to those followed when building a meaningful life. The lessons in this book are relevant to both.

I hope this book inspires and clarifies foundational steps toward your vision. I hope you find what resonates with your life and how you can build resilience.

I have three stories to share, a sampling of the many that encourage my writing.

The first is of a family that had recently come to the United States and tracked me down at an event. The mother had been following me for a couple of years, and every time she felt demoralized, she would read my posts and reread my story. She found inspiration in my life's arc, and it helped her family establish their lives in the United States. Even today, as they continue to face obstacles, they go back to my story for strength. The mother explained that she would often tell herself, "If she did it, so can I." We were all emotional, and I told them that they are this story's true heroes.

The second story comes from when I had to undergo an ultrasound. When I laid down on the bed, the ultrasound technician said, "I'm sorry if this makes you uncomfortable. But I have to tell you something. I know you."

I looked at her, puzzled. I couldn't place her.

"I mean, you don't know me. But I know you." She told me she had seen an article written about my life in a local magazine. After she read the article, she was inspired to make changes in her life. Until then, she had been a bit lost and working odd jobs. The article had inspired her to pursue becoming an ultrasound specialist! She had put her past behind her, and here she was—full circle—as *my* ultrasound technician. It was fantastic.

The third story involves an awards event I attended. I hadn't expected to win anything, but I did. As I got onstage to give a speech, I talked about my life story. When I returned to my table, an older white gentleman was crying. He told me a bit of his story, and I realized that sharing my own story had the power to encourage the most unlikely people to share their own.

These stories started long before my overnight shifts behind bullet-proof glass as a gas station attendant in Los Angeles. They started where all stories start—with the days of childhood. My life began in Iran with a loving clan, a village in the north, and then a move to Tehran. These were the years before the revolution and the ayatollahs, an Iran we have not seen since.

Shall we go there?

PART ONE

Love, Family, and Exile

CHAPTER ONE

From Astara to Tehran—
One Family's Journey

So that I would do my part in reducing the burden on my parents and family, I decided very early on to become competent. I guess you could say that I chose to become the CEO of my own life!

IT WAS A WARM, SUNNY SPRING DAY. I was a five-year-old with my long brown hair in a ponytail, happily holding my dad's hand. We walked in the park and practiced my times tables. My father, tall and with kind blue eyes, looked down at me with his warm smile and asked me multiplication questions.

"What's three times five?"

I bounced in my steps, giggling with joy at spending the afternoon with my dad. I was even more excited to show off how well I knew my times tables.

"Fifteen," I responded quickly.

"Hoorah. Well done!" He beamed at me with admiration.

My dad was my idol. He was kind, genuine, intelligent, and loving. I was the youngest of five children, with one brother and three sisters. My brother was the oldest—twelve years older than me. The rest were close in age to each other. Although I was only four years younger than my sister before me, I often felt like an only child. None of my siblings played with me; I was too young and too small for them. So by the time I was five, all my siblings would be at school during the day, and I would stay home with my mom. She was a kind person with special talents in singing, cooking, and poetry. I liked being home with her.

As was customary in those days, my dad often came home for lunch. Anticipating his arrival, I would put on my shiny new red boots, run to the kitchen, and pour a tall glass of water with no ice. I would carefully place it on a plate on top of a clean napkin. I would then run back and hide behind the front door as I heard his car. As soon as he opened the door, I would jump out.

"Surprise!" I would scream, laughing.

"Whoa!" He would jump up as he pretended to be startled. It never failed. He was always surprised.

I'd then run back and bring the water on the nice plate. He would drink it, thank me, and compliment me on something: my careful attention to not spilling the water, my choice of glass, or my thoughtful placement of the napkin.

Some days, he would encourage me to play music and do my special dance, which required footwork in my shiny red boots. I wasn't a skilled dancer. But he would make me feel like one.

"*Bah Bah* (loosely means "Well, well"). What a wonderful dancer you are!"

That was his superpower: his ability to find the good in people and connect with them by acknowledging their goodness. He found ways to point out even the smallest positive he could find in others.

Although he had a busy life providing for five children and running a company, he did his best to find time to spend with me. It wasn't always easy, and it wasn't nearly as much as I would have liked. But when he did, it was magical. One of my earliest memories is of how he would hold my hand and have me put my feet on top of his as I faced him. He would then dance with me as I stood on his feet. He had little rhythm but lots of heart. Those dances are etched in my memory.

My dad, Behzad Behzadi, grew up in a large family with seven living siblings, in northern Iran in a city close to the border with the Soviet Union. The name of his city was Astara, which means "star." His father, Pasha Behzadi, was the mayor of the city and had founded the first school for girls in that area. They were an intellectual, active, and loving family. Pasha died young at the age of forty-two, leaving his family with the monumental task of creating a life for themselves. Pasha had died trying to do good in the world when he traveled through the thick forests near Astara to negotiate a peace agreement between anti-government revolutionaries and the guards. His goal had been to make sure there was no bloodshed. In that, he was successful, but he caught pneumonia in the process and passed away. Having the courage to stand up for good in the world was a quality that was passed on from him to my dad and then to my generation. These were people who sacrificed to make our world a better place.

After his father's passing, my dad, who was sixteen at the time, had to find ways to earn a living. He traveled from his home to adjacent cities and looked for work as a teacher. He was exceptional at math, and it paid off—he became a math teacher.

Behzad continued to work and send money back home to his younger siblings and mother in Astara. He lived alone and, while working in the rural areas, ended up contracting malaria. The fever that is the hallmark of malaria comes at the same time every day, like clockwork. Rather than feel defeated, my dad would prepare his sleeping area before the fever struck to get through the fever and deal with it as it came. His tenacity paid off: he did not succumb to malaria. I wonder if that resilience was what I tapped into during my health ordeals. It's fascinating to learn how trauma travels through generations, and perhaps resilience does too.

As he built his teaching career, my father realized that his best chance for professional growth was to move to the big city of Tehran, the capital of Iran. In fact, in 2024, Tehran had a population of 9.5 million and counting. My father not only dared to move to this city that was new and strange to him, but he also moved his mother and his younger siblings there too. Although they were Iranian, my dad's family was from a region of Iran that did not speak the state language, Farsi.

Iran emerged from the Persian Empire, which expanded from India to parts of Europe. For centuries, the Persian Empire was the superpower in the world. As a result, it included many ethnicities and languages. Contemporary Iran comprises regions that speak languages vastly different from Farsi. The language my dad's family spoke was Azerbaijani, which is close to Turkish. Looking back, it's clear that my dad and his family didn't simply move from one city to another within Iran; they migrated from one part of the world to another. They had to learn the language and how things were done in this new place—a skill I would also learn when I immigrated from Iran to the United States.

———————

Before he could move his family to Tehran, my dad moved by himself. He found an apartment to rent through a friend he had met a while back. His friend was a smart, funny, and politically active person. He was married to a beautiful, elegant woman, and his younger sister, Heshmat, who hailed from central Iran, lived with them.

Heshmat was petite with lustrous black hair, deep black eyes, and a remarkably fair complexion. Although she was undeniably beautiful, her appearance was a stark contrast to the women from my father's home region. She was essentially the antithesis of my father in terms of physical attributes. He was tall while she was short. His eyes were light but hers were intensely dark. He had blond hair, whereas hers was black. Despite these differences, they shared the experience of losing their fathers at a young age, and both possessed a keen intellect and insatiable curiosity, which ultimately led them to fall in love.

Heshmat went to school in central Iran. There weren't many opportunities for higher education, especially for girls, in Heshmat's hometown. She was born to a young mother and a relatively old father who started his second family after his first wife died. He was a physician by trade and, though he didn't get to experience it when he was alive, earned many accolades and awards for his dedication, service, and gifted approach to medicine. Unfortunately, he was afflicted with an illness that went undiagnosed at the time but that we now believe was Parkinson's. His speech and movement deteriorated, but he never lost his passion for helping his patients, for whom he was the only option for care. So, rather than give up, he commissioned my mom to help him communicate with his patients. Heshmat was smart, by all accounts. Though options for education were limited, she took to school like a sponge. She had a fantastic memory and retained what she learned very quickly. It was no wonder that when her dad needed someone to communicate for him, he picked her. Heshmat was not even a teenager then, but she would attend her dad's visits with patients, and since he couldn't write due to his condition, she would take notes, write prescriptions, and communicate diagnoses.

When her brother and sister-in-law moved to Tehran, they brought Heshmat with them. The whole family knew how smart she was, and they wanted to give her the best shot at pursuing her education.

My dad met my mom when they were both young. He was ten years older, however. He was friends with her older brother through organizations they had joined. They were intellectuals who sought a better future for people, especially the people of Iran. They wanted freedom of speech, freedom of the press, and freedom to be. They opposed the hierarchal class system that was prevalent and powerful in Iran.

A person would have difficulty moving up the social ladder if they were not from an already affluent and prominent stock. My father and uncle (my mom's brother) believed this was fundamentally wrong and spoke against it.

My mom and dad shared many of the same points of view in that they believed people from all walks of life deserved the chance to become who they wanted to become. They believed that the arbitrary barriers of class made no sense. Their passion for this cause, their shared traumas of losing their fathers at a young age, and migrating to Tehran bonded them. This was a bond that was sealed many years before my birth and lasted until my father's passing fifty-five years later.

"It's a girl!" my dad cheerfully told my brother and three sisters.

I entered the busy world of a household of five children with still relatively young parents. My mom worked until child number four. My dad had moved on from teaching to working at an insurance company and was moving up rapidly because of his exceptional talent and competence. He had also studied law and earned his Juris Doctor. To say that my parents had worked hard to this point is an understatement. Although Dad maintained his passion for equality and freedom, he'd lost his taste for politics and anyone who made lofty claims of being a freedom fighter. He had learned that, as a citizen, it is hard to truly understand the power dynamics of a government. His conclusion and how he lived his life from that point on was to be truthful, empathetic, and just, and to contribute to the well-being of others by being a productive member of society. This mindset, coupled with his exceptional intelligence and competence, put him on the fast track to success.

Having moved up very quickly through the ranks at the insurance company, my dad was noticed and recruited by a company in the business of warehousing. As imports and exports entered and left Iran, goods would have to be warehoused for inspection. The company that recruited my father in the late sixties owned a few of these warehouses and employed ninety employees. During his nine-year tenure at the company, my dad expanded it to tens of locations around the country and employed 10,000 workers and corporate employees. He was one of the founders of the International Association of Warehousing—a feat, since Iran was one of the few non-Western countries represented in the association.

I was born into a crowded family on its way to financial affluence. Not only was my dad successful, but through his recommendations, his brothers also earned prominent roles in banking and insurance in Iran. The Behzadis had arrived!

But there was a cost to all of this. My parents, their families, and our young family had endured significant challenges. I was number five in a busy family that had survived years of trauma.

For most of my infancy and young childhood, I felt the weight of all those experiences, though I had no conscious awareness of it. I also learned that growing up in a busy home as the last child of immigrant parents who had overcome so much adversity meant that I had to make do with divided attention and fragmented attachment. To do my part in reducing the burden on my parents and family, I decided very early on to become competent. I became hypervigilant as to people's emotions and took care of others—even those many years older than me. I guess you could say that I chose to become the CEO of my own life! It wasn't an easy entry, but how I chose to react to it and to embrace it left its mark on who I became. Some traits turned into strengths and others into patterns I would have to overcome. But, in spite of it all, the foundation of love was there to carry me through.

CHAPTER TWO

Taking to School

*Although my exposure to the arts and creative projects was lim-
ited, their existence in a time and a society that didn't embrace
their significance . . . influenced my creative thinking, future
business skills, and self-confidence.*

"SHE'S SMART, VERY SMART," my father told one of his friends.

"How can you tell? How old is she?" his friend asked.

"Three."

Average three-year-olds can run and jump, feed themselves using
a spoon, and climb stairs alone. They're beginning to be aware of
themselves and their bodies and minds. I'm not sure what my father or
his friend saw in me at that age, but there must have been something.

"I'm telling you, she is brilliant," my father told this colleague.
His pride in me showed through his passion and desire that I get the
best opportunities for learning.

In time, the friend came by the house, and we met. Maybe he
figured that since I came from smart, accomplished parents, I really
was as smart as my father insisted. After meeting me, asking me questions, and talking for a while, he told my father he agreed. "Yes, she's
really smart."

Of all his children, my father's friends and family said I was
indeed the most like him. The admiration was mutual. He had a

little desk in the basement office where I would sit and draw while he worked. I didn't know how to read or write yet. He would work long into the night, but he would still find time to walk with me and teach me. Later on, he even signed up to be a member of our version of the Parent Teacher Association (PTA, or the Association of Home and School in Farsi), something almost no fathers did then.

He was an intellectual, encouraging my sisters and me to speak our minds; we weren't any less than anyone else. We mattered. He treated us that way. It's no surprise that he was the one who, very early on, decided that I was gifted and looked for a school that was the right fit for me.

Shortly after I turned five, I was taken to a school for more testing. I was accepted and started my education at this new alternative, state-run pilot school. Iranian schools were always strongly academic. What made this school different was its focus on educating gifted children in both academics and the creative arts, though the latter were limited and only a pilot program. In addition to a rigorous academic program, the school offered classes ranging from the arts, theater, and music to hands-on lab experiments. It was an elementary school with just a few students—not radical in today's world, but certainly so for its time.

I was one of the first students to ever attend the school, so there was no existing culture into which to assimilate. We created what we could in the way of culture but were still restricted by society's norms.

Being in a new school meant that I was placed in a small group of fewer than twenty students. We not only grew up together, but we also worked, played, created, and formed strong and intensely close bonds. This closeness and learning to work, collaborate, and create with others of like minds and creativity taught me some of the soft social skills I would use later in life and business.

The rigorous academic demands remained front and center in every grade. Although the exposure to the creative aspects—the music, the plays, and the access to creative thought—was limited, their very existence in a time and a society that didn't embrace their significance was, to me, the magic of the school. My time there, the education I received, and the relationships I formed significantly influenced my creative thinking, future business skills, and self-confidence.

These things may have lain dormant for a while when I was a teenager, but they flourished later in America as I entered the workforce and began to shape my vision for myself. In second grade, my music teacher decided to form a choir. I was all in! I remember standing proudly in the second row with about two dozen girls and boys from various grade levels. I basked in the joy of singing and creating harmony with my friends. The girls wore starched, white button-down tops and navy A-line skirts. The boys had complementary white shirts and neatly ironed blue slacks. Our coordinated uniforms matched our well-coordinated sound.

My passion for performance and public speaking was born in that school. I developed a love of performing, talking, and speaking before audiences of all kinds and ages. Little did I know the degree to which performance and music would become vital in my life.

———

Even at our special school, the ability to pursue performance and public speaking was relatively limited. Society engulfed us with messages that were counter to "showing up." This was especially true for girls. We weren't taught or encouraged to stand out. In fact, standing out was often viewed as shameful. The narrow opportunities presented to us at our school were, therefore, significant. They opened our minds and hearts to possibilities.

At the age of eight, buoyed by my newfound love of theater and music, I approached my best friend at the time, Azin, with what would become one of my first original creative ventures.

"What do you think about writing a comedy play and performing it?" I asked.

She smiled at me and said, "Do you think the school will let us? It isn't science or math."

"Do you think they care?" I asked.

There was only one way to find out. In the Iranian academic world of math and rigor, spending time on writing plays and practicing them was just not done. But we ignored academic tradition to create something different and exciting. We went to work focusing on the success of what we were doing, not dwelling on the possibilities of failure.

We completed the first draft of our play some time later. Then, we walked into the principal's office and asked to talk to her. I clearly remember my sweaty little hands trembling as I handed her our script. We were nervous but well prepared. We had already made the rounds in the class, recruiting the actors we would need. We just needed her permission.

To our surprise, she loved the idea.

"I love your initiative! We've never had student-created plays at school. I love it . . . let's do it!" she said with a smile. Her years of pursuing her doctorate in education, built on her firm belief that children learn best by being exposed to various ways of learning, had yielded fruit—in the shape of a comedy routine written and acted out by eight-year-olds.

Not only did she support the endeavor, but she also invited the entire student body to watch us when we were ready to perform it.

We were ready after weeks of writing, recruiting our actors, and practicing. Though we didn't need much room, the school had a large lunchroom that could fit more than a hundred people. At the end of this room was a stage with curtains, used when the student body would gather to hear speeches or announcements from the principals. It was also the place where families could attend and watch the choir perform. This was going to be the setting for our theatrical production.

On the day of our first performance, the actors put on their make-shift costumes and got ready for our play. We walked around and prepared the stage behind the long curtains. When the lunchroom doors opened, we could hear students walking in, talking, laughing, and making noise as they sat. I was both excited and nervous—excited to finally showcase our work and to deliver my lines, but nervous because this was a large stage, and every student at our school would be watching. But I never thought we were going to be a flop. The thought of failure never occurred to me. I don't know why. But from that experience that day, I learned the value of expecting success.

As the lights went on, all the other actors went to the sides of the stage, which would be out of sight when the curtains opened. We had practiced this many times. I was going to deliver the first lines by myself, so I stood front and center as the curtains slowly opened. Lights were in my eyes as I stood still until it was my time to speak.

I stepped forward and delivered my first line. It had a funny punch line. Staff and students alike burst out in laughter. Our new drama team was born! More importantly, the seeds of confidence and persistence were planted. I learned valuable lessons from this experience that would carry me through many more challenging and significant projects in my life. I learned that following my interests could pay off. I learned that asking for what may seem impossible can *make* it possible. I learned that I could create, manage, and perform.

The boys and girls at our gifted school enjoyed lots of different arts, along with music and theater. We learned in a fast-paced academic setting substantially more accelerated than our peers in other state schools, and we had enough creative exposure to expand our minds and souls. We grew up and grew closer until our worlds, and the worlds of everyone in our community and country, were turned upside down just before I was to start middle school. The revolution had begun.

How much of the life we knew would be shattered?

Chapter Three

The Five Walnut Trees of Jaujrood

A large, close-knit family is a microcosm of the larger world.
Spending my formative years in such a family gave me a chance
to understand how to find my way through society.

MY GRANDMOTHER ON MY DAD'S SIDE, whom we called Khanoom
Joon (meaning "dear lady"), was beautiful, kind, and very round.
Unbelievably, she had given birth seventeen times! Unfortunately, as
it went back in those days, only nine of them survived to adulthood,

and one died at the age of twenty-two. So, for most of her life, she had eight living children.

Every Monday night, she served dinner at her house. Several of my dad's siblings lived in Tehran, and they all had children. I have many cousins, with many of them being closer in age to my dad than to me. Those Monday night dinners were always chaotic but beautiful. My three girl cousins, two of them sisters and one from another uncle, were all about my age: Farnaz, Niloofar, and Shadi. I loved them.

Farnaz was a girly girl with very light hair and a very light complexion. "Look, my hair is almost to my waist," she once told me.

"I know! Mine is getting there." My hair was light brown with streaks of auburn, and it was growing to be as long as hers.

Niloo was more like me. A bit less of a girly girl but by no means a tomboy. Her thick, long hair had deep sections of golden blond. Niloo was a few years younger than me, but we *got* each other. We talked a lot and were sassy together.

My mom and dad loved to be with family, and they also loved nature. They had bought land outside of Tehran in an area called Jaujrood. They planted lots of fruit trees and built a beautiful villa with a nice big pool. They welcomed everyone to enjoy it with their families over the weekends. Many Fridays, we were awakened by my dad singing his wake-up song. And believe me, he was for sure tone-deaf! After much complaining and dragging our feet, we would get in the car and be off to Jaujrood. Road trips included my mom singing and telling stories. And I would almost always sit on her lap on the passenger side with no seat belt. That's just the way it was done.

We would arrive in Jaujrood, and most of the time, other family members and friends would start showing up too. People pitched in and brought food, cooked there, or just ordered it. My cousins and I would swim so much that it would feel like we lived in that pool. It was big and deep, built so that it would also operate as a reservoir for watering the trees. The water in the pool was very cold, yet we would stay in it for hours.

Then, there were the swimming contests. One of the most popular ones was to see who could swim underwater from one side of the pool to another (and back if they dared) without taking a breath. My middle sister, Shirana, was almost always the champion. No one could hold their breath as long as she could.

Sometimes, our parents participated in the swimming competitions too. Growing up in northern Iran, the beach was my dad's playground, and the ocean was his pool. So, his speed was stunning. No one could match him.

Niloo, Farnaz, and I would stay in the pool so long that our parents would have to drag us out, and then it would take me a long time to stop shivering. I was skinny, and the water was cold, especially since it was often nighttime by the time I would agree to get out.

There is nothing quite so dreamlike and timeless for a kid than to frolic in a pool with friends and cousins on a hot summer afternoon. It was our domain.

Jaujrood was what my dad had built to someday have his children, their spouses, and their children enjoy. He had specifically planted five walnut trees that you could see as you drove up the driveway. "This tree is Sherry's, this one is Shirana's, that one is Yashar's, this one on the left is Shani's, and the little one over there is Shirin's." He would tell us stories of how when the trees were mature, we would all have lunch under them with our families.

This was our piece of the land—the land our ancestors had lived on for centuries. The land where Cyrus the Great had delivered the first scroll on human rights. The land that supported our bloodline for millennia. The land that held the history of humanity with its rich art and culture. My father had designated a piece of that land to bring our family together. Sadly, we never saw that land and those trees reach maturity.

My mom's side of the family wasn't as busy but was still pretty big. The common trait on her side was kindness. My grandma, Khanjan (kind of like my other grandma's name, "dear person"), was petite and light-skinned. When my parents built the building we ended up living in in Tehran, they intentionally made it into an apartment building. Each floor had two apartments, and we had the top floor, which was the sum of two apartments in size. Almost every apartment was occupied by family members. Khanjan lived on one floor. Next to her was my uncle from my mom's side and his family. The other floor had my sister Sherry, her husband, and their two children; and on the first floor, my brother Yashar lived with his wife and three children. It wasn't just an apartment building; it was a community.

My cousins Kati and Keynoosh, two sisters close to my age, lived in our apartment building with their younger brother. I was almost exactly in between their ages. Kati was the older one, and Keynoosh was the younger. They were both skinny and dark and funny and kind.

Kati and I walked to school together. Our schools were adjacent and not far from home. We would come home at different times, but almost always, I would sit in her room after school and do my homework. Although I was a very good student, I didn't really love doing homework, so it was nice to be in the same room as my friend.

I was buddies with Kati and Keynoosh, and a couple of their cousins too. We often spent time together on weekends, attending our version of parties. A distant cousin of theirs was a boy named Ali. Ali was beautiful. Every time we crossed paths with him, all of us girls would look at each other and say, *"Acha cha cha cha"*—which meant nothing but that we were in love. Ali eventually became my first official boyfriend, which only meant that we talked on the phone.

A large, close-knit family is a microcosm of the larger world. Spending my formative years in such a family gave me a chance to understand how to find my way through society. My extended family taught me how to navigate the challenges and opportunities in interpersonal relationships. It wasn't easy to be heard and seen in a large group. So, I naturally learned how to make connections and find ways to showcase my unique place in the system. I'm not exactly sure how I developed those skills—I guess this is part of the mystery of how we choose to react to our environment. But I am grateful to have found ways to develop those skills, as they would later help me thrive—and save my life. Little did I know then, as a child, how far away that future was.

Chapter Four

No One Is Safe

*These images and experiences remained in my mind, con-
sciously and unconsciously, as reminders of threats to safety
and survival. I had already learned that the bottom could fall
out at any time.*

"Run! Run!"

A group of young men turned the corner onto our street as I
watched from the window of our apartment on the fourth floor. It

was apparent that they were running away from the military police. I had seen and heard about the confrontations between university students and the police during this movement, which started in Iran in 1978.

Pow! Pow!

Gunshots filled the air. The men ran even faster. I knew that if they didn't find a hiding place, they would be at risk of being shot to death. Reacting as fast as I could, I ran to the garage opener and clicked it open. With an agile reaction to the opening, they ran into the garage, and I closed it again. My heart was pounding. Were they safe? Would the police follow them? Would anyone know I had opened the garage door? Blood rushed into my face. Breathlessly, I peeked out the window, trying not to show my head in fear of the soldiers.

Within a few seconds, the police, entering our street with their guns drawn, kept running past the building. The young men were saved! They walked out after a few minutes. They were alive. But I didn't know for how much longer.

————

When I was born, Mohammad Reza Shah was the king of the Imperial State of Iran. Ruling from September 1941 until his overthrow in the Iranian Revolution in February 1979, he was the last westernized shah of Iran.

Referred to by the world simply as "the Shah," he oversaw and implemented economic and infrastructure enhancements in the country. However, as with his predecessors, he repressed political dissent and restricted political freedoms. He also pushed the country to adopt Western-oriented secular modernization over conservative Islamic laws. Socialization, clubs, bars, music, and creative areas were mostly allowed. Political challenges were not. When I was born, and later when I started school, women could wear shorts and short skirts.

They went to music clubs and danced when they felt like it. They drank with each other. They sat outside bistros and restaurants and shared meals, conversation, and laughter.

Men and women could interact publicly with each other. The hijab was optional but highly discouraged, and for all intents and purposes, Iran was growing more powerful.

During the Shah's thirty-seven-year rule, Iran spent billions on industry, education, health, and the armed forces. However, the regime did restrict freedom of speech, expression, and the press. Any criticism of the Shah and his regime was met with punishments. And the political and economic divide continually increased. I later began to realize that the real seeds of the revolution of 1979 had been planted years prior. Many underlying factors and foreign influences, including a nationalist movement in the 1950s that succeeded in nationalizing Iranian oil and was subsequently quelled by a coup, played a pivotal role in creating the fertile ground for the upheaval. The economic, cultural, and societal tensions and oppression finally boiled over in 1978. The movement started in universities and institutions of higher education. The initial focus and the cries of the movement in colleges and universities were around justice, and freedom of expression. However, Ayatollah Khomeini and his cabal hijacked the movement that started with these sentiments. They took advantage of the movement and the gap in leadership to eventually steer the revolution and claim it to be an *Islamic* revolution.

The rise of Khomeini and his crew was not just about religion, though it pretended to be. It was about the lust for power and control hidden behind religion. Islamic law was what the conservative class used to disguise their true agenda for power—a lust that continues to plague Iran and the entire region to this day.

This was the world I lived in when I entered middle school. I witnessed a bloody revolution with our basic survival at stake. As a preteen, I saw images of dead bodies, tortured faces, and acts of cruelty. My life and the lives of everyone I knew and loved were in danger daily. These images and experiences remained in my mind, consciously and unconsciously, as reminders of threats to my safety and survival. I had already learned that the bottom could fall out at any time.

———————

Demonstrations on the streets of Iran grew in size and momentum throughout the year. Over the next few months, we witnessed and experienced anxiety, sadness, confusion, and rage. As a child, I had to interpret the world and its safety based on the reactions of the adults around me. The ongoing battles with the police and the continued uncertainty of the stability of the Shah's regime pushed the adults into a state of fright. The blood-filled tide continued to rise.

In February 1979, it was clear that the Shah's regime was in mortal danger. Khomeini had already been back in Tehran, and the Shah had fled the country. There were sounds of sirens, screams, and the occasional pop of gunshots everywhere around Tehran. I could see plumes of smoke in the distance.

We watched the news on TV, listening intently and eagerly anticipating the latest. Suddenly, a man sat at the anchor's desk. We had never seen him before. Out of breath and a bit disheveled, he announced, "We are the new government of Iran. The monarchy has been toppled. Long live the revolution!"

Everyone at home looked stunned. It had felt like there was going to be a shift, but once it happened, it was shocking. I felt confusion and fear. It seemed, at the time, that some people cheered this change. Since then, I've learned to be skeptical about political movements and changes. I now know we never really discovered whose interests were being promoted with this revolution. I know many innocent, well-meaning people lost their lives in pursuing what they believed to be a better life. I also know that the lives of Iranian people turned substantially worse over the next few decades and even now. But then, at that moment, as a twelve-year-old, I witnessed uprisings, bloodshed, bravery, and a toppled government.

My cousins and I went to see what was happening on the streets. People were driving their cars, honking their horns, and many were cheerful—others were confused. Interestingly, the revolution and the temporary government that soon took power were not calling themselves Islamic yet.

While some cheered on the streets, looting and a rush occurred at police and military stations. There was absolute chaos.

Soon, the streets were riddled with young men, some as young as I was, holding machine guns. These were the newly installed Guards, who could stop anyone, anywhere, at any time for any excuse. Many told stories of people being gunned down or lost for good. My life and the lives of everyone else were in jeopardy. Any sense of security had been lost to the uncertainty of the times, filled with bloodshed once more.

We would either not leave home, or, if we did, it would mostly be during the day. Khomeini and other factions were building a temporary government, but it was nowhere near settled.

As the new regime took hold, it launched immediate and swift action against people who had previously held any position of power. This meant government officials, military personnel, and the like. But it also meant executives and business leaders. Mock trials were held, and mass executions were ordered and delivered in short order.

My father, who had worked his way up to be the chief executive officer (CEO) and grown his company to thousands of employees, was now at risk. He was part of the upper class in Iran. He was smart, educated, professional, talented—and dangerous because he was less likely to be compliant and support the regime than the ordinary man on the street. There were hundreds, if not thousands, of men and women like him—people with advanced degrees, influence, and critical minds.

My father decided not to wait for the regime to ask for changes in his company. He voluntarily stepped down.

I remember the day I came home from school to a couple of men in our living room. As I learned later, they were with the new regime and were asking my father some questions. We had heard stories of executives being arrested and taken to prison immediately. We had also heard many stories of executions. I wondered if this was going to happen to my dad.

But soon, the men left, and they never arrested my dad. Not then, not ever. What had happened was that once the word got out that my father might be interrogated (we're not sure how it had leaked), his blue-collar, dedicated employees went on strike. This was an unheard-of turn of events, especially during the post-revolution chaos. Most workers would want to see their bosses punished or, at a minimum, removed. As it turned out, my father's years of honest, genuine concern for the employees of his company had resonated with them so well that they went on strike to have him stay free and declared clean. His care for others ended up saving his life. What a valuable lesson for me to learn so early in life! I saw in action the values of integrity, compassion, and honesty . . . and how these core values are lifesavers.

The sad truth, however, is that many honest, truthful men and women were unjustly targeted, imprisoned, and murdered by the Islamic regime then and since.

Chaos grew during the first few years of the revolution. Factions that had come together to help topple the monarchy were now prone to infighting. Khomeini and his team, having the majority and the might of their supposed religious leadership, consolidated power in brutal ways. Khomeini's thugs and assassins arrested, tortured, and paraded on TV many of the revolutionaries and prior allies of the new government to stop anyone else from resisting. The regime executed people in droves.

Resistance was forming in large numbers. People did not want another autocratic regime, and this one was proving to be exceptionally cruel—substantially more savage than the one it had replaced.

The Islamic Republic immediately dismantled the rights of women. The regime announced that women would have to wear hijabs. To implement this rule, they deployed men on the street—many of them on motorcycles—to attack and beat women without hijabs. This was a stunning development. The women of Iran were some of the most educated women anywhere. They had held many positions of power and believed they had much to offer. To take away this most fundamental right sounded unbelievable.

As a child, I was not involved in the revolution, and I did not understand it. I did not know the dynamics at play with history, society, politics, macroeconomics, and geopolitical forces. Iran has a complex history, with its unique position in the Middle East and its oil and mineral riches. As a child, my world was limited to mostly my family and the smaller community in which I lived.

After the revolution, I was still a very young girl. The experiences and the images of the uprising and the subsequent chaos accelerated my awareness of my surroundings. The new Islamic Republic's brutal treatment of its people became widely known. I didn't have to delve deeply into politics to understand that this regime was committing egregious violations of basic human rights. Despite having a relatively secure home and the privilege of leading a relatively normal life, I couldn't turn a blind eye to the suffering around me. In my own small, teenage way, I joined the resistance against the oppressive rule of the Islamic Republic to defend our fundamental human rights.

Nobody in my immediate family was that politically active. My sisters and brother certainly were not. But my first cousins, my mom's sister's sons, were drawn to activism because they were university students.

My cousins were extremely bright. They questioned everything. The older cousin was studying engineering. His brother, two years younger than him, was the same way—talented and smart. I don't know how or why the Guards found and arrested them. I do know the Revolutionary Guard randomly went to universities and pulled people out of class. In university, you're supposed to be questioning the way of life, culture and politics, and even God and the meaning of life. But with the Islamic regime in Iran, anybody who seemed to question anything was targeted.

My cousins were arrested together. They were placed in the same jail and went on "trial" together. The trial was nothing but a guy sitting behind a desk with two other guys on either side of him. There was a line of prisoners to be "tried." The line moved very quickly, as only two questions were asked of each prisoner.

The younger cousin that came out told us about the entire experience. He explained that all the judge asked him was, "Do you believe in God?" and then, "Are you Muslim?" The cousin who was freed and told us the story said yes to both questions.

His older brother was more of an intellectual; he was only twenty-one years old and exploring the questions many ask at that age: What is God, and what is life? The questions in the "trial" were existential ones that he was still exploring. So, rather than lie, he simply said no to both questions. They jerked him out of the line. They had cranes set up in the courtyard of the detention center. My cousin, the smart, loving, kind twenty-one-year-old poet who was just discovering life, was immediately hung in front of his brother with no ceremony, no hesitation. He was simply hung from a crane. We were told that his body was then later buried in a mass grave, one whose location we will never know.

Arrested, given a two-minute mock trial, sentenced to death, and executed minutes later. His body swung from a crane for daring to question the regime. That's how quickly death came to rebels, thinkers, activists, and those only suspected of being anti-regime. Unbelievably, this is still happening in Iran today with the new generation of youth.

No one was notified of his death. If his brother hadn't witnessed it, we never would have known what happened to him.

Their mother lived with depression for the rest of her life and died a difficult death. A lot of people have no clue about what went on in Iran. The media reports on some things but rarely on the myriad kinds of cruelty inflicted upon people like my cousin, who dared to speak the truth.

Who else in my family and community might vanish without a trace?

CHAPTER FIVE

School Days

My point of view was my limitation, not my abilities. Every problem has a solution; if you can't find a solution, define the problem differently.

MY WORLD WAS SHAKEN once more when I learned that my school, where I had grown up and which I considered a family, was to be split up. Boys and girls were no longer allowed to be in the same school.

Some of my very best friends were boys, and I was heartbroken to learn that I could not see or play with them. We were only twelve years old.

Since our school was already small, they transferred our group to a new school that had been established only a few years before to accommodate the split. The new school was originally a private institution aimed at fostering accelerated academic achievement. Students were expected to study and pass all of the state-mandated curriculum for their grade within the first quarter of the school year. The rest of the academic year was dedicated to highly accelerated education. The aim was for students to be the top performers in their respective grades, and the school was modeled after institutions in Russia. So, here I was, entering middle school during the chaos of the revolution, having to deal with the loss of my friends who were boys, and now having to catch up with the new school, whose students were substantially ahead of the small group of us who joined. My education at our previous school revolved around academics and the arts. This school only taught academics. I was soon very lost.

We were required to choose a track, so I chose math and physics, both of which had always interested me.

My physics teacher was a college professor. As I sat in her class, I couldn't comprehend a word that she said. My classmates were so far ahead of me that I almost did not understand anything she was talking about. I struggled with the class for a few weeks and became very stressed. I had always been a good student and thought I was smart; now, I was failing. I started having breathing issues because I was so anxious. I was devastated and ready to quit.

One day, when I got home from school, I found the courage to tell my dad, "I don't think I can do this. I want to change schools."

My father was reading a newspaper. He gently folded it, peered above it with his reading glasses halfway down his nose, and looked up. He looked casually into my eyes and said, "It's up to you. You can change schools, but I assure you that nobody in that class is smarter or more competent than you are." And he went back to reading.

His words clicked in my head—switched the light bulb on, as the saying goes. I considered his words and pondered: *He's right. Why am I thinking this way?* Instead of avoiding it, I faced the challenge head-on. I resolved to succeed, and I knew I could. I would study every night and re-review chapters and concepts until I felt I understood them. Whenever I found myself demoralized about my progress, I would repeat to myself that I was as competent as anyone else. I would remind myself that I had chosen to do this. I believed it was a foregone conclusion: I would do very well in my physics class. It worked. By the end of the semester, I had the highest grades in the class.

I consistently excelled in my assignments and set the grading curve across the board. For years, that same physics teacher went around the school telling my story. I learned a lesson. My point of view was my limitation, not my abilities. Every problem has a solution; if you can't find a solution, define the problem differently. I wasn't bad at physics—I was just new to it. What I needed to succeed was to expect to do well. The rest was good old-fashioned hard work. It was a lesson I remember to this day. The later wounds I would receive of misplacement, chaos, and the after-effects of the revolution ended up creating resilience and confidence as I navigated them with my father's belief in me. I could still achieve despite my environment.

I only needed one person to believe in me. What a lesson! For years, I leaned on the understanding that one person's belief can make a remarkable difference. Much later in life, I found that this one person had to be me.

CHAPTER SIX

Arrested and Kicked Out

I learned that there was a cost for bravery but also that there was a way out. Gaining the courage to stand up for my beliefs has been an asset in both life and work.

"STOP!"

The command came from behind us. It wasn't a surprise. Anytime anyone was on the street or in public, regardless of age, gender, status, or destination, there was a risk of being stopped, arrested, challenged, or killed. The Revolutionary Guards knew most of the protesters and activists in Tehran were teenagers and young adults. We knew we could be stopped, and now we had been.

We stopped and turned around to see two soldiers behind us. The shorter of the two looked about sixteen or seventeen, not much older than I was at fifteen. They both had machine guns and were driving a jeep when they pulled up behind us. They exited the vehicle and swaggered confidently toward us, knowing we wouldn't run.

It was a gorgeous spring morning in northern Tehran, and we were walking on the sidewalks of a main street in an affluent neighborhood, passing by people's backyards, where we smelled spring flowers. These were relatively large yards, and these people had a keen sense of pride in their ownership. Fruit trees peeked above the walls in each yard. Iranians love flowers, and the smell was in the air. This area would generally feel safe, but at that time in Iran, nothing was.

Outwardly, we were just high school friends, compliant teenagers wearing the mandated hijabs and walking home to our families. We were young girls. How were we a threat to these men with guns or the regime?

But secretly, we were indeed a threat. We were activists who met and talked about the regime and what we could do to regain the freedoms we'd recently lost.

While the men with guns were right to suspect us, it was up to us to convince them of our "innocence." Citizens and the Guard played a cat-and-mouse game all over the country every day. Millions lived, but hundreds of thousands didn't.

We were activists and revolutionaries, not because we could no longer socialize or live as we once had, but because we had watched the horrors and atrocities already committed by the relatively new Islamic Republic of Iran since they took power in 1979.

Being arrested in Iran was and is very scary. Under the Islamic Republic of Iran, you have few legal rights, few human or civil rights, and indeed, very little due process. Often, and certainly back then, you are (and were) at the mercy of the Revolutionary Guard. They unsling their machine guns, wrap the gun straps around their arms, and point their weapon at you. Whatever they tell you to do, you comply or die. According to Amnesty International, Iran currently holds second place for the highest number of recorded executions, behind China.

With little recourse and no one to rely on to protect you, your survival is influenced by who you are, who you know, or how gifted you are at telling a story they will believe. This is the Iran I came of age in.

We were activists because, at any time of the day or night, we were at risk of becoming the next martyrs. We rebelled against the thought of that. We knew there were already many political prisoners. Our clandestine, activist-oriented meetings at different homes were not legal, and we'd be in trouble if the Revolutionary Guard discovered where we had been and what we had been doing or saying. So, when my friends and I left the house where we'd been meeting, we were prepared for the Guards should they stop us. We created stories to tell them if we were stopped and interrogated. You had to be ready if you didn't want to die or be arrested, but sometimes, even the best of our preparations wasn't enough.

Walking in Tehran was normal. Like the cities of Europe, Tehran was a walking city. People of all ages, especially teenagers, walked many places—even long distances of a mile or more to shop or visit family and friends. It was not unusual for us to be on the streets.

However, knowing that the Revolutionary Guard would randomly stop people, we decided ahead of time on a safe story to tell if we were ever to be stopped. We knew from other friends that the Guards always asked, "Where have you been? What have you been doing? What were you talking about?"

We didn't want to say we were talking anti-regime politics at our friend's house. So, we both agreed that we would say we were at the hairdresser getting our hair done, even though we were wearing the mandated head cover—the hijab. We knew the Guards wouldn't be able to see under the hijab to see if we were lying. Even if we had to remove the hijab for the female Guards after an arrest, it would be difficult to tell if we'd had our hair done or not. We also knew that the Guards would separate us and interrogate us separately to see if our stories matched.

It was terrifying to think that our stories, if told unconvincingly, could get us killed. But that was the world we lived in.

When the boys with machine guns asked, "Where are you going?" we said, "We're going home." Immediately, they separated us because that was their method of operation. They asked me questions before turning to question my friend. They compared our answers and checked our stories to make sure we were telling the truth. They were afraid of the youth getting together and encouraging each other in some uprising. Uprisings happened regularly, so their fears were justified.

Questioning us all at once wasn't enough. They kept going back and forth, hoping to intimidate or trip us up and get a confession of some sort. Our plan was just to continue to play dumb, making sure that they didn't think we were smart. Thankfully, we played our parts well. I don't know exactly what my friend said, but we both stuck to our visiting-the-hairdresser story.

Suddenly, they told us to get in the vehicle. They blindfolded us and forced us into their jeep, filled with what looked like sixteen-year-old boys with machine guns and all the authority lethal weapons can bring. We were in a vehicle and didn't know where we were going. We hadn't been charged or accused of a crime. I could tell from the conversations between them that they were still trying to figure out why they'd arrested us. That didn't mean they wouldn't kill us. It just meant they hadn't killed us yet.

They drove for a while, then stopped outside an unfamiliar building. They pushed us inside. After they removed our blindfolds, we could see what looked like the basement of a hospital. They handed us off to two women in hijabs because men were not allowed to body search women. These women would be able to not only ask us to take off our hijabs but also to make us remove our clothing so they could search us for booklets and weapons.

They didn't force us to remove all our clothes, just most of them, so they could search them for contraband. They also looked in our backpacks. I had made notes of the things we discussed at our meeting, but I was smart enough to take those notes in English, hoping none of them could read English and that they wouldn't find someone who could.

It was obvious that most of the teenagers associated with the Revolutionary Guard were not educated. Most barely had a high school education. They looked through everything, even flipping through the pages of our textbooks.

They searched us from head to toe, patting us down everywhere. They couldn't find anything, so they couldn't pin anything on us— not that that mattered.

What saved us, I think, was that we were obviously upper-middle-class girls, which made our visiting-the-hairdresser alibi plausible.

In the end, it was in their best interest to believe us, as they found no hard evidence against our story. We couldn't tell if it was due to youth, inexperience, or perceived social status, but they accepted our explanation with minimal questioning. Their ineffective interrogation was repetitive, as if they thought we would change our answers under pressure. "Where were you? What were you talking about? Who are your friends? When do you get together with your friends? What do you talk about? Where do you go to school?"

I told my prepared story: "I've been at the hairdresser's."

"What did you do?" They asked such questions to see if there was any detail they could extract from me. They wanted to see where I would trip up and say something that didn't fit my explanation. It was easy for me to lie, as I felt nothing, so I had no emotions, guilt, or fear to trip me up.

That emotional numbness is not surprising for anybody who's been in a traumatic situation. When you find yourself in a situation that could be a matter of life and death, often your body's natural response is to shut down emotions. You may not be able to fight or flee, so you simply freeze. I mechanically stuck with my story, with no feelings one way or the other. I didn't have any fear or anger. I didn't have any feelings because there was no space for them. The Guards finally gestured to each other in a "throw them out" gesture. They told each other, "We're wasting our time."

It was nighttime when we left the building, and we had no idea where we were since we'd been blindfolded when they'd brought us in. Tehran is not just a big city—it's a vast one. And we were fifteen-year-old girls. There were no Ubers or cell phones. No one knew where we were because we did not know where we were. I have no idea how we got home. That memory has left me. We had no money or other means to get home, so I assume we must have hitchhiked.

My dad was pacing back and forth when I finally got home around ten o'clock that night. He must have thought that I was gone for good. Under the new regime, those things happened. People just disappeared. No one was safe, not even children, teenagers, adults, the disabled, or the elderly, whether rich, poor, or middle class. We were all at risk. It didn't end when or if you could flee the country. If one person left, their family was targeted.

My parents never blamed me for the arrest. My father never showed anger toward me. He understood the situation. However, he was very upset from worrying about me, so he didn't exactly comfort me when I finally came home. But he understood.

He listened to my story and said, "Okay, okay." The next day, I had to go to school as though nothing had happened. But it had.

The trauma from the arrest was profound, leaving me feeling unsafe even at home. I lived in fear that someone could come for me at any moment, just as it had happened to people I knew. My best friend in elementary school—I won't use her name in case she is still alive and in Iran—was very much an activist in high school. She was arrested just like that—a knock at her door. She ended up in prison for ten years. She was my age, fifteen. She was arrested at fifteen, sentenced to ten years, and imprisoned for ten years. My point is that just because they let you go one night didn't mean they would let you go forever. I knew I could be arrested again—and less than a year later, I was.

Although we were dealing with unimaginable stress and violence, my fellow high school classmates and I were still just young teenagers. "Let's put on a show," I told my friend one day.

"What do you mean?" she asked.

"You spread the word around campus that they can come to our classroom to watch a show, and we can charge them a quarter to get in. We can then use that money to create even more shows," I said.

"Haha. What kind of show do you have in mind?"

"A talent show!" I exclaimed. "I know we can't play music, but we can have different groups come in and perform whatever they want. I'll do an act myself."

"That's hilarious. What's your act?"

"Hijab striptease. I'll sing and create my own music as I slowly take my hijab off for the girls that get in."

"Ha! It better be good. Let's do it!"

Just like that, we had a weekly show in our classroom during the morning recess. After the first show and my act, other girls started participating. There were hilarious group dances, comedy acts, and other fun routines. We would cry laughing. We used the money we collected to buy snacks and sodas for our audience. It's amazing how humans can show such resilience and the ability to play, even in the direst circumstances. The restrictions made us even more creative and playful. To this day, I crack up when I think of those days.

The school principals from our school and the boys' school collaborated to create academic contests between the boys and the girls. The original idea was to create some more rigor. What no one expected was that the girls would beat the boys in every subject every time! It's no surprise, knowing what I know now. Boys were more active and less mature then. It wasn't a contest for us at all. But it did ruffle some feathers with the noise it created. Around this time, a new principal had arrived at my school: a twenty-five-year-old, clearly an agent of the regime. Our young school principal decided it was time for us to learn our place in the world . . . as girls.

She invited a senator from the Islamic Republic government to speak to us. Knowing that all elections were sham elections, we all knew this senator, like others, was nothing but a puppet. Of course, we were required to sit and quietly listen to him and absorb his words of wisdom. But except for a few zealots, we had little respect for him.

He shattered what little inkling of respect we had when he started talking. The theme of his speech was that girls have brains half the size of boys and, therefore, they're half as smart. He was clearly a genius!

Fuming when his dumb speech was over, I went over to our principal and asked, "Why did you bring someone here to tell us we're half as smart as men?" She replied, "Because we are." I stared her in the eyes and said, "Maybe you are, but I'm not!"

The next thing I knew, my dad was called into the office, and I was kicked out of the school I had attended all my life—up until the eleventh grade.

The principal said to my dad, "She is a thought leader and a leader of the anti-government movement." Of course, she had no evidence, just a simple accusation.

"At sixteen? She's a child!" my dad exclaimed. "But never mind. This is clearly not the place for her. I'm taking her out of this school." He came to my defense quickly so that he would not have to argue with the principal. Luckily, my dad had always been active in the PTA and remained active even after the revolution. He had earned a lot of respect from everyone, including the principal. This respect may have saved my life.

Nonetheless, this experience reminded me once again that speaking up to defend myself and standing up for what was right had a cost. Taking a righteous stance would mean sticking my neck out and singling myself out of the group. I hadn't said or done anything inappropriate or incorrect, and yet I was the only one asked to leave. This message resonated with the prevailing larger societal expectations of being invisible and conforming. My father's supportive reaction to pull me out of the situation with dignity also sent me a message: even though standing up can be dangerous and isolating, it's respectable. I learned that there was a cost for bravery but also that there was a way out.

Chapter Seven

War Comes Home

I learned that even in the direst times, . . . being a guide and a beacon of hope to help others is vital. Often, resilience comes from kind actions.

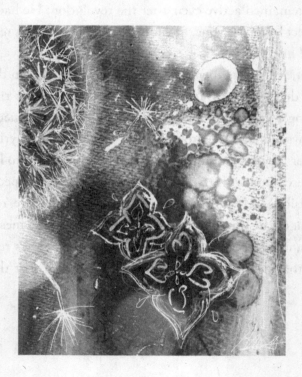

IRAQ SHARES A BORDER WITH IRAN. During the transition of power between the monarchy and the Islamic Republic of Iran, Saddam Hussein was the leader of Iraq. In 1980, Iran was dealing with the aftermath of the power transition that had resulted in lots of posturing among its ruling group. Clearly an enemy of the West, the Islamic Republic repeated strong rhetoric against the United States. In an unprecedented act of aggression, the Iranian state supported a siege on the United States embassy in Iran, holding fifty-two people hostage. Tensions between Iran and the West, as well as its allies in the Middle East, were boiling over.

I was too young to comprehend the magnitude of these developments. Witnessing the images of the hostages on the screen was unsettling. I had been to the United States a few times by then. I had also visited and stayed in England. I had firsthand knowledge of the Western people and didn't understand the animosity spewed on the Islamic media. What I did understand was that the tensions were increasing.

Iraq invaded Iran with force. The surprise and strength of the Iraqi invasion pushed back the Iranian forces immediately. The news of daily bombings and the forward movement of the Iraqi army on Iranian soil added to our already fragile sense of safety.

Before long, we met people who had left their homes and all their belongings in the border cities of Iran to escape to the central parts. These families had worked and lived in those regions with love and dignity. Suddenly, they found themselves with nothing—no home, no employment, and lost family and connections. The newly installed Iranian government didn't have the wherewithal or the resources to support these families—even if they had wanted to.

Young men died in droves as Iraq progressed farther and farther into the country.

"You tape the windows in your room. I'll do the family room," my mom said as she handed me black paper and masking tape.

Iraqi jet fighters had started invading Tehran's airspace. We had already heard bombing the previous few nights. As a safety measure, the residents of Tehran were required to cover their windows with thick black paper. We learned about the sirens and that once we heard them, we would have to leave everything behind and take shelter. At night, if the sirens went off, we would have to quickly turn off all the lights before seeking shelter. The black paper was to shield any light from the Iraqi jetfighters so that they would not be able to view the city clearly. We were taught to walk quietly down the steps of our apartment building to the basement for safety.

Sirens went off almost nightly. Without hesitation, we would turn off any remaining lights (and there were generally none, as we would make it a habit to not turn on any lights at night) and march quietly down to the basement as the sound of the sirens wailed, creating a deafening presence. Most of the parents would bring lanterns and flashlights. We would sit in the basement quietly as the sounds of bombs and anti-aircraft missiles filled the air.

Before the revolution, Iran was one of the best and closest allies of the West in the world. Tehran was considered the "Paris of the Middle East." My dad had formed and forged meaningful relationships with US companies. We had traveled and stayed in many parts of the United States. My sister Shani lived in Los Angeles. On my previous visit to LA, only two years prior, our American friends had called me "Strawberry Girl" because I loved strawberries back then.

Wars don't make sense. This war especially did not make sense to me.

Bombings continued and delivered severe damage and human casualties in Tehran. My good friend's entire family died in a bombing. They were upper-middle class and lived in an upper-middle-class neighborhood. No one would have ever expected that she would become an orphan because of a bombing.

The entire city became war-torn. Lines for food were common, and news of casualties and deaths were ubiquitous. Saddam dropped chemical bombs on a few border villages and cities in Iran, and the images from those cities were horrifying. We saw videos of entire villages with dead bodies of children, men, women, and animals all over the streets. The strange thing was that the buildings remained intact. Burned victims who survived were interviewed on TV, and some were sent over to Germany for testing.

Fear for survival was my daily life. I was a new teenager with all the teenage changes and challenges. And I was reminded every day that my life could very well end at any minute. The threat was sustained in our lives daily and for years afterward.

We soon learned to find ways to cope with the circumstances. Though aware of the possible doom and often afraid, we weren't about to succumb. Since we went to the basement almost every night, and since many of the people in that basement were family, we figured we could find ways to calm our nerves.

After the shock of the first few nights, we started playing games. Our little lantern lit up the windowless basement. We would play cards and dominoes. Since I didn't like playing cards much, I would perform, encouraging everyone to sing a song. Most often, I would go into a comedy routine as my dad would call out a family member's name, and I would pretend to be that person.

He had seen this act before, so he knew which characters were the most entertaining for me. My uncle (my mom's sister's husband) was our favorite character. He was a jolly, short, chubby man who loved to eat fruit. His favorite was tangerines. My specialty was to sit just like him with my legs crossed and pretend like I was popping tangerines in my mouth as I spoke really fast, just like him. Some nights, the adults would cry from laughter.

Through humor and games, we collectively softened the harshness of the sirens and bombs. Our ability to adapt to environments—as harsh as they may be—is, to me, the main reason why humanity has grown so much.

I learned that even in the direst times, reaching within to gain perspective was crucial. I also learned that in such circumstances, being a guide and a beacon of hope to help others is vital. Often, resilience comes from kind actions. These are lessons I've used often since then.

The war lasted eight years. But the attacks on Tehran didn't last as long. Through lots of sacrifice, Iranian forces pushed the Iraqis back. This was done mostly by sheer manpower and hundreds of thousands of Iranian lives lost. By the end of the war, Iran had taken back all its territory. Iraq had lost its invasion. What a tragic, unnecessary war. I was then and remain to this day against aggression and against war. I have seen what it does firsthand.

It has taken a generation and will likely take more for Iran's people to process their trauma from this war. I can only steadfastly pray that the future holds hope for peace and reconciliation.

Chapter Eight

The Gathering Storm

My oldest sister, Sharareh, nicknamed Sherry, was already married, had children, and had moved away from home to a place outside of Tehran. My middle sister, Shirana, who was twenty-two then, and I made a trip to visit Sherry. Two other girls, Sherry's neighbors, decided to return to Tehran with Shirana and me. So, there were four of us girls. I was sixteen, and the rest of them were in their twenties.

We left to return to Tehran on what was called a luxury bus. Traveling from Isfahan, where Sherry lived, it took about eight hours to get to Tehran. On the way back, we had to pass through Quom, a town that was a hotbed of very conservative, fundamentalist, religious people.

The Revolutionary Guard stopped the bus as we were passing through the city. They didn't need any search warrants. They didn't even need a reason to stop the bus. They were the Revolutionary Guard. They could arbitrarily stop anyone, anytime, anywhere, using any vehicle—from bicycles to buses to walking.

They boarded the bus and surveyed the occupants before they began shouting.

"Get off the bus! Quickly!"

Some passengers immediately left the bus. Others sat and waited as the Guards began to pull out everyone's bags, suitcases, and personal belongings. They threw the bags on the ground and piled them outside the bus, then turned their attention back to the passengers.

"Whose bag is this one?" They were met with silence.

"Whose bag is this one?" They would hold up a bag and glare at the passengers as they shouted.

"Whose bag?!" Their anger grew with each bag they seized.

One after another, the person whose bag they held would step forward or leave the bus and go stand by the bag. Men, women with children, women traveling alone, people with families—no one was exempt from the Guard's demands.

As each person left the bus and stood by their bags, the Guards would open the bag and go through it while we all watched—some, like me, watched from the bus, looking down from the window where I was seated. If the Guards found something incriminating, they would arrest the owner of the bag—or, depending on exactly what they found, kill them right then and there.

"Whose bag is this?" They asked the same thing with each new bag they picked up. My arms and legs grew cold, my hands trembling, as irritation gave way to fear.

When they picked up my bag, before I could stand to leave the bus, Shirana stepped forward. She did this because she was older, but more so to protect me. I had a book in my bag—not something that was okay to have when the Guards searched your belongings. The book had something to do with socialism. It wasn't radical or extraordinary, just informational, but it certainly wasn't something the Guards viewed as acceptable to have on one's person, especially if you were female.

Sure enough, the Guards opened my bag and found the book. I looked out the bus window at my sister standing there as they searched through my things. She turned white. Until then, I had forgotten I had the book in my bag. Although I was confident the boy with the machine gun who had taken the book out was illiterate—he was holding the book upside down—it was still a book.

"Whose book is this?" a guard shouted.

"It's mine." Shirana took responsibility for my book and my bag. She knew it was a dangerous situation and volunteered herself for the potential punishment. She threw herself on the sword to protect me. She knew I was watching her but intentionally ignored me to signal me to be quiet. So, I was.

There was a split second of silence as the Guards realized their mission to find someone violating their twisted version of Islamic law had been successful. Then, all hell broke loose.

"Why do you have a book?! What is this book?!" Their yelling and aggression escalated. They told us all to get off the bus. Then, they had the four of us girls stand together. The two other girls traveling with us, who had nothing to do with my book, also got into trouble. Guilt by association.

Once again, we were all put into their jeep. This was so much worse than the first arrest because this time, we had a book. Therefore, we were clearly activists or worse. A lot of my memory of this arrest is patchy and unclear because of the trauma of it—even after all these years. I have since learned that memory loss is common for trauma survivors. With many years of focus and work on my memories, I still can't remember the finer details of this day, a clear indication of the severity of this life-threatening ordeal.

What I remember is very hit-and-miss. The next thing I remember is that we were taken to another facility and placed into rooms intended to be used for solitary confinement. Maybe they'd run out of rooms, but my sister and I were both placed in the same room. The other two girls were separated, and each one was put into their own room.

It wouldn't have been a problem if the two girls with us were just innocent bystanders. But it just so happened that the two other girls were activists themselves. We were all worried that they would be in real trouble if the Guards were to dig deeper and discover who they were. Thank goodness the Guards had no way of searching for our personal information in real time—the internet and social media did not exist then.

We stayed there in silence. I couldn't imagine what was happening to the others until I heard strange sounds coming from one of the other cells, a random *thump, thump, thump*—the sound of someone hitting the ground and thrashing. The stress of the search and arrest had triggered a seizure in one of the girls, who had epilepsy and was prone to seizures. We could hear her in the cell next to us, alone, in the middle of a seizure, and with no one to help her.

"Guard! Guard!" we yelled. "You've got to get to her, you've got to get to her. She's having a seizure!"

I wondered later, *Did we hasten our friend's demise or save her life?* There was suddenly a lot of commotion, people running around, and the Guards responding and taking her away. I still don't know what they did with her, how they helped her—if they did—or anything about what happened to her after we got the Guards there. And then, things were quiet again. There were only the three of us left to wonder about our future.

They still had all our bags. For those of us with purses, they had gone through them looking for more evidence of our "crimes" against the regime.

Unfortunately, my book was not the only contraband they would find. One of the other girls had written a letter to a friend, waiting to be mailed. In her letter, she had badmouthed Khomeini, the regime's leader. Her badmouthing was just her words to a friend. It wasn't exactly a manifesto of hate to a rebel group intent on overthrowing the government.

But if all hell had broken loose when they found my book, hell exploded when they found the letter.

"You are a communist!" they screamed at her. "We're going to keep you! We're going to kill you!" The Guards were practically frothing at the mouth in their excitement at discovering someone they believed was a dangerous activist.

"We're going to keep you here! You're going to be executed. This is the end of your life! You are going to die!" The threats kept coming.

We were terrified. Executions happened regularly. These weren't false or baseless threats from the Guards. They did kill people on a whim and often for much less than possession of a letter or a book.

They kept us the whole day.

Again, like my first arrest, the Guards, for whatever reason, let me and two of the other three girls go. Suddenly, we were once again on the road at night, in a strange part of town with no money and no way home. However, they detained the other girl who had been with us—identified as an activist and slated for death based on her letter and my book. I was sick to my stomach.

I do remember we hitchhiked home that night with a stranger. I don't know if he was a taxi driver or if he chose to drive us. For whatever reason, he took pity on us. He drove us all the way to Tehran, which was many hours away, and dropped us off at home.

I have very little memory of what happened next. I do know that I told my parents what I knew—that the Guards had thrown us out of jail and had kept one girl with threats that they were going to kill her because of a letter they'd found.

We wondered what was going to happen now. I'd been arrested twice.

Over the next few days, I gradually learned what had happened while we were imprisoned. When our bus arrived in Tehran and we weren't on it, my family learned from passengers on the bus that four girls had been arrested.

No one knew where we had been taken. My parents in Tehran and my sister Sherry and her husband in Isfahan were terribly worried because nobody knew where we were. I think Sherry and her husband, Reza, or both, drove from their city to Quom—looking for us along the way. They were terrified but undaunted.

The Guards kept the other girl for another three weeks. We don't know what happened to her during that time. She doesn't ever talk about it now, but at the time, she did share bits and pieces.

She said that the Guards would wake her up—wake all of them up, all the girls they'd arrested for being "enemies of the regime." Sleep deprivation is a form of torture, and they used it without mercy. Just when she would manage to fall asleep, the Guard would wake her up again to talk to a judge at 11 PM or midnight. The judge and the Guards berated her and repeatedly told her she was going to die. I think that may have been worse than the sleep deprivation. Those kinds of words are burned into your mind and heart forever.

"You are an enemy of the state. You are going to die. You are going to be executed. We are setting a date for you to die." The threats were malicious and repetitive and designed to scare prisoners into confessions.

She truly believed they were going to kill her, and why wouldn't they? They'd killed so many others. She wasn't sure what they wanted to kill her for, so she would just cry and get confused.

"Tell us. Tell us about your connections. Who do you know? Are you a communist or a socialist?"

"I have no idea what you are talking about. I don't know anything about any of this." She would cry, and they would continue to berate her until they were tired of it, or became bored, or had a new prisoner to harass.

After three weeks, they released her, realizing she didn't know much about politics. Despite the pressure, death threats, and mental and emotional torture, her lack of knowledge convinced them that she wasn't an activist. As a result, they released her. We never discussed this incident again. This experience made it clear that Iran was not safe. It wasn't safe for many, and especially not for me. Having been in prison and having experienced the loss of my freedom, I knew I did not want to live with that threat anymore. And yet, almost nightly, I had expectations of someone coming to our house and arresting me. This was not an idle threat . . . it was possible, and it had happened to many.

CHAPTER NINE
Leaving Iran

Through it all, he had witnessed that I had it in me. That I had risen to the smaller challenges in life and perhaps, I was ready for a bigger one.

BY THE TIME I WAS SEVENTEEN, I had been arrested twice and expelled from my school. My father had barely escaped arrest. We had learned of many unjust imprisonments. We witnessed atrocities, including when my cousin was executed. We knew my good friend was in prison and sentenced to ten years. We were living with war and continued chaos and persecution. We were afraid that if I stayed in Iran any longer, I could be arrested again or killed. The Guards might not be accommodating and release me without harm the next time. The gathering storm was on our doorstep.

"She's got to go."

When my parents finally decided, I don't remember the exact wording they used to share their decision with me. But I know that I learned that summer that I would get on my mom's passport, since I was still a minor, and leave Iran. The revolution had happened a few years prior, and the war with Iraq was still raging. There weren't many countries that accepted Iranians then. But my parents had decided that they wanted to have me leave as soon as possible. Therefore, the destination they chose was a neighboring country, Turkey.

There wasn't much discussion about this. The overwhelming danger and unpredictability were hard for my parents to process. They couldn't pause or share their feelings with me as they planned on sending me to the unknown. They had a hard decision to make. Should they keep me at home and risk losing me to the Guards? Or losing me to the lack of opportunity and freedom that could adversely affect someone like me mentally and emotionally?

Should they send me away from Iran, leaving behind everything I knew, in the hope that I would find my way? Would they dare send this small, skinny girl, who was full of love and had grown up with her close-knit family and friends, to live on her own in a new country where she knew no one? This meant that their youngest girl, the apple of her dad's eye, who had never been left alone, who had no notion of how to shop, cook, make money, or fend for herself, would have to live alone in a country where no one knew her. Would she make it? Would she be kidnapped, lost, murdered, raped? Would she lose her mind because of the stress of abandonment? My parents wrestled with these questions.

They had to make agonizing decisions quickly. And they did. I was going to leave Iran soon.

Without letting many people know, my parents asked me to say goodbye only to people I trusted. I called some of my friends and saw a few more. I don't remember how and when I said goodbye to my sisters and their children, my brother and his family, my cousins, or the rest of my family, but I must have.

I don't remember exactly what I packed or how I packed it. My short life of seventeen years would have to be packed in a suitcase that was to be my only belonging. I was still a child. I loved my room, picture frames, toys I had kept over the years, clothes, and memorabilia a teenager keeps. I had to take clothes for warm and cold weather. I only had room for a couple of pairs of shoes. I had no space for anything else. No photos, no toys, nothing to remind me of home and my life. It was so sad I couldn't even allow tears to form.

Who would be my mom?

Who would cook for me?

Who would welcome me home from school?

Who would be my dad?

Who would rub my back as I sat for an afternoon snack?

Who would guide me?

When would I ever see my sisters, my brother, my nieces and nephews, my cousins who lived in our apartment building, my extended family who got together for Monday dinners at Khanoom Joon's, or my grandma who lived in our building? Also, when would I be able to see my friends again? When would I sit under my walnut tree my dad had planted all those years ago?

The emotional toll was too great for me to process, and it was too overwhelming for me to remember most of what happened.

Our departure from the Tehran airport was intimidating. The Guards scrutinized us while asking questions, and they conducted body searches to ensure we weren't taking excessive money or assets out of the country. Expecting that I would have to live on my own, my mom had brought a small bag of gold jewelry with her. She knew that taking jewelry out of Iran was prohibited, yet she had decided to take a chance. This was our only hope, since the amount of cash we were allowed to take wouldn't last very long.

They searched me first. I don't know how, but without talking, my mom and I communicated. Somehow, this little middle-aged woman moved more quickly and stealthily than most drug smugglers. Before the Guards could blink, she had passed the jewelry bag to me, as I was already in the clear. We successfully smuggled it. This was my one and only experience doing anything like this. But now we knew we would have some money to hold me over.

I don't even remember how I finally said goodbye to my dad and how he kept it together to see me, his precious daughter, take her small seventeen-year-old body off to the gates to leave him. The fear of being arrested or facing worse consequences consumed his thoughts, as he was responsible for making this daring decision. Dad had raised me to speak up and strive for a better life. He led a life of dignity and honesty, which resulted in our family not experiencing the financial success that many of his peers had in Iran. With his position at the helm of a large corporation, he, too, could have accumulated more substantial wealth, as many in lower positions than he had, through collusion, bribery, and the like.

Therefore, he was responsible for having to send his seventeen-year-old girl to a foreign country with little or no money. Later in life, he told me of these facts in his letters. I am so very proud of him and grateful for his dignity and his courage. My departure from Iran left him shaken and afraid. But he also knew that he had raised me to be competent, that I had talents, and that I deserved to live an authentic life. He could have succumbed to fear and made me stay, be quiet, get married, and live a small life in conformity. But he was a thoughtful, caring man who had witnessed my abilities and believed in me. He had raised me to stand on his feet and dance with him as he guided me. He had instilled confidence in me to put on my red boots and take the figurative stage. He had encouraged me to believe in myself when I didn't think I could. He had supported me when others singled me out and kicked me out of school. Through it all, he had witnessed that I had it in me. That I had risen to the smaller challenges in life and perhaps, now I was ready for a bigger one.

So, he took a monumental risk. He took a risk on me, offering me freedom and a chance to build a life. However, this risk could result in tragic outcomes. For all he knew, he might never see me again. And he didn't . . . for ten years.

As we finally settled in our seats and the plane took off, I felt relief and sadness. Outside the window, I could see my country falling away as the plane passed over the Iranian landscape. I swallowed hard, a lump forming in my throat as I realized that I was safer but had left all I knew behind. I remembered my sisters, nieces and nephews, cousins, friends, home . . . and my dad. My mom was sitting next to me, but I had a feeling it wouldn't be for very long. I couldn't process all that I was leaving, but sensed that I was leaving all I knew.

Iran, with all its political challenges, is a country with a rich history and culture. The tapestry of ethnicities, religions, customs, dialects, and languages had been formed for millennia as people of various backgrounds shared many common traditions. Neighbors watched out for neighbors. The elderly were respected and revered. The rich language and life lessons taught through the poetry of Rumi, Hafez, and others delivered the wisdom of generations to the young. No one was alone. There was always a sense of community, even in the hardest times. The resilience of the Iranian culture, as told by

Ferdowsi, showed up in everyday life. Despite the violence, atrocities, and unjust cruelties committed by those in power, and despite the war and its savage toll, the people maintained their strong culture. They found joy and love in many small but significant ways. I did not have the words or the emotional bandwidth to acknowledge the loss that I was about to experience. But, somehow, I knew. I was somber, confused, and scared.

That innate ability I had to believe in and expect good to come made this transition tolerable.

As we were leaving Iranian airspace, I took off my hijab, looked out the window, and thought to myself, *I don't think I'll ever see this beautiful country with its tall mountains and rich nature again.*

And I haven't since.

CHAPTER TEN

Alone in Istanbul

MY MOTHER AND I arrived in Istanbul on a sunny day in 1983. The airport was vast and filled with hustle and bustle. Passengers, porters, and staff were walking and talking all around me. I had just stepped off the plane, having left everything I knew. I was grateful that my mom was with me, though I wasn't sure for how long. The pace of it all was dizzying, and I continued to feel dazed and disoriented as we found our way to a taxi and off to a hotel. I'm not sure how we had decided on the hotel, but it must have been through other Iranians, as this hotel was filled with Iranian men and boys. It was soon clear to me that the area wasn't safe. We had left Tehran, Iran's capital city, and found ourselves in a place not much safer than the one we had left. Instead of political violence and turmoil, there were drug and sex traffickers in this run-down area of Istanbul—dangerous for anyone, let alone unaccompanied Iranian women.

Istanbul was Turkey's most populous city at that time, with more than six million residents, and today remains Europe's most populated city at fifteen million plus. It's a beautiful city with so much culture. Yet, much like most urban areas, it had a rough and dangerous underbelly. That underbelly was where we, like many other Iranians fleeing the regime, ended up.

Istanbul was a bustling metropolis with heavy traffic, crowded alleys, and a mix of new languages and ancient landmarks. We knew of many Iranian refugees in Turkey, almost all men. It was highly challenging for men and boys to leave Iran, mainly due to the military draft that was in place. However, we soon learned that many of them had managed to escape the country through illegal means.

We saw a few Iranian women at the hotel but no young girls. I was a rare breed. We soon got to know some of the women and men staying at the hotel. There was no shortage of highly educated, sophisticated intellectuals who could not or would not live under the tyranny of the regime in Iran. Almost all of them hoped that Turkey would be a short stay before they settled in countries in Europe. Many wanted to end up in the United States, but that seemed unlikely. Due to the hostility with the Iranian regime, the United States had all but frozen granting visas to Iranians.

My mom and I spent our days talking to other Iranian hotel guests about everyone's plans for leaving Turkey. One attractive middle-aged woman bonded with us. She was there alone, awaiting a response from the French embassy to receive her visa for France. She was a respectable, meticulously dressed woman with a proper and polite demeanor.

"My brother is a major figure in space exploration in the United States. He's lived in the United States most of his adult life," she told my mom in the hotel lobby as we sat and chatted. "My parents sent him to America to earn his PhD, and he stayed there. You may have heard his name. He's pretty famous in Iranian circles," she said.

Her brother was an example of the Iranians of the generation before the revolution who had found their way to the United States and shined through their incredible intelligence and work ethic.

"What an inspiration!" I told her. "I want to do something great too. I'm good at math, and I love physics," I told her with confidence.

She smiled warmly, with a twinkle in her eyes. "What a smart girl! I know you'll do something great. I think you're very mature for your age," she said kindly. Her encouraging words were heartwarming and much needed.

Our connection with her lasted only a few days, as she did end up receiving her visa to France. I don't know where in the world she is now, but wherever she is, I hope she's well.

Most of the other Iranian residents of the hotel were young boys about my age who had escaped Iran. Unfortunately, most of them didn't have valid passports. During the day, they would congregate in the lobby, exchanging ideas. Some would talk about how they had obtained a legitimate passport from the embassy, and some would share their contact information for counterfeit ones. Almost all of them hoped to leave Turkey through connections they had in Europe or the United States. Many of them, unfortunately, had succumbed to the difficult environment of the area we were staying in. Many had become drug users and pushers.

I remember focusing on understanding what was happening and orienting myself in this new place. I befriended a couple of the boys from the hotel, and we remained friends while they were there and I lived in Turkey.

After only a few days in Istanbul, my mom informed me that she would soon leave me and try to get to the United States. I don't recall the conversation. Frankly, knowing the level of stress we were both under, I wouldn't be surprised if we didn't have much of a conversation at all. Nevertheless, I held out hope that she would try to get me to the United States too. This was the understanding of a highly traumatized seventeen-year-old child leaving her world behind. The prospect of being left completely alone in a foreign country with no parents and little money was so daunting that I couldn't process what was happening. In the dire and risky situation we were in, there was little assurance for me. This lack of assurance is what made this experience especially traumatic. Had my mom had the wherewithal to explain to me that although I was going to be left alone, it would only be temporary, and no matter what, my family would always look out for me, I would not have felt as confused. This lack of assurance and any expression of love and support left a hole in my psyche—a hole of abandonment that I carried and nursed for years to come.

Mom then introduced me to a woman whose house I was going to live in. The house was small with low ceilings, and it was dark and dank and smelled like a combination of cigarettes and old, stale moisture. The owner of the house was a pretty, small, middle-aged woman with light eyes. She seemed proper and clean. She spoke little English, but my mom could communicate with her. Over the years, my mom had learned Azerbaijani, my dad's mother tongue. Azerbaijani is very close to Turkish, so the two of them could understand each other. As my mom explained to me, the agreement was for me to stay at this woman's house for as long as I was living in Istanbul. Apparently, she rented a room for girls. She could room three girls, and I would be the third one.

After a short conversation and a cup of tea, the woman offered to show us her house and the room I would share. She showed little emotion as she gave us the brief tour.

The small room had three beds, each positioned in a way that allowed all three to fit. Due to the beds taking up most of the space, there was very little floor space to walk around. We shared two closets, but they were essentially armoires with some drawers, and there were no wall closets. We put my little bag of belongings, all I had in this world, in the small bedroom.

My mom gave me some of her remaining money and the bag of gold jewelry we had smuggled. She then paid the woman cash for rent. Then, with little emotion—most likely out of her emotional numbness for having to leave her child behind—and even less explanation, she hugged me goodbye and left.

There I was. Within a week of entering a new country, I was left alone. I had very little money, no connections, no friends, no experience living on my own, and no knowledge of cooking or grocery shopping. I had never been to a bank, I didn't speak Turkish, and I had no guidance. Furthermore, due to the war, communication with my home country was severely impacted, so I couldn't even call home.

I was a petite, young, emotional girl who had grown up in a busy household with siblings in a close-knit community. I had always had friends and family around, but now, I found myself in a cold, disconnected place with no way out. I didn't even have a passport since I was on my mom's, and she had to take it with her.

I couldn't even feel sad in the midst of this severe trauma; I felt numb, a sense of dissociation.

The older, emotionally cold Turkish woman my mother found to "care" for me lost any remnant of warmth once my mother left. I was not a guest or a friend of a friend. I was a business commodity, a form of income.

As soon as my mom left, things started feeling very different in that house. Having never cooked or gone grocery shopping, I had to learn how to find ways to eat. There was a limited amount of food in the house, and I can't remember what I ate—only that I didn't eat often.

The landlady did not allow us to shower because running water was expensive. So, she would make us use pots that we would fill with water to wash ourselves. I was only allowed to use the little bit of water in the pot to clean myself. I didn't have a shower the entire time I was in Istanbul. Was it cruel? I couldn't say. I *can* say it wasn't how I'd grown up.

There was a lot of coldness in that house—and I don't just mean a lack of heat. So, I left the house as often as I dared. The landlady was not only stingy with physical resources but also with emotional and social ones. She wouldn't help me learn Turkish, so fleeing the house became my mental and emotional escape, as well as my classroom.

I couldn't always telephone my family in Iran. It was very difficult. Bombs and the Iran–Iraq war had destroyed or damaged most of the infrastructure. Getting a phone call through was a miracle that took hours or days. The landlady was not happy about my calling. "Everything costs money" was her motto, whether it was water, food, or phone calls. I would sit by the phone for eight hours straight, trying to get through to my dad. Sometimes, an overseas operator would take pity on me and do the repeated dialing herself until we connected.

I had two roommates. One was a girl who was only a couple of years older than me. She had grown up in Germany, although she was originally Turkish. She had been kicked out of Germany for reasons I never learned about. The other girl, who was more of a woman at age twenty-eight, was from Bulgaria. I don't remember their names, and I barely remember what they looked like, but that's what time and trauma do to one's mind. They leave holes in your memory, holes you don't know are there, holes that contain a piece of a memory that seems to make no sense—the smell of someone's cologne, the color of their hair, or their favorite dress, but no more. Yet sometimes, you fall into one of those holes, and everything comes rushing back with such force that you believe, if only for a few seconds or minutes, that you're back there, living it all over again. It's a cruel trick the brain plays on those who survive trauma. I'm fortunate I don't remember much of my time there.

Although I can't remember the Bulgarian girl's name, I do remember that she was tall, had black hair and green eyes, and was kind. She took me under her wing a little bit, perhaps to her capacity. The German girl, however, was out of control. She drank and probably did other related activities. I didn't talk to her much, but we did share a room, so we crossed paths.

I didn't care much about why the other girls were there, but I wondered sometimes about the owner's story. What made this woman, who was clearly educated and beautiful, become hardened, cold, and uncaring? She had reluctantly promised to take care of me and did the absolute minimum to ensure that happened. It was up to me to figure out the rest—shopping, money, language, food, how to get around, and anything related to my doing what I needed to do to get out of Istanbul.

When my mom left, she took the only identification I had—my name and photo on her passport—with her. I had no passport of my own, only copies of my mother's. I needed to find an embassy, get my own passport, and navigate the issues of visas, knowing nothing about those things. I could curl up in the fetal position, cry, and wait to be rescued, or I could take control of my situation with the only resource I had—my passion for learning.

I didn't speak Turkish. I spoke Farsi, my native language, and I knew English fairly well but not great. And most people, especially those with whom I needed to communicate to live in Istanbul, didn't speak Farsi or English. It was their country, so I had to learn this new language, Turkish, quickly. As it turns out, I have an aptitude for languages. Or maybe it was my sincere desire to navigate this society that pushed me to learn Turkish. Either way, I learned to speak Turkish fast. Learning Turkish wasn't like taking a leisurely class. It was a necessary survival skill if I was to live there.

I made a habit of asking questions of everyone I met while searching for answers about things I didn't know or understand. These questions helped me learn how to shop and feed myself. People and their insights were crucial for my survival. They gave me the most important thing I needed: a plan to leave Turkey. There is nothing wrong with the country. I just wanted to get to the United States. That was my vision.

I had been to the United States as a child. I remembered how I was welcomed and included by some kind people we had met. It was clear that freedom of speech and freedom to build the life one desires were values held dear by Americans. The United States was viewed as the land of opportunity. Having lost so much to the pressures in Iran, I craved those freedoms and those opportunities. The United

States was my destination and my new home. I had to find a way to get there.

Prior to being on my own, I had never fully grasped the value of money. I was a teenager, and I had little understanding of how long the money I had would last! I had never been responsible for paying for my living expenses. To make matters worse, I didn't understand the Turkish currency. Now, I had to learn how to handle budgets and finances and stretch my limited funds with an entirely new currency. I was drinking from a fire hose and had to learn quickly, or else I would be out of money in a new country with no one to watch out for me. What would I do if I ran out of money? Who would rescue me? Where would I live? The Turkish landlady would surely not let me stay if I didn't pay. I had to learn and learn fast.

And I did. I remembered how when I transitioned to the new school after the revolution, I felt lost. My dad reminded me then that I was no less smart or competent than anyone else. I had learned that applying myself and depending on myself had paid off in that experience. This was a much bigger scene with much higher stakes at play. But the principles were the same. I knew I could apply myself, and I knew I could make it through. I asked, studied, and applied myself. I learned the new currency and used my math skills to figure out how to spend my limited funds. Therefore, I survived.

My sister Shani, who was twenty-one at the time, was already in the United States. Ever since she was a teenager, Shani had attended boarding schools in Switzerland, followed by high school and college in the United States. As a teenager and prior to the Iranian revolution, Shani had fallen in love with Europe after a visit. In that era, many affluent families sent their children overseas to continue their education. Shani was one of those children. Her departure from Iran and her life in Europe and the United States were significantly different than mine. That being said, the changes and challenges post–regime change in Iran had negatively impacted her as well. While she was safe and secure in the United States, she had to work to make up for the disruption of financial support from my family due to the restrictions implemented by the Islamic Republic of Iran. But knowing she was in the United States was deeply comforting to me.

————

At some point, I met and befriended a Turkish cop. I naively thought he had some interest in me or was concerned about my well-being like a brother would be. Nothing romantic happened between us. But he was good at helping me find my way around Istanbul, and I grew to trust him and would go to him often for advice.

I was embarrassed and intimidated at times, but I needed to know things, and there was no other way to learn them. I needed to figure out how to take care of myself. I needed to know how to get my passport. I did not want to live in Turkey or that house. I had a clear goal: to leave Turkey and pursue my college degree in the United States. That goal mobilized me to stay the course.

One day, the Turkish cop asked me to meet up with him. We were friends, and I trusted him, so I agreed. I found the address he gave me. It was a small building with two stories. He had told me to go up to the second floor, so I climbed up the metal stairs outside the building, somewhat confused.

Where is this, and what is this? I thought. I reached the top of the stairs, found the right apartment, and knocked on the door. The cop opened the door, and I looked past him, surprised to see a room full of strange men I'd never seen before. There were a number of them in a room filled with smoke. I only took one glance but could see they were sitting on the floor and drinking and smoking.

"Come in," he said.

Startled, then scared, my instinct kicked in. This didn't look safe. Without saying anything and with no hesitation, I turned around and sped down the metal stairs without stopping—feeling that I was running for my life.

I never saw him again. Just like that, I had lost the primary person who was helping me navigate Istanbul.

Looking back, I am grateful I listened to my gut and didn't step into the apartment. I'm also grateful that I didn't let his betrayal dishearten me. He was the one friend I thought I had. It took a bit, but I quickly recognized that who he was would not define who I was or who I would become.

I took the information I'd gleaned from our friendship and combined it with everything else I had learned. I found the embassy, went there, and told them I didn't have a passport for myself because I'd come to Turkey on my mother's. I had copies of her passport, so they eventually issued me my own passport because it was clear I'd left Iran as a minor.

That process took some time, but once I got my passport, I started thinking of ways to get out of Turkey. I had an uncle in Germany who would call me occasionally and try to get me to go to Germany, but I couldn't get a visa to go. That discouraged me, but it didn't stop me. I contacted everybody and anybody I knew. I kept trying. I had limited funds and didn't know how long I was going to last where I was.

Meanwhile, my mother, who had left me in Istanbul, had found her way to the United States as she had hoped. There, she had connected with a cofounder of the gifted program I had attended in Iran. He had left Iran after the revolution but was still passionate about his legacy and what he had built. When he found out about me and that I had managed to escape, he became my advocate. He worked with a connection he had in academia and found me admission to a California college.

Once I was admitted to college and the paperwork was sent to me in Turkey, my mom left for Iran. From our separation in Istanbul until the next time we saw each other, it was a few years. I didn't see my dad for another eight years. Even after our reunions, we had limited time together. I didn't know it then, but I essentially lost my precious life and time with my parents when I left Iran.

———————

Even when we can't formulate a plan, there are events going on behind the scenes to bring us out of our impossible situation and help us realize our vision. I can't count the number of times this has happened in my life—the right person, an innocent comment or conversation, a friend who knew someone who knew someone. All of this happened because I had a vision. I've learned that in life, taking steps, steadfastly pursuing your vision, and then trusting the process works.

Admission to a US college might have seemed like a free ticket to escape Istanbul, but it was not—and I knew it. It was just the first step. I accepted the admission, and then I prepped for the interview I'd need to have at the US embassy in Turkey to get my visa.

Every Iranian I knew at the time who sought a visa to the United States was rejected. The United States had a hostile and complex relationship with the leaders in Iran. The US government did not want Iranians to enter. It was an understandable policy, but one that also seemed strange, considering that we had fled that regime because we were very much enemies of the Iranian Islamic State. It seemed like for those of us who were against the Islamic regime in Iran, there was no place to go. The rich or well-connected Iranians and those with significant investments were able to emigrate, of course, but everyone else was not welcome.

Knowing what was happening in the world, I went to the US embassy in Turkey with my recent college admission and a storyline I stuck to through the interviews. I stuck with what was authentic and genuine to me—that I desperately wanted to pursue my education.

I had been a math major in high school. My grades proved that I was a good student and that I cared about learning. Having been at risk of not being able to pursue higher education in Iran due to college closings, I knew I was going to do my very best to finish college. Because math and physics came to me naturally, I was excited about pursuing a field that allowed me to focus on my math abilities.

I walked to the US embassy with one of my new friends, a boy from the hotel. We stood in a long line for hours to wait for my turn.

Finally, someone called my name.

"Shirin Behzadi."

I walked up to what looked like a counter and stood there. In a few minutes, a short woman walked out.

"Are you Shirin Behzadi?" She said my name perfectly. "*Hale shoma chetore?*" She asked in Farsi, meaning, "How are you doing?" She was clearly fluent.

She was also clever, stern, and tough. The interviewer tried to derail me by asking about my political beliefs rather than my educational goals—perhaps to determine whether I was one of those revolutionaries who had caused the hostage crisis and other anti-American movements.

"What do you want to do in the United States?"

"What are your political beliefs?"

"What are you going to stand for?"

With every question, she stood on the other side of the counter silently, stone-faced, waiting for me to answer. She continued to press me. She displayed great expertise in keeping me off-balance by intimidating me with her stern demeanor while asking the same question in various ways to catch me in a lie.

With each question, she would remind me in some way that I was "from Iran" in a tone suggesting that I was a terrorist and a threat to the free world. I did not allow myself to get drawn into that line of thinking. That wasn't me, and I was confident that my true essence would come through. I responded, "I'm all about science and technology, and *they* don't have borders."

After a long interrogation, she realized that I was being truthful. My passion for learning resonated with her.

"Wait here," she finally said.

She walked away after the long interview, leaving me standing there motionless. Cold sweat trickled down my spine as I realized this was my one chance. Having lived on the streets of Istanbul for a while, I had encountered drugs and other dangerous situations. I had even endured cruelty from my landlady and faced hunger and poverty. I couldn't afford haircuts or new clothes, and I was probably not very clean because I couldn't take showers. But despite all this, I was intelligent, hardworking, and resourceful. I knew I could be an asset to the United States, having visited there before the revolution and having stayed for months at a time. All I wanted was an opportunity to show them what I could do and build a better life for myself. I wanted to be productive and make a difference, and the United States could give me that chance.

This woman would make a very important decision about me and the rest of my life. She should know, I figured, that I would be a useful, contributing member of US society because I knew what it was like not to have opportunities. I would seize every opportunity, and I would make her proud. She just needed to let me in.

Those were my thoughts as I stood there at the counter, nervously waiting for her to come back. I didn't allow negative thoughts to enter my mind. I was worth a chance, and I knew she knew that too. So, I expected the results I wanted.

It felt like I stood at the counter for hours, but I'm sure it wasn't that long. After the wait, she walked back to the counter. She was shorter than me, which was strange since I'm not tall. So, she looked up at me and smiled. This was an unexpected smile from someone who had been so tough in questioning me.

"Welcome to the United States," she said as she handed me the paperwork and my passport. I was stunned. I had been granted a visa. I was going to the United States! I didn't have the words or the emotions to express my relief. But I knew I'd made it. I was finally able to leave. And I was finally able to look forward to building a life.

That was Turkey for me—danger and opportunity at every turn.

With each small victory, my resilience and courage continued to grow. By the time I left for Los Angeles, I was ready for anything I thought life could possibly throw at me. Who knew that the shootings, protests, bombs, and violence I'd left in Iran would prepare me for the violence and darkness in Istanbul?

My experiences in Istanbul left their mark on me. What I would have never asked for or wished upon anyone, from loneliness to displacement to hunger and poverty with little connection, was undeniably difficult—and yet, these were valuable lessons that helped shape me. I learned to be resilient, self-reliant, and steadfast in the pursuit of the life I desired. These lessons would prepare me for a new life in LA, working behind bulletproof glass in a neighborhood almost as dangerous as the ones I'd left behind.

Looking back at everything now, I tell myself, decades later, that everything does happen for a reason, including war, betrayal, murder, and injustice. You must believe that things will change because they will. You have the power to change them.

PART TWO

The United States

CHAPTER ELEVEN

All-Night Gas Station Attendant

That realization, the expectation of a better life, the hope, and the promise of more goodness to come are the reasons I survived those days.

I HAD FINALLY MADE IT to the United States, where I would start my journey, my new life. I knew I had to find a way to support myself quickly. So, when someone mentioned that there was an opening for a gas station cashier, I jumped at the opportunity. I didn't drive yet and knew little about being a cashier, but I was eager and a fast learner, and I would be getting paid!

The gas station was in a poor and violent area—shootings, muggings, drugs. As the cashier, I stayed in a bulletproof enclosure where I would process payments. I had enough room to be comfortable and had access to a bathroom. Later, I stashed my textbooks in a drawer under the cashier's tray. I would arrive for my shift, one of my coworkers would unlock the booth, and I would run in and quickly deadbolt the lock from the inside. There I had some safety. This was definitely not Istanbul or Iran under the Revolutionary Guard, but it had its own flavor of danger. By then, I had endured so many versions of danger that I could fairly easily handle this type of threat.

Although taking money, making change, and running credit cards through a machine wasn't exactly high finance, my math skills served me well. I got a good sense of the ebb and flow of business and the practical side of money exchange: reconciling, inventory, and similar tasks. This was yet another opportunity to learn.

The tray we used to pass credit cards, cash, or the few small items we had for sale was installed under the bulletproof glass, with a small opening for the tray to pass through, enabling transactions. The tray was designed to be too small for a gun or even a gun barrel to go through.

Still, my supervisor trained me to ensure that if I put change in the drawer, I did not put my fingers in the tray to push it forward. If I did, the person on the other side could grab my fingers and not let go. That wasn't a skill I'd take with me when I moved through my career later in life, but I did learn that there are many things in this world that you don't know you don't know—and they can jump up and bite you if you aren't open to learning how new things work.

We used an intercom to talk to the different gas pump users so we didn't have to leave the secure room. We had to ensure that customers weren't pretending to have an issue to get us out of that room, so we only talked to them via the speaker. In the rare situations where I would have to go out, it was scary. I would run out and then run back in. Although muggings and robberies were common at the station, I was fortunate enough to never be a victim.

As the new girl and the youngest, I was always given the absolute worst shifts because I was at the bottom of the ladder. I worked all the major holidays and any shifts no one else was willing to do. I would get to any assigned shifts early to ensure I was there on time or before my shift started. My ability to make a living depended on being responsible and showing up on time. As I had only sporadic contact with my mom and dad since I had left Iran, I found ways to parent myself. Like a good parent, I would remind myself to be on time and do my work right. Those skills would prove valuable throughout the rest of my life.

One Christmas morning, I woke up early in the dark and drove to the bulletproof booth for my shift that started at 6 AM. Strangely for LA, the roads were empty and silent. I knocked on the door, and the night-shift worker let me in. We quickly deadbolted the door behind me. Once he counted his inventory and cash, he had me sign the card we kept for every shift change.

"Merry Christmas, Shirin. I'm going home to my family. I hope my kids aren't up yet. I want to see them open the presents," he told me with a sweet smile on his face.

"Merry Christmas. I hope you enjoy it," I replied, not quite understanding what all of that meant. I had never celebrated Christmas in the United States until that time. My usual Christmas experience involved visiting our family friends in Iran, where Mr. Hakoupian and his family would play music, enjoy food, and celebrate together. Mr. Hakoupian would usually encourage me to sing and generously shower me with gifts. I loved it.

My coworker was ready to go home for Christmas after we exchanged our cash drawers and agreed on inventory and cash balances. I unlocked our booth, let him out, and relocked it as quickly as possible.

I sat alone in the tall booth chair, my feet not touching the floor, with a bleak view before me.

The neighborhood didn't offer much solace. Bits of trash drifted down the empty streets. The gas station was at an intersection where I could see the traffic lights turn green, yellow, and red. There was another gas station across the street, a strip of rundown houses, and the freeway above us. No one seemed to be driving that morning. The sky was still pretty dark. It seemed as if the only light in the neighborhood emanated from my booth.

It doesn't really get too cold in Southern California, but as cold days go, that day had brought a chill. I sat at my desk, and my young eighteen-year-old eyes looked around in the deafening silence.

I'm sure everyone, even in the rough neighborhood where I was, was either asleep or about ready to wake up to celebrate the day. I had woken up early that morning and rushed to get to my shift, but now, I had silence.

Images of my parents, siblings, family, and friends, thousands of miles away, came rushing back. I thought of the Monday evening dinners at Khanoom Joon's. Although the air in the booth was stale, I somehow smelled the sweet smell of my grandmother's fantastic cooking. I felt the warmth of her home as my girl cousins and I were running around. I felt the noise and the giddiness of so many people talking, eating, and laughing. In my mind's eye, I could see the beautiful flowing hair of my cousin Farnaz, who encouraged me to keep growing mine. I was there. And I wasn't there.

In that moment, reality set in. I was not home. I was not near my cousins and my family. No one was cooking sweet-smelling food for me. I had no parties to go to. What would this Christmas bring beyond longing?

As the cold winter day dawned, the sun rose, bringing comfort. Time passed slowly, almost pausing as it does when you have nothing to occupy you. A few cars appeared on the street as the city was slowly waking up. I had been up for a few hours, reflecting on what I had already lost. As a young teenager, I had experienced so much loss. I had been arrested in Iran. I had learned about the execution of my first cousin. I had witnessed my best friend sentenced to ten years in jail. I had endured the bombings and the war. I had lived in a new country by myself. I knew abandonment. I had experienced abject poverty, hunger, displacement, and loneliness. So, sitting at a desk in a bulletproof booth in a rough neighborhood didn't seem all that strange.

I had spent most of the morning feeling sad and cold. As the sun showed its warmth, my heart began to warm up.

"Sad that I'm here. And fortunate that I'm here," was the epiphany I had. With all the sadness in the cold winter morning, I felt the warmth of hope.

I have made it against many odds, I thought. Sure, I was a poor gas station attendant with no parents around and little money, but I had made it out of Turkey and to the United States. I had made it!

What's going to stop me now? I thought. I felt that if I had made it this far with all the challenges and adversities, building my life from here on out would be much easier.

"I'm going to do it!" I decided. I would find my way out of there and build a meaningful life. This was not my destination, I realized. Instead, this was the beginning of a road I would travel with dignity, tenacity, and passion.

I got increasingly excited as I dreamed about where I was headed. I knew . . . I just knew that someday I would run a large company. I don't know exactly how this belief arrived. But it was a clear vision. I don't know why a poor, lonely, immigrant brown girl would think of such a vision. But I did. It was already there. I knew it was real. I knew I had it in me, and I would work relentlessly to create it.

Though it had been a day with sadness in it, it was also a day with reflection. I realized that I'd had a good life and would see to it that I would have an even better one moving forward. That realization, the expectation of a better life, the hope, and the promise of more goodness to come are the reasons I survived those days. They are also why I endured being without parents, money, and help. I felt like I was the only one who could help myself. Years of messaging from the Islamic regime in Iran that I would have to sit in a corner and disappear were echoing in the background to defeat me. But I knew better. I knew that I had already endured chaos, cruelty, imprisonment, war, displacement, abandonment, poverty, and loss. I was grateful to have survived it all. I was thankful for the small but crucial support I had received from strangers. My belief in the goodness of people was unshaken.

There was no reason to believe I couldn't build the life I desired. I had become sturdy and was not easily broken. That meant that I was ready, willing, and capable of building the life I dreamed of. And there was no reason I shouldn't expect it: not being poor, not being alone, not being an immigrant, not being any other adjective that others would consider less than ideal. I was not going to break. And I had proven I wasn't. I was going to run a big company someday. And I would build a life I would be proud of someday. People might take me for granted, being a brown immigrant woman working at a gas station behind bulletproof glass, but I wasn't going to. I would believe, expect, and become who I was destined to become. I would do it with heart and with regard for others. I knew what it was like to be dismissed. I wouldn't dismiss others, and I wouldn't dismiss myself. World . . . I was coming to claim my place.

The wound is where the light comes in. And I had plenty of wounds to light up my life.

Within a few months, I finally bought a car, an ancient, dinged-up yellow Toyota Corolla. I bought it for only $300, so it wasn't that valuable to anyone else. Even so, I would park it right by the door of the bulletproof booth and keep an eye on it. When I started college, I would bring my textbooks to the gas station and study in between customers. The only way I could go to school full-time and still make money was to take all my courses over two full days. The rest of the time, I had to work. I would take my textbooks wherever I was and study.

One day, someone came by the cashier's window to pay to pump gas. He asked, "What are you studying?" pointing at my textbook in front of me.

"Calculus," I said, smiling.

"That sounds hard. What do you want to do when you grow up?" he asked.

Without hesitation, I looked straight at him and said, "I'll run a big company like General Motors."

He raised his eyebrows with an expression of both surprise and delight. "Good luck!"

I've often wondered how it was that a poor immigrant girl from Iran working at a gas station behind bulletproof glass would think that way. By then, I'd had more time to live with my vision. That vision mobilized me and helped motivate me through those tough days. It would also energize and excite me while I worked and studied.

One day, during the quiet time of the holiday season, a man drove up to a gas pump in a beat-up car. There was a little girl, about five or six years old, in the passenger seat. The man approached the booth and told me, "I've run out of gas and have no cash to pay. I have to take my little girl home to her mother. Can you help me?"

I thought to myself, *Me? Can you find someone poorer than me?* I didn't have enough money to pay my rent. I was eighteen years old, and for my eighteenth birthday, the only "gift" I'd received was a mug! I had not bought clothes since leaving Iran. I was a teenager who wanted to look good and be relevant like any other teenager, and yet, I didn't have money to buy new clothes. And here this man was, asking me for help.

I thought for a moment, then looked at the little girl.

"I promise I'll come tomorrow and pay you back," the man pleaded. "I just don't have cash on me now."

"Okay," I said. "I'll put my own money in the cash register because I can't be short. I would be fired. I'll put in ten dollars."

"Thank you. I'll be back." He pumped his gas and left.

He never came back. My good deed came out of empathy for his daughter. I didn't believe the man's story of having just run out of cash or that he had to take his daughter somewhere. He struck me as a liar even as he was asking me for help. In my eighteen years of life, I had already seen so much, and I could understand people well. I knew he was lying and that losing that ten dollars meant losing another lunch for me, but I did it anyway. And I would do it again if it happened again, except now, I would find more effective ways to help.

My passion for doing good for others was already in my DNA, and it was never for the reward or payback. It was always around the deed itself. I wanted and hoped that the little girl could find the safety of having a car with gas taking her to her destination. I hope she understood that another girl, not much bigger than she was, had given up her lunch money for her.

Chapter Twelve

Finding My Way

I believe our ability to bring lightness and joy to our hard days
was the reason we made it through and eventually thrived.

Working full-time to pay for my living expenses and tuition while attending college didn't quite pay the bills. So, I decided to apply for any financial assistance available to a California resident.

Because my GPA was high and I was working full-time, I received enough scholarships to pay for half of my tuition. I was golden!

Well, not quite. I had gone years without a friend, a true peer, a BFF, with whom to share dreams, challenges, adjustments, and fun adventures (not that I had any idea what those might be). But that was about to change.

I had been used to a busy and warm home life growing up. And I was fortunate that my sister Shani and her roommates had created a warm environment at home in our little LA apartment. Over time, my aunt and uncle and their families also immigrated to areas near LA, and my sweet cousin Niloo, with whom I had grown up, was now not too far from me. I had a few family members who made life feel more like home. But I still didn't have any friends . . . until I met Rozita.

Our meeting was serendipitous. Working and going to college classes full-time didn't leave much time for studying. Studying was especially challenging in a home filled with people. So, I often stayed at school and studied in the study hall between and after my classes.

One day, after a long study session, I walked out of the study hall and into a break area where students sat around and socialized. This break area was adjacent to the computer room, where we could use campus computers for studying, writing papers, or programming practice. Often, it was mostly occupied by students in the science, technology, engineering, and mathematics (STEM) fields.

I saw a thick zoology book on the table next to a couple of girls and declared, "I don't envy anyone who has to study this thick book!" Rozita turned to me and smiled her beautiful smile, "I know . . . it's mine." And just like that, we connected—a serendipitous connection that took us through the rest of our lives.

Rozita became my touchstone, a sister, and extended family. She was also Persian but had been here with her family for years. While I maintained a relatively active social life on the weekends with some of my cousins who had immigrated, Rozita became a significant part of my life, a constant presence.

Doing well in college and emboldened by my new friend, I decided, at some wildly exuberant moment, to have business cards made up with my name and "Investment Advisor" as my title. I didn't have the money to justify making the cards, but I did it anyway. And I handed them out to everyone, including Rozita.

Rozita had fair skin with black eyes and hair. I wasn't tall, but compared to her, I was. I had short hair while she had long hair. She had a curvy figure, and I was thin. Externally, we looked very different, with different styles. My style was edgier, and she was a girly girl. She always wore high heels and skirts, and I was a pants girl. She was pretty—very pretty. And she was also funny and clumsy. Rozita could easily trip and fall, even walking on a straight path or a clear carpet. Her clumsiness was truly endearing.

She loved to dance and laugh, so we listened to music and danced and laughed a lot. We were both immigrants, struggling financially and dreaming that things would improve for us both. It didn't make sense how happy we were together. And yet, maybe it does make sense. I believe our ability to bring lightness and joy to our hard days was the reason we made it through and eventually thrived.

Because I attended a commuter school, I didn't participate in college life much. I simply didn't have the time. I also didn't think I would fit in well. A newly immigrated Iranian woman wasn't exactly on top of others' lists of the coolest people to hang out with. However, having a keen interest in people and genuine connections, I made a few friends, although Rozita became my closest one.

While many college students and people we knew were bonding or commiserating over their clubs, alcohol, and lifestyles, Rozita and I bonded over Diet Pepsi and being broke. Even though she had way more money than I did, she was still not financially secure. I was lucky to find somebody close to me who shared many of my challenges.

During our early college years, Rozita worked as a waitress. When I landed an office job toward the end of our college career, I also found her a position in the same office. I would drive us to work and back, and we spent much more time together. We were inseparable.

We couldn't afford to go to most places, so when we decided to go on a trip, we picked Las Vegas.

"Are you guys crazy?" her mom asked, raising her eyebrows. "You don't have money to stay at a hotel. You don't have money to gamble. You can't drink. You can barely afford gas. Why go there?"

We told her we just wanted to see what Vegas was like and planned to spend one night there.

"We'll figure it out," Rozita said, begging for her mom's approval. "Shirin is a good driver," she added as if to help her cause.

"Are you kidding me? You're planning on driving to Vegas in Shirin's beat-up car?"

But eventually, she smiled and approved. She knew us well and was sure that we would find a way to enjoy ourselves and be safe.

We climbed into my beat-up Toyota, turned on our favorite radio station, rolled down the windows, and took off on our road trip. With no air conditioning in the car, we embraced the hot wind in our faces as we sang our songs out loud. We had our Diet Pepsis, and the world was our oyster. In hindsight, we were happier than many ultra-wealthy people I've met since.

We couldn't afford to spend the night anywhere, so we just stayed up all night walking around. Whenever we got too tired, we would go to a lounge or sit in the ladies' room to rest. Vegas hotels' ladies' rooms were some of the most luxurious places to sit around. We had found a way to enjoy the small things in life and were prepared to do so thoroughly. That trip was one of the best times I've ever had, in Vegas or anywhere else.

I love my biological sisters, and I'm very close to them, but Rozita and I shared a different kind of sisterhood. We were the same age and going through the same phase of life. She was either over at my house multiple times a week, or I was over at hers. We chose each other as friends and sisters to the end.

I was blessed to have her in my life at a very critical time for us both. Not a lot of people could understand our plight.

We were both math majors. I entered college as a math major, hoping to switch to engineering. At the time, freshmen from outside the United States were not admitted into engineering, but I wanted to be a software engineer.

I attended a state school because I couldn't afford more expensive colleges and because the school I was attending had a good reputation for its academic rigor. However, since it was a state school, we had to live with the State of California's rules. California wasn't exactly overwhelmed with STEM students at the time, but the administrators still wouldn't let me into the program as a first-year student. They told me to start as a math major and that I could apply to switch over to engineering later.

Regardless, I was killing it in math—making perfect scores, as in 100 percent across the board. Thanks to Iran's more advanced math program and academics, plus the school for advanced students that I'd attended, I was far ahead.

"I swear . . . I don't know how you get 100 percent every time. You're the only girl in the class. And you're not even Asian! If you set the curve one more time, I'm gonna scream," a funny Asian guy who sat behind me almost every class told me after one of our exams in our upper-division math course. He tapped me on my shoulder jokingly, lightly, but also seriously, to complain about how I was setting the curve very high in our class of fifty. With the number of math classes I took and aced, I could have easily finished as a math major. But I had my sights set on software engineering. I diligently followed the requirements to transfer into a different program in my sophomore year. I had not only taken on math but had also achieved the highest grades across the board. So, as instructed, I applied to electrical engineering in my next year of college.

My grades were excellent, and I had met all the requirements for transferring to electrical engineering. However, I soon discovered that all this was irrelevant to the college administrators, as they were not going to let me in. They didn't need a reason except that I was a foreign student. I begged them. I pleaded. I had recommendation letters from every professor I'd ever had and from deans of different schools, but they still wouldn't let me transfer into electrical engineering.

I had one of three choices to make. I could stay as a math major, switch to another major besides engineering, or quit. And I'm not a quitter. I thought, *Well, a math major isn't going to do me any good.* I wanted to be in business, grow a business, and someday run a big company. I decided that it would be best if I learned the language of business, so I switched my major to accounting.

Looking back, I'm convinced that pursuing my accounting degree set me up for eventual success. What looked like a major setback when I wasn't allowed to become an electrical engineer became a truly good thing that happened to me. It just didn't seem like it then. That's how true resilience is built, I learned. Not through avoiding challenges and adversities, but through embracing them and overcoming them with hope and the expectation of a positive outcome.

When I started accounting, I wondered, *Are you kidding me? This isn't that hard.* Soon, however, I realized that much of what I was learning was about how businesses operate. Accounting proved to be, indeed, the language of business. And I enjoyed it.

Rozita graduated as a math major. She ultimately got an engineering position. We'd talked about working together as engineers, but our paths took different directions.

Before we graduated, we decided to take another trip, this time to Northern California. We had a place to stay at our family friend's house, and a friend from elementary school in Iran had just moved up there. This was going to be our graduation gift to ourselves. With the little money we had, we packed into my same little Toyota. We still remembered the sweet taste of our one-day adventure to Vegas, our only trip during college. In San Francisco, we visited every touristy spot that wasn't expensive. We screamed, got scared, and laughed at driving the steep streets of San Francisco with a stick shift in a car with a weak engine. We were lucky we didn't roll backward!

One day, we parked the car to walk around Lombard Street, and when we got back, someone had completely smashed the driver's side of the car. It was so bad that I couldn't open the door to get in.

Whoever hit the car didn't leave a note to take responsibility. I was heartbroken and sad at the state of my beloved car, and I wondered how I was going to get it fixed. But after the initial surprise, I looked at Rozita, shrugged my shoulders, and laughed. I mean, it was almost comical. With everything I had already experienced in life, this was nothing.

Rather than fret or lose hope, I entered the passenger side, crawled over the stick shift, and sat in the driver's seat. I decided that the hit-and-run incident would not ruin my experience. And it didn't. San Francisco gave us lots of beautiful memories. Had it not been for the hit-and-run, we wouldn't have had that experience to laugh about it later in life. We drove all the way home with the driver's side not opening; at every stop, I would get back in by crawling over the center console. And we found the humor in that. That was fun!

A close relationship like what Rozita and I had doesn't just go away. You may not see each other as much, but you still feel like that's your buddy, your go-to friend. Whenever I experienced any kind of milestone in my life, she was always the first one I went to, and she did the same.

We often laughed, whispered, and shared secrets as friends. Rozita was my biggest fan. She always made me feel smart and competent. She believed in me and let me be who I was. It was always comfortable, genuine, and loving with her.

Rozita got married before I did, when she was twenty-two and I was twenty-one. Being still young, we had little money to spend on her wedding.

She took me to look at the dress a family friend was tailoring for her. It was a mermaid style, just what she wanted. Her short, curvy body fit perfectly into the lace dress.

"Do you like it?" she asked me with a sparkle in her eye.

"I love it!" I declared. It wasn't a dress that I would ever wear, but it suited her style and taste beautifully. She was a beautiful, young, hopeful girl, and this dress presented all of that well.

As we approached the wedding day, we knew we had to have some decorations. So, her sisters and I created the table decorations and flowers for the wedding ourselves.

On her wedding day, I helped her get ready. A friend did her hair and makeup and helped her put on her press-on nails, and we had a little beauty time between us.

It's what you do for a girlfriend, someone so close and dear to your heart. You do it because you're soul sisters.

Her wedding was another milestone, joyous in many ways, but sad in that it marked a time when we were parting ways to pursue our own lives.

Chapter Thirteen

A Place of My Own

Those years and experiences taught me how to assess situations and people's states and respond tactfully, timely, and with care. These lessons provided me with skills that were advantageous throughout the rest of my life.

COMING TO A NEW COUNTRY to make a life involves many fundamental transitions to find economic, social, and community connections. You have to go back to the basics. I was fortunate to have a family, education, and a best friend. Finding secure and comfortable housing took longer.

My first residence in LA was at my sister Shani's place with her roommates. I had a room and a hand-me-down alarm clock that was also a radio. That was my only possession except for the small amount of clothes I had with me. At this home with Shani and her roommates, there were four women with lots of differences in personalities. It was funny, beautiful chaos.

At first, Shani would drive me to my job at the gas station, but she finally got tired of it. "Just take the bus!" she told me. She was a young twenty-one-year-old herself.

I was new to the United States and didn't know the bus system. But how bad could it be? I looked up the schedule and set out to find my way from our home to Pomona, where the gas station was. Southern California is not known for its public transportation, and I soon learned why.

The first bus I took dropped us off at the station, where I would have to connect to another bus. I was stunned when I stepped out of the bus at the station. It was like a scene out of a scary movie. There were railroad tracks and very little civilization in sight. I did not know where I was or how to reach my destination. After waiting for what felt like an eternity for my connection in the sweltering heat, I started walking. I had a vague sense of the direction I needed to head in. As I gradually made my way, the sight of some homes finally came into view. Walking through those unfamiliar streets as an eighteen-year-old girl was a fear-filled experience. This was not the neighborhood you'd want to find yourself in, especially as a young girl, and the desolation only added to the sense of unease. With no cell phone or GPS to rely on, I decided to ask for directions. This proved to be a mistake, as the first guy I asked was not wearing underwear under his coat! This was my cue to start running, and run I did until I found myself on a familiar street, from which I now knew how to get to the gas station. My quick response had saved me again.

The bus ride back home took one and a half hours. When I got home, Shani was horrified.

"Where were you? What happened?" she asked.

To make matters worse, it was the day of our Persian New Year. The table was set, and I was supposed to celebrate the first day of spring.

After I told her of my ordeal, we both chuckled nervously.

"Yikes. That could have been really bad. Let's not do this again. I'll give you rides until we can find a way to buy you a car," she said.

This was when we started looking for a cheap car, and I had to learn to drive.

After my brother, his wife, and three kids arrived in the United States, Shani and her roommates moved out of the home, and my brother and his family moved in. I remained in one of the rooms. As immigrants, especially those fleeing places in disarray like Iran, you do any work that you can get. My brother and his wife were both architects in Iran. But they certainly couldn't do that work as new immigrants.

Then, my middle sister, Shirana, made it to the United States—a true miracle. We don't know how and why she was given a visa to enter, but we're so grateful she was. Shirana had already saved my life in Iran when we were arrested for the "crime" of owning a book. Shirana is the friendliest and kindest of us all. She had lived in the United States before the revolution and returned to Iran because she was worried about her family. She was then stuck. But when she returned to the United States, her prior experience in America helped her transition well into an office job. She was six years older than me and ended up renting a small apartment with one bedroom and took me in. She never let me pay rent—though she didn't have much herself. I was happy and grateful. I still had to work full-time, but now I could study more. Shirana saved me once more . . . an experience that was repeated years later.

We were invited to the wedding of a friend of Shani's, where Shirana met Kami. They bonded quickly and, before you knew it, were engaged. When Shirana moved out of our shared apartment, I knew I had to move out soon too. I couldn't afford the rent by myself, and the Iranian culture of the time didn't look fondly on a girl living alone.

My sister Sherry and her husband, Reza, finally arrived in LA with their two kids. They were married before the revolution and enjoyed a comfortable life in Iran, with Reza as a sales manager and Sherry as a banker. However, they left it all behind because they saw no future for their children in Iran. Like any new immigrant to the United States, they took on jobs and did whatever they could to support their families. Knowing that I needed a place to stay, they offered to let me live with them. I was to contribute to the household and share a room with my niece and nephew in a small apartment that housed all of us.

I had been without a permanent place to live or a room to myself for years. Navigating living with various family members requires understanding the complex dynamics of people and relationships. Although I knew these people, I had never lived with them as an addition to their families. And to make matters more challenging, the stress and anxiety levels were very high for everyone, as we were all navigating new lives. Those years and those experiences taught me how to assess situations and people's states and respond to them tactfully, timely, and with care.

By the time I was twenty-one, I had moved around and lived in many places. I was ready and eager to find and create my own home. This is when I met a young Iranian man, Reza, who was finishing his master's in software engineering and who had also fled Iran and was living with his aunt. Our traumas and displacements connected us, and we quickly decided to set up a home together. In a short period of time after meeting, we were married. I felt like I finally had a new home of my own.

My journey from Iran to the United States was difficult, but caring individuals showed me kindness and assistance. When I faced a severe toothache, I decided to visit a free clinic, which turned out to be the office of a practicing dentist who generously provided services to people like me. He treated me with care and shared stories about his family, making me feel comfortable during the appointment. I don't know why he decided to provide these free services, but I'm grateful he did. He fixed my teeth and found a small growth on the roof of my mouth. Even though he must not have been paid much for his work, the dentist genuinely cared for me. I also received help from other doctors under the same program. One of the directors explained that the doctors offered help because they wanted to care for each other and help people in need. This experience inspired me to commit to helping others and to pay it forward. Living without a permanent place and navigating complex family dynamics are extraordinarily challenging. Perhaps none of us can fully understand how small acts of kindness ripple forth to heal us unexpectedly.

CHAPTER FOURTEEN

Discovering My Vision and Upholding My Values

I set out to become the best, most focused, and most valued member of my professional team. I had already expected that treating people with genuine regard would bring out the best in them. Having experienced it, it became my guiding principle. This approach paid off throughout the rest of my career, both professionally and personally.

CAL POLY IS NOT KNOWN for its business school, and that's a shame because we had many good professors and dedicated students. I had decided that if I were to be an accountant, I would shoot for the highest license I could get: certified public accountant (CPA). It's funny how life comes together—my dad had also started his business career as an accountant, though not a CPA. I hoped and believed that this path would take me to my goal of running a big company.

To earn a CPA license, one would have to pass a rigorous, multiday exam followed by hundreds of hours of specific experiences in areas of the field as certified by a qualified company. I soon discovered that my years of studying accounting in college had only set the stage to take the CPA exam but did not prepare me for the test.

I visited the career office one day during my junior year. The career counselor told me, "Unfortunately, the Big Eight accounting firms don't really recruit from our school."

I asked, "How can I improve my chances?"

"You can meet the recruiters or apply for an internship," she responded. "But I have to warn you that internships are even harder to get than full-time jobs."

That small glimmer of hope—an internship—mobilized me. I resolved to get an internship somewhere. I researched, connected, and used any resources I had to prepare my résumé for the best success.

My hard work paid off. Ernst and Young (EY) invited me for an internship in the winter quarter. It felt like finding a new home. After gaining confidence and experience as an intern at EY, I aced all my full-time job interviews and received offers from all the Big Eight accounting firms. It was a great achievement for me!

Joining EY was the best fit for me due to my experience with the firm and alignment with its culture. I started as a new staff member and worked toward my CPA, which I passed with flying colors. Sitting there with my starting group at the downtown LA offices of

Ernst & Young was unbelievable. Looking around the room at these fantastic newly graduated students from reputable schools with lots of talent, ambition, and capabilities was awe inspiring. Little did they know that only a few years before, I had been working at a gas station. Little did they all know that, years later, they would be serving me and my company as a multimillion-dollar client.

Feeling excited and proud, it hit me that all those years of continuing to pursue my degree, with all the hardship and hard work, had earned me this place at this wonderful, well-respected organization.

Soon, I learned that there were specialized groups within the audit practice: health care, financials, and technology. I'm not sure why, but I gravitated toward the financial group. I asked around and was told that it wouldn't be up to me which group I would be assigned to and that as a new staff member, I would move around naturally.

Ask for the toughest, most rigorous assignments, Shirin, a voice in my head urged me. I remembered all those years when people had told me that I couldn't accomplish at high levels, when school and government officials had spread the message to both me and the culture at large that an Iranian woman should not be heard or seen. I felt that the message was wrong. People have different gifts, and allowing them to express them makes for happier people and better communities. Though I would struggle with the lasting damage those messages caused in my psyche, I had lots of excitement about the ability to learn. The challenging, long hours of work at EY felt like my playground. I loved the intellectual exchanges and learning about businesses from the inside out.

Perhaps it was my persistent and expressed interest; maybe it was the energy I put out. Perhaps it was luck; perhaps it was a combination of all these factors that eventually led to me being assigned to the financial services group. We took on large clients and worked outrageous hours—sometimes through the night. With Los Angeles being so geographically expansive, I sometimes drove two and a half hours each way to our big client. And then I would put in endless hours there. I worked so hard that I started having significant wrist pain. *Oh no*, I thought, *is my rheumatoid arthritis back?*

As a child, I'd had lots of joint pain. Looking back, and now having learned about trauma, it makes sense that I had developed and been diagnosed with juvenile rheumatoid arthritis. It's now known that an autoimmune response is one of the manifestations of trauma response in the human body.

I had this condition from the age of eight until I left Iran at seventeen. It looked like now that I was safe, it was returning with a vengeance. But I wasn't going to be stopped. This was my chance to build a good life—and I would pursue it regardless of the pain. I know in our current era that this wasn't a healthy response. But at the time, I was recovering from years of poverty and displacement. Once I had the opportunity to build a life, I was going to go at it with all I had.

I would put my wrists in wrist guards and show up to the client early in the mornings after a two-and-a-half-hour drive. The senior manager on the job noticed the wrist guards and inquired. I told him they just hurt. In his inquiry, he learned about my long drive and raised his eyebrows with surprise.

"We're not doing that anymore. We will get you a hotel room during the week. You'll stay near your job and go home over the weekend. The company will pay for your hotel stay and your meals. You don't have to suffer like this," he said with kindness in his eyes.

I was shocked, elated, touched, and emotional. Not only was this new plan a relief, but it proved that I mattered and was valued. I was committed to honorably appreciate the attention and care shown to me. I set out to become the best, most focused, and most valued member of my professional team. I had already expected that treating people with genuine regard would bring out the best in them. Having experienced it, it became my guiding principle. This approach paid off throughout the rest of my career, both professionally and personally.

I was twenty-six years old, married, and a CPA working on banking jobs for EY all around Southern California. I was working and connecting with executives at some of the most respected companies in the world—but I was worried. The track before me didn't look like what I wanted. I desired a life that included running a large company *and* having a family. If I stayed as an auditor, neither of those desires would be fulfilled as I had planned.

A couple of years before I joined EY and before I graduated college, I had married a twenty-five-year-old man who had also fled Iran. I was ready to set up a family. Maybe it was because I had strong parents. Or maybe it was because I had lost the presence of my parents so early in life. But I knew that if I were to have children, I wanted to be engaged and involved with them. I wanted to work hard but with flexible hours to be present as my children grew. Unfortunately, this approach and the possibility of working flexible hours were unavailable back then, and certainly not at a large accounting firm.

To top it off, accounting firms had few women partners at the time. It didn't look like there were many opportunities to become one—at least not without sacrificing everything, including having a family.

My vision was to run a large company someday. I didn't know what my path would look like. But I believed I had to understand operations. My continued growth as an auditor would not have made me an experienced operator.

I had a decision to make. I was finally at a solid company with a reliable path to success. I was liked and valued. But it was time to move on. Time to pursue my vision of running a large company while staying true to my values. If I were to be a mother, I would have to make a change.

Sitting in my car during a break from a banking audit job, I realized that my time at EY was ending. What a tough decision to make!

My sadness turned into sobbing while sitting in that car. No one was forcing the decision, but it was what I knew I had to do.

As it works when you make a decision, an opportunity came to me while sitting in my cubicle at the new Orange County, California, office I had recently transferred to. It was a client of EY's that was looking for someone with an understanding of banking who could run their loan servicing department. Because it was a client that had brought the opportunity to us, I was able to openly discuss it within the firm. Walking into a partner's office, I asked about The Hammond Company, The Mortgage Bankers.

"Tom Hammond, the CEO, is an intelligent and intellectual individual. He is a wonderful client, and you would love working with him," the partner endorsed.

My job interview at Tom's office was scheduled after my interview with his chief operating officer (COO), a woman who had recently joined them from a large bank. Sizing me up toward the end of the interview, she asked, "Can you be tough?"

"I wouldn't consider myself tough. I am assertive," I said.

She smiled; apparently, I had passed her test.

Tom's office was exactly as I would have expected. A spacious office with mahogany bookshelves at the back-end wall, with a beautiful seating area of luxurious fabric and dark wood trim. His office had huge windows and two large monitors facing the door that showed stock market tickers. They were creating mortgage-backed securities of loans the company originated, and they would sell them in secondary markets.

Tom was a tall gentleman with piercing, inquisitive, and intelligent eyes. Although his company, which bore his name, was growing very fast, and although he was the president of the Mortgage Bankers Association, he was attentive and respectful to the twenty-six-year-old me. I liked him from the moment I met him. Years of adversity had taught me how to gauge people quickly, and I knew he was a leader I could trust.

Having left my home and family earlier, I would become emotional whenever people left the companies where I worked. I was puzzled by those feelings, but I understand now. Leaving what had become somewhat of a home for me at EY was exceptionally hard. That sorrow was only mitigated by the thought of what I was now looking forward to: The Hammond Company (THC).

Loan servicing has various functional areas. At THC, we had scores of customer service folks who took and screened customer calls all day. We also had loan delinquency and foreclosure groups, loss mitigation, real estate owned, and others. The company grew rapidly, originating hundreds of millions of dollars of loans per month and maintaining over one billion dollars' worth of loans to service. It was a busy time.

Soon after I arrived, I was in charge of parts of the department. An older woman named Holly managed it all, and I reported to her. She was a friendly, wonderful woman—and a bit of a mother figure to everyone. Partially because of that maternal approach and partially because of the fast pace of growth, it was clear that the department lacked proper organization.

"Would you be open to me reviewing the department and documenting our processes? It's the best way to detect holes and areas of improvement. I did this many times as an auditor at EY," I told Holly.

Since she genuinely cared about the company and her department, she approved and supported my project. I was off to the races.

As companies grow, operations often fall behind. Processes and procedures implemented to ensure proper organization are changed, forgotten, or not done right—often unintentionally. I learned this while working on the project at THC.

Staying late most days to map the department after hours, I learned about the weaknesses in the processes and structures. It was time to fix them. The question was how to implement improvements while employees were already working at their capacity to keep up with growth.

I was eager to learn how to accomplish this. I had left EY to run a big company someday, and implementing change and improvement would be par for running a company. So, I knew I would have to find a way.

Chapter Fifteen

If You Don't Have a Solution, Redefine the Problem

I adjusted my view of the problem. As a new manager, I was trying to change many ways of doing the work without the buy-in from the people who had to do the actual work. It made sense to engage and include them in solving the problem rather than solving it for them. They had to buy into the plan.

ALL THOSE YEARS OF SELF-RELIANCE had taught me that I could solve problems. But no matter how much I thought about the problem of implementing improvements while continuing to grow and engage the teams already stretched thin, I couldn't find the solution. I was focused on a core principle in my life: doing the right thing. But what was it?

I'm looking at the problem wrong! I woke up to this thought. I learned then and have used that lesson throughout my life: Every problem has a solution. If you haven't found a solution, you may not have defined the problem correctly.

I adjusted my view of the problem. As a new manager, I was trying to change many ways of doing the work without the buy-in from the people who had to do the actual work. It made sense to engage and include them in solving the problem rather than solving it for them. They had to buy into the plan.

With Holly's help and approval, I gathered groups within the department to discuss processes and procedures. Having prepared in advance, I guided the conversations to ensure that team members were included and engaged. This exercise took an hour or two from each group's work, but the results were well worth it. Everyone felt heard, and some of the solutions they came up with were even better than what I had initially figured out. It was time to implement change, and we wanted everyone to be aware and be part of the solution. However, some motivation was still lacking. I realized that overall teamwork was weak.

"Let's do some activities that help people bond," I suggested to Holly.

As busy as everyone was, they welcomed our bonding efforts. Once a week, during lunch, we would do activities together. We kicked it off with funny mock Academy Awards with certificates describing each person's strengths and good characteristics. From there, we would take ideas from the team, and we enjoyed many experiences together. Having been an outsider for many of my formidable years, I knew the best motivator for people was to have them be included and seen.

This new approach worked. Our department made fantastic, measured improvements in results and morale in a short time. Despite our fast growth, our performance didn't miss a beat.

As we settled in with our new processes, interest rates rose, and there were concerns about their continued climb. As mortgage lenders, our business was susceptible to interest rate changes. We had to react quickly and effectively. Tom had to make some tough decisions and cut some costs.

One day, Holly came into my office with a calm but concerned look. She informed me that she had been laid off and that I would have to take on her role on top of mine.

I had only known her for a year, but I liked Holly. I went into Tom's office to hear the news from him directly.

"I would like to ask if we can keep Holly as a consultant for some time," I asked Tom.

He agreed. I knew Holly was a reasonable and solid person, but I also knew it would be hard for her to move on. So, I suggested that she stay on as long as she wanted as a consultant and that she keep her office.

"I don't need a new office, Holly. It's yours," I told her.

She loved it and stayed for another year. She enjoyed her office the entire time while I remained in mine. We worked well together and, in collaboration, continued to run the department. I accepted responsibility for that section of the business and learned a lot from the experience.

———————

Jon was our chief financial officer (CFO). He was sharp, experienced, and well educated. Jim, our controller, headed the accounting department, which was made up of a crew of CPAs, most of them with Big Eight accounting experience.

Jon took me to lunch one day.

"I have some news that I would like to keep confidential until it's announced. I'm leaving the company for another position. I've seen your work and your ability to organize your department. I think you'd make a good CFO," he said.

A CFO? Although I knew I had the competence to step into the role, I was still only twenty-eight years old, and many great accountants were ahead of me in the company's accounting department.

"I can do it. I can learn and apply myself. I know I'm able," I told a family member.

"No. This is too dangerous. There are so many people in the accounting department. Tom will say no, and you'll have many enemies at work," they said.

I realized that people were offering me advice based on their own limitations. I had no reason to be afraid—I was just going to note that I was interested in the position. It wasn't an ask against anyone. It was an opportunity to let Tom know about my interest.

To complicate matters, however, I was pregnant. I had not yet met a female CFO. It's incredible how the landscape of companies has changed in the past decades. But back in the late nineties, we didn't see a lot of women in C-positions. And I certainly had never seen a pregnant CFO. But if anyone was going to be open-minded, it would be Tom.

I decided on a principle I've carried with me since. You can hear people out, but you don't have to take their words to heart. So, I didn't. I decided to pursue the position with Tom.

"I think we both know that I can make a good CFO at this company," I explained to Tom.

"I agree!" he said.

I became the CFO of a relatively large mortgage bank with twenty-two branches and over one billion dollars in servicing when I was twenty-eight and pregnant. Jim and the accounting department celebrated my promotion, and we had a wonderful working relationship for the rest of our careers at THC.

I had to learn, and I had to learn fast. Every resource, experience, and hour I had was dedicated to being the best CFO I could be. I appreciated the opportunity and Tom and the company's confidence in me. I was not going to let them down.

When interest rates rose sharply and quickly again due to the Federal Reserve rate hikes, the bottom fell out for the company. As with most mortgage banks, we experienced a sudden drop in business. We knew we had to do something relatively quickly. After a thoughtful assessment of the market and our ability to generate business in the challenging environment, we realized that the best outcome would be to sell the company to a larger bank. By design, we had a limited product offering: home mortgages. When interest rates rose suddenly, the demand for mortgages dropped fast. A financial institution with a menu of products could weather the storm much better than we could. So, we decided it would be best for our mortgage holders and employees to find a new home. I was reminded once more of the lesson I had learned years ago. Every problem has a solution. If you haven't found the solution, you may have to redefine the problem.

Tom agreed and set out to sell the company. We started the process with a larger bank. While running the company, seemingly in a free fall, we underwent a rigorous due diligence process. As CFO, I was responsible for negotiating the best terms for the company and overseeing the smooth transition of our loans to this larger bank.

After a few years of growth for the company and me as a professional, it was time to say goodbye to THC. I had my son while I was there, and Tom allowed me to work flexible hours while my baby was a newborn. Tom was very much ahead of his time. The partner at EY was right. He was an intelligent, intellectual man, and his open-minded approach to allowing me and others to grow was a gift. I am and will forever be grateful for his presence in my life. The experience at THC taught me how treating people well and allowing them to blossom with their talents can be productive and create a rewarding environment. I cherished those years and those lessons. Thank you, Tom.

My career journey, from finding a position with my dream company to leaving it and creating opportunities at another, proved that you can pursue your higher goals. The key is to earn better positions by wholeheartedly applying yourself to them and asking for what you believe is reflective of your value.

Chapter Sixteen

Losing Rozita

Life, as stressful as it could be in college, was always fun with Rozita, always an adventure. With her, I learned not to take things I couldn't change too seriously. Be in the moment. Be grateful for what you have without losing the vision of where you're going. Make things happen where you can.

I missed the days we shared in college, but I assumed it was just age, marital responsibilities, and career opportunities that slowed us down as we got older.

Rozita married a man she barely knew. He was tall and handsome and swept her off her feet. I met Reza, her husband, at a quaint coffee shop on a rainy afternoon. As he walked in, a chill ran down my spine, and I couldn't shake it off. At twenty-one, I was still learning to trust my instincts, and something about him just didn't sit right with me.

When Rozita shared her decision to marry Reza after a brief six-month courtship, I couldn't help but feel a wave of unease. Naturally, I only wanted the absolute best for her, and this sudden development left me deeply unsettled. "I think she's making a mistake," I uttered to our coworkers at the office where she and I worked for a short time before college was over. I don't know where I found those words or how I found the courage to say them.

After her wedding, Rozita gradually stopped coming to our social events. She didn't call me as often. Although she attended my wedding a year after hers, she didn't participate in my pre-wedding plans. I was puzzled and heartbroken but assumed she was adjusting.

———

About four years after she was married and when we were both working, I realized things were just not right. By then, I was working at
EY with a very busy schedule, but I would consistently call her to
check on her. One day, I realized that she had not called me at all the
previous year. Sure, she was taking my calls, but she was never calling
me first. She had also found excuses not to attend any gatherings I
would invite her to. I thought that she didn't want to connect with me
anymore. I had given my all, so I figured it was time to stop bugging
her with my persistence. I had to stop calling her.

With a heavy heart, I would intentionally stop myself from dialing her phone. I would think of her and send her loving wishes. I
wished my friend would come back.

A month passed, and suddenly, I had a call from Rozita.

"Can I come to visit you?" she asked.

"Of course! I would love nothing more," I replied, feeling both
excited and worried.

She came over and broke the news that she was leaving her husband. She told me stories of how systematically and gradually she was
being cut off from the world by her husband. Sadly, she had not contacted her family—her mom, sisters, and brothers—for over a year
because Reza wouldn't let her.

She was a young, smart, beautiful girl with a loving family that
had been through so much together. And she had been forced to dis-
connect with them. This was emotional abuse.

"You were the last person to keep in contact with me because you
were so persistent. When your calls stopped, I realized I had to save
myself," she said.

I hugged her, and we cried together. I was sad to learn she had
endured so much pain and sorrow. She promised to leave and rescue
herself and go back to her family. I promised always to have her back.

Rozita had a good job and had bought a house for herself and her husband. When she left, he destroyed the house, including smashing the appliances and making holes in the walls. The financial devastation he caused her forced her to file for bankruptcy. She was still in her late twenties.

———

Before she got married, Rozita had had off-and-on issues with her health. After her divorce, she seemed a little more tired each time I saw her, but I thought it was nothing big. Maybe work was stressing her out.

One day, sometime later, she called me while working late and told me she didn't feel well.

"I think it's just my stomach," she said.

"Do the doctors know what's wrong?"

"No. It's like an upset stomach, but it's hard to describe," she replied.

We were young. We didn't worry about health issues or lingering illnesses.

Off and on, she wouldn't feel good. The energy she'd had when we first met slowed down, and we just didn't do as much. I attributed a lot of it to us getting on with our lives, careers, and jobs. We were getting older. It was normal.

Then one day, she called me again.

"I went to the bathroom and had a nosebleed," she said, her voice quivering. "It won't stop, and I'm freaking out."

"Go to the doctor, Rozita. You're in your twenties. That's not normal," I told her. Still, it didn't occur to me that it could be anything serious.

These bouts of fatigue started happening to her more often. She would get dizzy and feel unwell. We didn't know what was wrong, although she was still searching for a diagnosis. At last, she found a specialist and went to see him. She called me and told me what he found.

"It's lupus."

Finally, she had a name for what was destroying her, a diagnosis to work from. But I still didn't understand what it meant. Neither of us had any idea what lupus was. We were starting to figure it out, but I never really registered its gravity. I called around, trying to find someone who could explain it to me.

Now, I know that lupus is an autoimmune disease. An autoimmune disease occurs when your immune system—the body system that usually fights infections—attacks your healthy tissue instead. Lupus can cause chronic inflammation and pain in any part of your body. I don't know if the nosebleeds and stomach pain were early symptoms related to lupus, but I know the fatigue was.

When I found out I was pregnant, Rozita and I decorated my nursery together. I bought a blue crib with dinosaurs on it because I knew I was having a boy. There wasn't much—just some pictures, decorations, and a few pieces of furniture.

When she came over, she'd just had surgery, and she was a little bit lopsided, but I couldn't imagine decorating a nursery without her involvement. It was a subdued time, but I enjoyed seeing her again and sharing this experience with her. I didn't realize then how little time she had left.

Rozita visited us after Sam was born, but she did so a lot later than I would've liked. She came over when he was about a month old. At the time, she would often be in bed all day long.

While Rozita had finally gotten a diagnosis, it was too late. Her lupus was out of control.

"It's like you're driving a car in a twenty-five-mile-an-hour zone," the doctor said. "Only you're going eighty miles an hour. Your immune system is in overdrive, and we can't stop it. We can't even slow it down."

Her doctors had to put her on powerful medication, and that's when she became increasingly fatigued. We were in touch, but not nearly as often. I would call her, and she wouldn't pick up. This was way before cell phones, so I would call her on a landline. It would take her days to return my calls because she slept most of the day.

Eventually, she decided to quit her job due to her fatigue. We couldn't see each other as much because I was working longer hours. I was raising a baby, and she was very sick, unable to do the things we'd loved to do—travel, hang out, and visit with each other and friends.

Then, she started getting sicker. I went into denial about her having a serious disease. I preferred to think that she was tired and sleeping a lot but healing.

Rozita was stoic and did not talk about her pain, what she was experiencing, or how bad the lupus was. Her silence only fed my denial about how sick she truly was.

I remember calling her and calling her. She wouldn't pick up the phone; if she did, she sounded so tired. "Oh, I was sleeping," she would say.

Sleeping in the middle of the day? I would get pissy and frustrated with her. Looking back, I think I was also scared and unwilling to admit reality to myself or her. "Oh, Rozita, it's the middle of the day!" I'd say, exasperated. "Get up!"

One day, when she came over, it looked like her doctors had done some sort of procedure. They had cut into her throat. I could see the scars, and she looked strange. But the scope of her illness still didn't register with me, and she still didn't tell me how bad things were. Never.

Even though she was growing sicker and sicker, I believed she would shake it off, get better, and we'd be back to the way we were—laughing and having good times, looking forward to raising children, and growing old together as good friends should.

Rozita always believed in me and supported my dream of running a big company someday. She never had the same vision for herself.

Instead, she told me and anyone who knew me or met me what an amazing, intelligent, accomplished woman I was and how I was destined for greatness. She was my true champion.

I've since learned not to assume or tell myself a story I've made up about something or someone, thinking I know what's going on. I've learned to ask and to press for details and the truth. I've learned to create an environment that welcomes expressing one's feelings. Rozita must have been overwhelmed and scared and found it easier to pretend to be okay.

She deteriorated rapidly in the last year and a half. At one point, she went to her doctor, who told her to go to the emergency room. They rushed her in because she had water in her lungs and around her heart. She had a few surgeries, and her vision was impacted, but she was alive.

Afterward, she met a nice man at an event. Although she didn't have much energy, she had enough to date him. He was exactly what she needed: a loving companion who accepted her exactly as she was, even as sick as she was.

So, when she told me she would travel to Europe for three weeks with him, I was excited. I was a little worried about her, of course, but also happy.

After she left for her trip, a voice kept coming into my head, saying, *Call Rozita, call Rozita.* I would answer that voice and say, "Why would I call her? She's in Europe." I would argue with myself when this happened. I didn't heed the voice.

Almost three weeks after her supposed trip to Europe, I received a call from Rozita's sister on a Friday morning. She told me she had been trying to find me. She had gone through Rozita's belongings to find my phone number and finally found that card—the business card I had printed so many years ago in college when I had dreams of being a CEO while working as a gas station attendant. The card that I'd printed, even though I had little money to feed myself. The card I'd made that read "Investment Advisor," believing that someday it would come true. The card that everyone had thought was funny, with my name, made-up title, and my old phone number. She had called that number, which had given her a recording of my new number, and that's how she found me.

"Shirin, Rozita has been in the hospital with severe infections ever since she was supposed to leave. She has been in a coma since Monday. We're told she is going to pass. I have been trying to find you for days. Come quickly!" she said.

I could not believe my ears. I screamed in sheer pain when I hung up. Somehow, Rozita was trying to find me. Somehow, she did. And I had to go be with her.

I got to the hospital as soon as I could. Knowing I was in no shape to drive, my two sisters, Shirana and Shani, took me. Rozita was in an induced coma and had been for some time. She had been with her boyfriend when she checked herself into the hospital on a Friday, three weeks before the day her sister had called me. Doctors told her she had pneumonia and started administering antibiotics, but she just got worse and worse. Days before this incident, doctors had started an aggressive chemo plan to help tame her lupus. As it turned out, her system could not handle that chemo and the infection that followed.

When I showed up, the doctors, nurses, and her family told me, "This will take some time," referring to her dying. "You guys go home."

My sisters had taken me to the hospital, and so we all drove home together, but I couldn't rest. I told them, "I have to go back." They were kind enough to take me back to the hospital after a couple of hours.

When we returned to Rozita's room, not much had changed. The monitors showed her heartbeat and vitals, but they couldn't show what my heart was doing.

I bent over in pain and disbelief, collapsing into a crouch of grief, witnessing my best friend, my only friend since I had arrived in the

United States, my sister of thirteen years, my confidant, lying there in a coma. She had ventilators mechanically moving her chest to breathe for her.

Every hair on her arms was standing up straight. Her breathing was violent and shook the bed. The heart rate monitor showed her heartbeat at over 150.

"It's been like this for hours. I don't know how much longer her body can handle this. Her heart is beating as if she's been running for hours," the nurse said.

I knew she was running. I felt like she was trying her very best to save her life. She had so much to live for. She had her mom, her brothers, her sisters, and me and my sisters surrounding her with love. She was beautiful, kind, funny, smart—and only thirty-one years old.

This woman was the only person who had experienced the same pain of being displaced, thrown away, and poor as I had. She was my light on dark days and someone who had laughed with me and brought so much joy to my life. Now, she was lying there fighting so hard to live.

I kept standing up and then bending down to breathe. My sisters tried to comfort me, but they were stunned themselves. None of us had seen or experienced anything like this.

Suddenly, the heart rate monitor started showing a dip in her heartbeat, which got slower and slower.

"It's time," the nurse said, announcing Rozita's approaching transition.

We all started crying in unison.

"Stop! Everyone step away and stop!" her mother yelled over the din we were creating. "We need to let her go! Take your hands off her . . . stop yelling . . . don't scare her . . . she has to go!"

This brave woman who had immigrated to the United States with five young children and then buried her husband after cancer while having lost all their family funds had such a brave and giving heart to allow her child the dignity of passing in peace.

We all stood there silently, crying and giving Rozita our love.

The monitor dropped from 150 to 125 to 100 . . . to 35, and then she was gone. An indescribable silence and a palpable peace filled the room. I had never seen anyone pass away. I had never witnessed anyone cross from life to death.

I had little spiritual or religious training or faith then. But I learned that night at about 1 AM that there was something there—that Rozita was more than what we could see. There was a quality that lifted up and away from that hospital bed. And then there was peace.

I never wished for this, but I've thanked Rozita many times for the gift she gave me by allowing me to be present. I'm convinced she guided her sister to find me and then held on until I was there. She gave me the gift of her presence in my life and the privilege of being there when she passed.

Rozita died that night without regaining consciousness, without my being able to talk to her, to tell her how much I loved her, or how much I valued our friendship. I didn't realize things would happen so quickly. I got there in time to say goodbye, but not much else.

Even as she lay still, the machine designed to imitate her breath continued to rhythmically expand and contract her chest. It was a hauntingly surreal sight, a stark contrast to the absence of life within her. The nurses entered and gently urged us to step out of the room.

After some time, having skillfully detached the tubes and machines from her, the nurse kindly allowed me to step back into the room, the stillness and silence almost unbearable. Her mom was still sitting there, stunned.

Rozita was lying on her left side, facing the door. She had a hole at the base of her neck, where her throat was. I'm sure that was where the tubes had been put in.

I gazed at her as she lay there, the air heavy with solemnity. The silence enveloped us briefly before I exchanged a few words with her mother, bid Rozita farewell with a blown kiss, and quietly exited the room. A part of me had died with her. I stood there trying to absorb all that had happened. I wished I'd been there for her more often.

I was devastated and numb. But almost immediately, I thanked her. I said out loud, "Rozita, what a gift you just gave me."

Chapter Seventeen

Motherhood

Having core values that I held close helped me make difficult decisions.

Oɴᴇ ᴏꜰ Rᴏᴢɪᴛᴀ's ʟᴀꜱᴛ ᴀᴄᴛꜱ of love was helping me decorate my nursery. Although she wasn't feeling well, she took the time and energy to help me create a loving space for my son. She did this because she knew how important having a child was to me.

I don't know how, but somehow, I always believed I would have children. Even as a young girl, I seemed to gravitate toward and feel protective love for little boys and girls and took care of them any chance I could. And when someone told me they had named their daughter Sara, I knew that it would be my daughter's name too.

Though I had always had lofty career goals, especially since I had been on my own since I was seventeen, I was more passionate about my values. My top values are honesty, hard work, and caring for others. Above all, however, the idea of being a dedicated mother always prevailed. Even before I had children, I knew I wanted to be engaged with their lives and that I wanted them to blossom, which meant that I had to be physically, emotionally, and mentally present in their lives. My commitment to being the best mother I could be was even more significant than the drive to run a big company. That was my driving force in making many decisions about my career path.

It's unfortunate that society undervalues parenthood. In the nineties, professional women felt pressured to prioritize their careers over childcare, often losing out on promotions if they took time off for their children. In that environment, and understanding those dynamics, I decided a career within established corporations was not the route for me. I was not willing to make the sacrifice moving up the corporate ladder would require of me if I couldn't also be an engaged mother.

Having core values that I held close helped me make difficult decisions. As I sat in my car, sobbing in the parking lot of the bank I was auditing that fateful day when I decided to move on from my position at EY, I was mourning the loss of my beloved place of work where I felt valued. What motivated me to take action and move on was the gravitational pull of my desire to be an involved mother who would someday run a big company.

I found out I was pregnant early on. At twenty-eight, I was still building my life, and though I had a good job, I was worried about the future. Often, I played around on my spreadsheets, plugging in scenarios of raises and promotions, and it would still not look like there would be a time on the horizon when we would be in a great place financially. I was determined to change that.

While pregnant, I had asked for and received the promotion to CFO of THC—a great accomplishment. Now, I was standing before a board of directors of all older men—not one with even brown eyes—making a case for the company when suddenly I felt like I might need to step out.

"You can finish your presentation, but then go straight to the hospital," my doctor said. I had used the couple of minutes during the break we had at the board meeting to call him.

Reflecting on who my son, Sam, has grown to become, it's so appropriate that he wanted to participate in a board meeting to help negotiate a deal. He would have been proud of how I handled the meeting and the deal. The meeting was a resounding success, and no one suspected I was in labor. But I was! From the moment Sam was born, he did his best to raise his head and his eyes to look around. It was almost as if he had been waiting so long to see this world and was going to take it all in. Knowing who he has turned out to be, this all makes sense to me now. I believe we have innate qualities and gifts that we're born with. Curiosity is one of his.

I loved being Sam's mom, as I still do. Tom, the CEO of the mortgage bank, graciously allowed me to work flexible hours while Sam was an infant. This was simply not done in the nineties, at least not often, and certainly not as an opportunity afforded to a CFO. I was able to deliver the expected results at work while also bonding with Sam. What a gift!

Sam had a unique view of life. He was a joyful, active, and smart boy. He said his first word when he was nine months old, and it was *mah*, the Farsi word for "moon." Once he started talking, there was no stopping him. Full sentences in both Farsi and English came very fast. He would talk to anyone and everyone, and I would encourage it. I would give him the floor to talk, and he would welcome it. Cashiers at grocery stores, gardeners, and random strangers in lines at stores and restaurants would have interesting conversations with Sam. He would often ask them questions that brought a smile to their faces and an expression of surprise to their eyebrows.

"Where do you live?"

"Why do you buy that?"

"You just cut in line!"

"Call me."

These are some of the lines he would say as I held him in my arms. There was no sitting in strollers. He would either run around or have me pick him up. I don't think he walked until he was ten years old. He *ran* everywhere.

I was passionate about allowing Sam to speak up, to explore, to express himself. My approach may not have been conventional or easy, but neither had been my upbringing. I had grown up learning to rely on myself, and though I had yet to experience significant success, my out-of-the-box thinking had saved my life, and it had helped me set up a home. I was CFO because I had followed my path. Someone with my background was not expected to achieve what I had already reached. I had arrived there by staying true to my inner voice. I could only imagine the richness of life that my son could create for himself if he were allowed to learn about and follow his passions in a safe and protected environment. I believed it was my job to help him explore, as well as to create the guardrails that provided him with safety and do my part as a diligent observer. I used the skills I had learned throughout my life to instill discipline and ethical and moral values while still providing Sam with freedom. What a tricky balance to strike!

I've followed Sam's lead regarding what he wants to do all his life. From having lots of reptiles as pets to carrying a flyswatter for years (yes, most children have binkies, but Sam liked his flyswatter), to learning how to swim (he just jumped into the pool and swam across at three years old), to playing water polo and piano, to creating businesses from childhood to adulthood, Sam has been a fascinating, creative person. And I've been his supporter and advocate. It's been my pleasure and joy to be close to him all these years. I'm grateful that I took the time to step away from the path I was on to create a new one that allowed me to be his mother, who also happened to work.

As he grew up, I continued to build a career that allowed me to work flexible hours. I didn't work less; I worked around my chosen schedule. I could pick him up from school most days of the week. On some of those days, I would have to drive back to work afterward, which would take me an hour each way. But it was my pleasure to take him home and talk to him about his day. I was his room mom for all his years in school, for as long as they allowed room moms. I was his number-one cheerleader at his games. I was his homework buddy and his private tutor. I ensured he was heard, but I was also his disciplinarian, teacher, and guide. And he's been the bright light that has brought me joy.

My life as a mother who worked was very challenging. Most days, I felt like I would work from morning to night. Some of that work was related to my profession, and some as a mother running a household. I endured many exhausting days and nights between the confusion and challenge of raising children while working full-time to build a company, often running at full speed and without breaks.

Knowing what I know now, I am confident that my decision to prioritize motherhood, as hard as it was, was one of the main reasons why I ended up succeeding in my career. Defining my core value of motherhood as one of my most important values created a clear path for my life and career. I made decisions about where to work, how to work, and what to build based on my desire to be an engaged mother. As a result, I left jobs and took on career choices that resulted in my eventual achievements. Had it not been for my eagerness to stay close to my children, I would not have made the creative choices I did. I am confident that I've been richly rewarded because of the decision to put motherhood first.

One day, when Sam was eight years old, we were walking after we had come home from school. He was talking about his swimming at school.

"Isn't it great to be good at something? You're good at swimming. Doesn't that feel good?" I asked as we walked by our house on a beautiful, sunny afternoon.

"Yeah. It's nice. Doesn't it feel good to be so good at being a mother?" he asked in reply.

Of course, that touched my heart. Those beautiful words made all the hard work and long nights worth it.

When Sam was eighteen months old, the company where I was the CFO was sold to another, larger bank.

During the mortgage banking heyday at that time, the company snowballed. However, the economic downturn led us to consider being acquired to protect stakeholders, employees, and the business due to the impact of rising interest rates on our mortgage-dependent infrastructure.

Finding a partner with a larger portfolio of offerings made the best sense because they could weather the storm more effectively. Our servicing portfolio was strong, with well-paying mortgagees. Our underwriters had done an excellent job, and therefore, our mortgages had fewer delinquencies and foreclosures than most. This was a great lesson that validated our hypothesis, which I carry to this day. When markets were robust during low interest rates, many lenders extended credit beyond what mortgagees could reasonably pay. This strategy was based on a shortsighted view of the markets.

Those lenders were simply interested in making a buck while they could. They weren't focused on building a sound book of business. We, on the other hand, did not subscribe to that mindset. We built what we believed was based on the chassis of good business practices. Because of that approach, we ended up with a strong portfolio of loans, even considering the interest rate increases. Although, in hindsight, our dependence on a singular product offering created a weakness for the system, our strong loans and processes made us a good acquisition target. It was time to sell.

I helped negotiate the sale of our mortgage bank to a larger bank while managing the company's financials and responding to due diligence requests. This was all happening while I was under thirty, raising an infant, and mourning the loss of my best friend. Both boards approved the transaction, and agreements were signed after due diligence. We began transitioning operations and mapping out where various departments and people would be absorbed within the larger bank. It was clear that I would be moving on, since the acquirers had an entire staff at the bank. It was also clear and negotiated that our CEO, Tom, the intelligent, intellectual, forward-thinking man who had given me a fantastic chance and trusted me, would also move on.

Tom had founded his company years before, persevering and growing it. He wasn't always the easiest person to deal with. Some feared him, some disliked his style, some liked him, and some were his fans. I, of course, was one such fan.

He was a good man who had done some good work and had touched many lives. He now had to say goodbye to his company, which was bittersweet for him. I hoped that, given time, he would realize that and celebrate his successes. So, I hugged him goodbye and farewell. And I knew I would stay in his life and he in mine.

My final bonus wasn't generous, but it was sufficient. It would give me enough runway to focus on Sam and find what I wanted to do next. Both my husband and I had been working hard, and we had managed to accumulate a little bit of savings. But we also had a mortgage and bills to pay, and we were keenly aware that raising children—and especially providing for their future—would require much more. I could not afford to not work.

By then, I had worked full-time since I was a teenager. I had been a CPA and an auditor with the most prestigious group at one of the most esteemed accounting firms in the world. I had risen to CFO of a medium-sized bank and managed its financial operations. I had been a part of negotiating and transitioning a successful sale of a business. At thirty-one, the most logical next step would have been to search for a secure, lucrative CFO position or something similar at another company. But how could another job inch me closer to running a big company?

Even more challenging, how could another job with a company help me stay true to my core value of wanting to be an engaged mother? Surely, another CFO position would require long hours of work, especially if my goal was to climb up high enough to run a company someday. I was not going to pay that price. So, entrepreneurship was to be my path. Little did I know how hard that was going to be.

Chapter Eighteen

Next Crossroads

Yet now, here I was, questioning whether following a secure path to another CFO position was right for me . . . The time had come to take my next step. It wasn't going to be easy, but since I was going to run a big company someday, I took a leap of faith. I was going to go out on my own!

AFTER I LEFT IRAN, I dealt with abject poverty for years until I landed a job after college. And even then, I wasn't well off. Being poor is painful. For most of my formative teenage years and young adulthood, I couldn't afford to wear what I wanted to wear, go where I wanted to go, or be included in groups I wanted to be a part of. I had to weigh groceries so as not to go over budget, and I spent many days on the edge of hunger. I had little I could rely on for guidance and support while growing up in the United States. Those experiences created sinister financial insecurity.

Yet now, here I was, questioning whether following a secure path to another CFO position was right for me. Having already had a child, I knew the kind of involvement I wanted to have with him as he grew up. My core principle of being a mother who happened to work, rather than "a working mother" (the phrase frequently used back then), guided me to my next decision. The time had come to take my next step. It wasn't going to be easy, but since I was going to run a big company someday, I took a leap of faith. I was going to go out on my own!

Every company, big or small, needs a CFO. I don't care where an organization is in its life cycle—understanding and managing finances is essential for any company of any size. This means that there are many companies in Orange County that can use the services of an off-site CFO. That's what I can do. Companies that are not large enough to hire a full-time CFO or companies that want to add to their bench can use someone with my background. Why not do that? I thought to myself.

The challenge was that an off-site CFO was not a well-known service. Many reputable, large firms offer this service today, but in the late nineties, it was not common. Being a full-time mother and not having many dollars to market my services made providing this offering hard to do. I didn't know how I would find clients. To make things more challenging, unlike in my previous jobs as an accountant, I wouldn't have a support team. So, I would have to be up-to-date and good at resourcing, and I had never done that before. Luckily, I had a strong network of friends and present and former business associates. I started contacting them one by one.

I also needed to find a caregiver for Sam. After many trials and errors with different people, I placed an ad for one. I wouldn't allow anyone to stay with my child without my supervision until I was comfortable with the caregiver, so all those trials and errors had happened right under my nose without any problems for Sam.

Gosia showed up at the house after her sister had called me in response to the ad in the PennySaver. She was a blond Polish woman with stern but kind eyes. She walked up to Sam, and they struck a bond at once. She was it! She was to come every day for me to observe and gauge whether she was the right fit to care for my child as I built my practice. She stayed for the next twenty-three years as my children's caregiver and surrogate mother.

I had stayed in touch with Tom, my former CEO, and after a break, he was now building his new consulting practice. He was not interested in building a company that operated as a bank, but he was focused on consulting in commercial real estate financing. And he was very good at it.

"You can be our off-site CFO. Our lenders would like that, especially since you were my CFO at the bank," he declared.

It was my pleasure. Teaming up with Tom and some of the old team that he had brought with him sounded wonderful, so I was in. And before you knew it, I had a practice.

Chapter Nineteen

Here Comes Sara

Motherhood taught me how to help nurture people's unique talents—a skill that paid off in spades both in raising children and in growing teams. Follow their lead.

I KNEW I WANTED A DAUGHTER. Sam was two years old and quite a handful. He wasn't a difficult child; he was just very active. I had my clients and Gosia. If there was a right time to have another child, this was it.

"You're in labor and only twenty-five weeks into your pregnancy. She won't survive if she's born now," my doctor said after I went for a visit with what felt like contractions. As it turns out, they were. I was not having it. I called my clients and planned remote work to the best of my ability. There weren't many options then, but I decided that I would make sure my child lived. I focused even more intently on being healthy and helping my child.

I was to slow down and embrace quiet, restful moments to allow for a calm environment for Sara. I've since learned that those quiet moments of slowing down are precious gifts that allow for reflection and growth.

My tenacity paid off. Sara was not only not born early—she was born late! As soon as she was born, she started looking for me. I took her on my chest and saw a patch of dark hair on her arm.

"Does she have a mole?" I asked the doctor.

"No," he said, laughing. "It's her hair. We had to pull her out, and some of her hair fell out in the process. She had so much!"

And she did. She had beautiful hair and beautiful eyebrows. I asked the nurse, "Isn't she pretty?"

"Oh my God. She's gorgeous!" she said.

Then, the nurse accidentally dropped a tray. The sound startled Sara, who made a jerky move and cried.

"Wow! She has sensitive ears! I'm surprised how much she reacted to this. How did it bother her?" the nurse asked.

I didn't know it then, but that was a sign of things to come. Sara did have very good ears. No wonder she became a talented musician as she grew up.

Sara was sensitive, intuitive, and liked by her peers. Her preschool friends loved her. And she loved me. She didn't want to go to school without me. So, I attended three hours of preschool three days a week for a year until she was comfortable.

Sara loved a good mess. She loved the mud. Maybe it was her way of creating art, or maybe it was to be a little rebellious or to feel the texture of life in a way that people don't often take the time to do. Or maybe it was for all those reasons that she liked to play with the mud and be messy. She has certainly grown up to have all those qualities of creativity, rebellion, and connectivity.

"Let's make a mud pile for her," I told Gosia one day when I got home.

Many good parents want to allow their children to learn various skills. To me, the best way to learn where their talents resided was to allow them to explore many opportunities, from sports to music to other interests. My only exposure to music had been through my participation in choir. I knew the only way to know whether Sam and Sara liked music was to have them take some lessons. So, I signed them up for group piano classes when Sara was three and Sam was five. I had to attend those classes with them—especially with Sara, since she was so young. They both enjoyed it, so I later enrolled them in private lessons.

One day, five-year-old Sara walked up to me. "I want to play the violin," she announced.

What? Where did that come from? I thought to myself. *We know no one who plays the violin. We've had a few family members play the piano. But the violin? Who does that?* I smiled and figured the thought would pass. But it didn't. The next day, she grabbed a toy guitar and pretended it was a violin. She put it on her shoulder and pretended to play.

I had my work cut out for me. I had to find her a violin teacher.

Once I found one, Sara took to the violin like a sponge. She performed then and continued to perform on many stages. She has since traveled the world, even performing at the Sydney Opera House when she was fifteen. It's been a beautiful experience. She's become a talented, competent artist and person. It's been my absolute pleasure to support her through her journey.

Motherhood taught me how to help nurture people's unique talents—a skill that paid off in spades both in raising children and in growing teams.

Follow their lead.

PART THREE

Success

CHAPTER TWENTY

Navigating Naysayers
and Building Value

*I was excited to embark on an entrepreneurial journey. My
gut told me I would be good at it. So, I took another leap of
faith. I decided to join them.*

SARA STARTED WALKING when she was nine months old. She would
hold my hand and walk around to practice. So, when she finally took
her first steps by herself, she would hold her right arm up as if she were
holding my hand. That is how she had learned to balance herself! And
as she learned to balance her body, I learned to balance this new life
with two children. Like many young parents, I spent my days running
between children as one napped and the other needed an activity. I
was teaching new words and skills as I was learning motherhood.

Life was busy at home, but it was also time for me to find ways to
acquire new clients. My engagement with Tom had come to an end
when I got pregnant with Sara. I understood and respected that he
needed someone full-time. I still had other clients, but they offered
fewer hours.

One day, I received a call from a company looking for someone to
look at their accounting system and its setup. I knew I wasn't exactly
a systems person, but I thought it wouldn't hurt to talk to them.

The initial conversation with one of the founders was easy and straightforward. It seemed like they had a solid accounting system in place, but they were unsure about how to properly set it up according to best practices. They were also confused about developing a chart of accounts, among other things. The founder also mentioned that they had some tax-related questions. The company was called Budget Blinds (BB). It had been created a few years before to sell window coverings franchises. The five founders had worked in a similar company before BB and had decided to create the same concept once the predecessor went out of business for personal reasons. They had seen the concept work and wanted to build on the same chassis.

Franchising is an interesting business. It's an art and a science. The idea is to create a concept and system that can be taught to others. Interested parties invest in the system and acquire a license to operate a franchise. The license provides them with the right to operate the franchise business if they follow agreed-upon processes, systems, and protocols. And of course, franchisees pay franchisors royalties and other fees.

Therefore, a franchisor effectively operates in at least two businesses: the business of being a franchisor and supporting franchisees to success, and the business of making sure the products or services offered by franchisees are designed and marketed correctly so that consumers buy those products. There are many more facets to being a franchisor, but these two are the most prominent functions.

When I first met with BB in the late 1990s, there weren't many franchisors in the home improvement space. Most were in the food service businesses. Therefore, the company had to create its own systems and go-to-market strategies because there were few best practices to emulate.

Having been exposed to various types of businesses at EY, the bank, and in my consulting work, I had developed the ability to quickly understand the setup of a business. Understanding the developmental stage and size of the company, I was confident it would be a short engagement that would be useful to the company, so I agreed to stop by their office and bring my seasoned tax accountant friend, Patty, to help them with their tax questions.

Their office was nice and appropriate for the company's size. They had recently brought in a general manager (GM) to help them grow the company. This GM was one of the only people who had an office to himself. Most everyone else shared offices. It seemed like an intimate space with a group of people who had known each other for some time.

Patty and I were guided to a small conference room where we met the GM. He was a big imposing man and had clearly chosen the spot and the posture to show authority. As I approached him, I extended my arm to shake his hand before sitting down.

"Do you have children?" were the first words out of his mouth even before I had bent my knees to start to sit down.

Surprised by the question that seemed to come out of nowhere, I replied, "Yes. I have two, a three-year-old and an infant."

"I believe women should stay home to take care of their children," he said in response. It was clear he wanted to push my buttons.

Little did he know that for most of my career to that point, I had experienced countless adversities related to my gender and ethnicity. Even in the professional settings where I worked, I had been exposed to many inappropriate comments.

"Go get me coffee . . . that's what women do," one of my managers had ordered me a few times.

"I only want to answer questions from a pretty girl like you," said one audit client's CFO.

"Aren't women from your part of the world used to getting kicked?" a superior once asked when he accidentally kicked me under the table.

I'd already developed a thick skin and had learned a calm and diplomatic way of responding in such instances. It was clear that if I—or any woman or minority—were to respond as most people would do, I would be tagged as difficult, emotional, and aggressive. And I was not going to let anyone tag me unjustly. So, I had taught myself ways to respond assertively but not emotionally.

The social climate and my upbringing in Iran during the Islamic Republic had engraved messages in my psyche that it was improper for a woman to speak up. And the social norms in corporate America didn't favor women who spoke up either. I knew that, often, I had just and reasonable reactions to improper and unfair comments. But I took many of those comments and experiences on the chin and accepted them with a form of "It is what it is." Luckily, despite those negative messages, I maintained my belief in my abilities. I had seen them in action and how they had paid off in my life. So, although I didn't always respond as I really wanted to—and as I now know would have been perfectly appropriate—I didn't allow those comments and behaviors to affect my focus. I continued to focus on doing good work to the best of my ability and always doing my best to do the right thing. I chose this as my path to showcasing my capabilities and contributing positively. I was going to succeed, and that success would be my best response.

"That's great. I hope it's worked for your family," I ended up replying to the GM, not at all playing into his hand.

The rest of the meeting went well. It was clear to me that the GM had claimed he understood how to deploy accounting systems. Judging by the little bit I saw that day, he did not. As the meeting adjourned, the GM walked out, and two others stayed.

"I'm sorry. I don't know what that was," one of them said.

"Thank you. It was uncalled for. If we decide to work together, I will not work with him," I said, pointing to the GM's office.

"I promise you, you won't," he said.

A few days passed, and I thought more about BB and its founders. I felt compelled to give them good advice regardless of our decision.

The project wasn't big, but my moral compass was active. I felt like they had to get good financial management in place.

The company's stakeholders had collectively decided that they wanted to build it to sell for $50 million someday. At the time I met them, the company had a number of franchisees and showed promise, but it was nowhere near a $50 million valuation. The GM had made claims about how he knew what it would take to build a $50 million company. He had offered to take the guys to tour a company that size.

"What does that even mean?" I asked. "What's a $50 million company? A manufacturer looks very different than a restaurant chain than a technology company. How would a tour of any company worth that much be meaningful to you guys?"

Clearly, the company's management had some experience with the products being offered and some experience with franchising. However, it was also clear that the company had a long way to go to create valuations close to the numbers they wanted. They needed good, experienced financial and operational management. Though it was much smaller than any company I had audited, managed, or advised, something about it intrigued me . . . it was entrepreneurial. And I was excited to embark on an entrepreneurial journey. My gut told me I would be good at it. So, I took another leap of faith. I decided to join them. I felt excited and a bit nervous—but not much. I was ready to roll.

CHAPTER TWENTY-ONE

Growing the Company

The fact that we had to "do or die" and that no one could res-
cue us . . . mobilized us to do what we needed to do to survive
and thrive.

I TRANSITIONED FROM CONDUCTING a thorough review of their accounting system to taking on the role of financial manager for the organization. From my perspective, it became clear that we needed a deeper understanding of how to drive the company's growth. We saw our initial growth slow down considerably, and the team diligently worked to unravel the mystery of accelerating our growth. Often, entrepreneurial businesses experience initial growth from sources known to the entrepreneur. The first batch of clients and customers are those within the relatively close network of people who start the business. The challenge is to find ways to sell the company's products and services to those beyond the founders' initial network.

The question of how to find prospects interested in buying one of our franchises often occupied our thoughts and was the subject of many of our meetings. I became an integral part of the executive team. Ours was an agile and entrepreneurial group. We held impromptu meetings covering relevant topics all focused on growth with agile execution. Our approach to problem-solving was thoughtful and quick. We made many decisions—including some bad ones.

But we learned quickly and course corrected. I was the CFO but oversaw, contributed to, and managed many parts of the company. I was joined at the hip with the guys, especially the CEO. We were soon all friends and comrades.

The first few years at BB were very challenging. In franchising, especially in its early years, it's necessary to expand the network of franchises to grow. The organization can improve its marketing efforts with more franchises, leading to better results. As marketing and sales grow, franchisors can negotiate better pricing and more favorable terms with suppliers. This results in better products being sold at better margins and more efficient marketing efforts, leading to better profitability for franchisees. Successful, profitable franchisees support the franchise system by paying their fees, allowing it to grow by bringing in new franchisees. This growth cycle can continue if managed properly. However, this formula has many complexities, so only a small percentage of franchisors in the United States reach over one hundred units. Our franchise system, though small, was a pioneer in its field, operating in a space not well known for franchising: home improvement. This lack of awareness meant there were not many, if any, franchise systems we could study and emulate. However, it also underscored the need for innovation and adaptability in our approach, allowing us to pave our path in the industry.

We tried many strategies and tactics. We looked at every aspect of the system, including how we trained and supported franchises to elevate our offerings and build the best systems we could design. Unfortunately, our work and well-planned systems did not attract more franchises yearly. We began to struggle to pay the bills.

As we coped and planned, the guys and I spent lots of time together. We would go to lunch almost daily and talk about our personal lives quite a bit. We became very close, and being the only woman in the group, I became the go-to person for a lot of personal conversations. Personalities varied a lot. A couple of the guys were considered to be at opposite ends of the spectrum based on some personality quizzes they took. As these relationships grew organically, and as the stressors in building a company—that was taking so long to build—continued to mount, everyone used every tool they had. That meant that roles and reactions became complex and, in some cases, rigid. One's ego would step on another's. One's inability to process information in the same manner and at the same speed would frustrate another. There was affection and care among us, much like a family. But frustration and misunderstanding were brewing, too, also much like a family.

The GM was a polarizing personality. My take on him was that he had some sales experience but not much more. He had found these guys who had a nice concept and were executing but didn't have much experience outside of their own company. The GM had, therefore, easily positioned himself to be an expert in growing companies—which clearly wasn't the case.

Once I started working with the company, I ensured that we had measurable expectations. It took us some time to walk every executive team member through creating those measures and then having them accept responsibility for them. The GM was no exception.

"He misses his goals every month," I told the guys. "Isn't he here to generate franchise sales? We haven't seen the results he's promised." I was frustrated. Unfortunately, arrangements had been made to issue shares to the GM, and despite our reservations, those shares were issued.

Before we knew it, all hell broke loose. The GM used his superpower of understanding people's weaknesses to pit the guys against each other. There were days when we had all-out shouting matches in our meetings.

The environment had become toxic. It took a lot of effort, patience, and methodical performance measures to finally part ways with him.

Later, when I was on a short vacation at home, my phone rang. The guys, sounding desperate and scared, wanted to meet me at a restaurant ASAP. The GM had just sued the company.

"His lawsuit is seeking to dissolve the company for misman-agement," they said with a combination of fear and anger. They felt betrayed.

"You guys . . . lawsuits come with all kinds of threats. We've done nothing wrong and have lots of good recordkeeping to protect us. I am sure he will not succeed." I repeated this many times, yet even those assurances were not quite comforting.

We started a legal fight that lasted for the next three years and just about bankrupted us.

But while the former GM's lawsuit was very difficult for all of us, his position vacancy created the space we needed to gel better and move forward in unlocking how to sell more franchises.

We used many approaches to recruit prospects. Like most entre-preneurs, our journey of discovering what worked was filled with tri-als and errors. But we just kept at it. Everyone contributed with all they knew and had—including me. It just so happened that between my prior experiences and my life lessons, I had become an effective problem-solver and builder. I had learned about and could manage or help manage many aspects of the company.

Our franchisees sold custom window coverings. We provided sys-tems for earning customers and helping them design custom window coverings for their space. We had little success convincing manufac-turers and suppliers of window covering products to take us seriously. Our franchisees could use innovative products and thrive on better pricing and warranties. But like most manufacturers, our suppliers didn't care much about our future vision. They based their terms and their desire to innovate for us on the existing volume of business and not on what we thought, believed, and hoped we could do. Therein lies the philosophical separation between entrepreneurs and other, more established companies. Most entrepreneurs live with the poten-tial, and most corporations live with the historical. I believe neither is exactly right. But the question is how to close that gap. We were all a bunch of relatively young, albeit experienced, folks who had yet to prove we could build a large company. Our suppliers were seasoned companies, having been in business for decades, who had stakeholders to whom they would have to justify their decisions. The gap between the two points of view was large.

Or was it?

We started problem-solving. We wanted to partner with suppliers who understood our vision and could innovate to match our customers' demands. We wanted them to provide our franchisees with unique products, prices, and warranties that helped separate them from the competition. We knew—just knew—that we were going to be able to deliver substantial results if we could find the right partners. But those same suppliers struggled with giving a relatively small company the chance.

"We need to earn their confidence," we discussed at one of our many weekly meetings.

"Maybe we should find a respectable, gray-haired man who would speak on our behalf," someone suggested. And like magic, the light bulbs went on. Who did we know that we trusted and liked and that our manufacturers would take seriously?

"John!" one of us called out.

John used to visit the company and its franchises on behalf of one of our main manufacturers. He was exactly the respectable, gray-haired man we needed: knowledgeable about custom window coverings, likable and trustworthy, and someone we enjoyed working with. Although we were knee-deep in the lawsuit with the former GM, we still had a business to run and grow. To make matters worse, the insurance company through which we had our coverage that should have helped with our defense in the lawsuit refused to pay for that defense. (They were eventually proven wrong and had to reimburse us after we had settled the lawsuit.) Hence, we had to fund the defense with our own cash.

The fact that we had to "do or die" and that no one could rescue us from this unfair lawsuit mobilized us to do what we needed to do to survive and thrive. I had been here before. I had faced "do or die" many times in my life up to this point. I already knew that by leaning into challenges, we could overcome them and grow from them. I was ready, willing, and eager.

We decided to hire John. Considering that we were still struggling to grow as well as under attack, this was a bold move. But it was also a calculated one. If our hypothesis was correct, John could help us create a tangible separation in the marketplace to help our franchises become more profitable. More profitable, satisfied franchises would allow us to market and bring in new franchises. It would be an excellent win for us.

Luckily, John was up for the challenge. He came into my modest office and reviewed our financial statements. Our overall revenue from rebates was minimal.

"We can do a lot better than this. We can generate so much more business for franchisees and, as a result, a lot more for our financial statements," John said.

I know! I exclaimed silently to myself.

It had been almost four years since I had given up a lucrative career as an off-site CFO to focus solely on BB. I had two children and a personal commitment to be available to them—and I was. But was the cost too high? I mean, I had been at the top of my class at EY, promised upward mobility based on reviews and accolades. I had been the CFO of a respected bank in my twenties. I could have looked for jobs that provided me with a clear path to financial and career success. And yet, here I was. I had been trying to unlock how to grow a small entrepreneurial company for years now. It wasn't due to lack of effort that we hadn't yet cracked the code—but the code was undoubtedly not cracked. We were struggling financially, and we had a massive lawsuit that threatened our very being. Having been away from a full-time position for a few years, my résumé was no longer as attractive for another job. I was digging myself deeper and deeper into a point of no return.

But I had a fire in my belly to build this company. I was passionate about the future that I could see and feel but wasn't yet here. I was witnessing the blossoming of my peers. And I was still trying to figure out how to help our company blossom.

John's words resonated with me. I knew we had the potential to grow the system, but we needed the right partners. I became excited and hopeful when John validated those thoughts.

"But we need to create an agreement that we can offer to our suppliers," I told John. "The agreement must spell out what they receive and what we get. I don't want them to think they have the upper hand and can do with us as they wish."

I interviewed John and other stakeholders in the company. Using the information gathered from them and adding my thoughts as to what we would have to require from suppliers, we formalized what we had to protect: our proprietary systems and the investments we had made to acquire them. Since we were battling an extended lawsuit, we decided we were going to write this agreement and then run it by lawyers to make sure we hadn't misrepresented anything.

That agreement became our template, used for another seventeen years with edits over time. It was built on our new approach to negotiating with our suppliers—one that would put us in the driver's seat.

CHAPTER TWENTY-TWO

Secret Sauce

We didn't know it while we were going through our tough years, but it was exactly because of our setbacks and challenges that we became very good at creating solid, reliable systems, support, operations, and an overall company.

To bring in new franchisees that would invest in buying one of our franchises, we had to figure out the best way to recruit prospects.

And, of course, we had to learn how to move those prospects through a process that earned their confidence in investing in our systems and becoming licensed franchisees. For years since I had joined the company, we'd had limited success with prospecting. Of the few prospects we recruited, we had a reasonable success rate in having them invest in our concept. However, that success rate could be improved. It was no wonder that the problem of bringing in more and better-qualified franchise licensing leads was at the top of our list of issues to resolve almost every week.

Though we had many promises of franchise activity, we had not seen the results. We depended on others. It was time for us to explore on our own. We tried many options to generate leads for franchise licensing, from advertising to participation in shows to online activity. We had also talked about using business brokers to generate leads, but we had yet to do that well.

Realizing we had to move things along faster with our lead generation, we brought in a new franchise licensing team with broker relationships. We took the time to learn what those brokers looked for and created assets, pitches, teams, and plans to attract them. And the plan paid off! We started seeing new leads coming our way.

Although the franchise licensing team did well with the lead flow, our closing rate remained suboptimal.

"What are we missing?" someone asked at one of our executive meetings. "We've improved everything. We've upgraded our marketing, support, and training. And we even have new products and pricing thanks to our new efforts with our suppliers. We know people can make money if they invest in our franchises. Why are they not? We should be getting interest in droves!" This was everyone's shared and expressed sentiment.

For years, we had focused on creating a reliable system that would allow franchisees to make a consistent return on their investment at BB. I was keeping track of franchisees' sales and profits based on their reports and comparing them to the fees they paid. This was a profitable and good concept. What were we missing?

Our CEO attended a conference to learn more about franchise licensing, but he returned a bit puzzled. "Our franchise is less expensive than most. I know we operate in the home improvement space as home improvement franchises, so there aren't any other concepts to compare ourselves with . . . but we're priced really low," he said.

Collectively, we agreed to raise the price of our franchise. This was a scary and risky move. If we raised the price and could not sell any more franchises, we would be dead in the water. In reality, we were humming along and doing okay, but we wanted to do better. We also knew that with the cost of the lawsuit, we *had* to do much better.

We agreed to take the difficult but calculated risk. We raised the price substantially.

Pricing is interesting. People associate low prices with low quality. And conversely, they often consider high prices as a sign of high quality. Going too high with pricing, however, can backfire depending on the product being offered. We had to do it just right.

It worked!

Years of trial and error had paid off. The new pricing for our franchise helped investors understand that we were not offering a passing opportunity. Ours was a reliable, profitable, and sustainable concept. We hit the mark and started selling franchises fast. At that time in franchising, selling ten to fifteen units a year was considered great; we started selling that amount per month! We maintained that pace for many years. The best news was that the people we put in business during those years thrived. We had a renewal rate of 99 percent, which means that as agreements came to maturity, our franchisees were so satisfied that they renewed their contracts 99 percent of the time.

We had figured out our secret sauce. It was the perfect result of creating robust, reliable systems. Systems that we had established throughout the years we had not grown as fast. We didn't know it while we were going through our tough years, but it was exactly because of our setbacks and challenges that we became very good at creating solid, reliable systems, support, operations, and an overall company. Removing a bad apple from the helm, though it created lots of chaos with the lawsuit, allowed us to understand the dynamics of how to grow our concept well—and raising our price, as risky as it was, positioned us well. All those challenges and difficult times forced us to embrace a "do or die" mindset and, with it, the creativity we needed to unlock our secret to success.

———————

It was hard to believe. We had been struggling to pay the bills for years. We had made some improvements and enjoyed some success after the GM's departure. We then had to defend ourselves against his lawsuit using our hard-earned dollars. The necessity to generate funds to defend ourselves mobilized us even more to create a new approach with our suppliers through our new vendor alliance and to succeed with our franchise lead generation and closing. We were growing very fast, tripling our franchise count and making many lists as one of the fastest-growing franchise systems in the United States. And we did all of this while we were still dealing with the lawsuit.

Many of us spent countless hours accumulating data and evidence to support our actions regarding the company and the GM. The time had come for depositions, and I was going to be deposed on video since I oversaw and measured many aspects of the company's operations.

Our lawyers spent hours prepping me for the upcoming deposition, which they believed would last a day.

"You're already well prepared," the lead lawyer said to me.

"Of course—because I'm telling the truth," I said simply.

I was confident in my abilities. I knew that if BB were to fold, I would be okay. As a CPA and former CFO with years of experience, I was familiar with operations, negotiating exits, managing large transactions, establishing companies, and building brands. Plus, I was only in my early thirties. I was fairly certain I could find another job if I needed to. However, what mattered most to me was doing what was right. Standing up for these individuals against an unjust lawsuit was the right thing to do. The founders at BB may not have had a lot of experience running other companies, but they did have a strong commitment to growing this one. This was an unjust lawsuit, and I was not going to stand by and let the former GM ruin the company and all the stakeholders' dreams.

As I was driving to the offices where the depositions were to take place, I decided to pump myself up by listening to one of my favorite artists, Missy Elliott. When I parked in the garage of the fancy highrise office of the opposing counsel, I felt the car shake with the beat of my uplifting music. I felt like a boxer ready to enter the ring.

This boxing match of words and accusations being videotaped lasted not one but two whole days. The plaintiff's attorneys tried many ways to catch me, only to hear me respond calmly and with conviction. I had tracked the GM's performance, as well as everyone else's. I had reports and information that supported our approach. I was telling the truth—no one could ever catch me.

"Wow! I've practiced law for thirty-six years and can honestly tell you I've never had a witness as strong as you, Shirin," our lead attorney told me during a break.

I knew my stuff. I was telling the truth and had all the evidence I needed. Still, knowing I was being recorded and deposed by a team of aggressive lawyers sounded intimidating. The voices from the past as to how a respectable girl should behave were still in my head. But so was the image of my dad's approving smile as I told him about my stance against our principal at my high school in Iran. I had stood up to authority, defending what I believed was right.

"I'm not any less smart than anyone else," I had told that principal, who'd been installed by the Islamic regime. And my dad not only didn't get upset with me, but he also admired me. That was the message I took away—that it was my right and responsibility to stand up for the good. That voice was much stronger than anything society had tried to push on me. I had no fear. I would tell the truth assertively, strongly, and with conviction.

Our lead lawyer's continued vote of confidence and admiration motivated me to keep it up. The sixteen hours of grueling deposition backfired on them. It was the nail in the coffin of this lawsuit that we needed. This boxing match was over, and we were the victors.

Three years after we were sued, we received the final judgment and were informed that we owed the GM ten dollars . . . ten single dollars, and no more. This lawsuit was finally off our backs!

The stress and pressure this adversity had brought us had also moved us to unlocking our potential.

After we succeeded with the lawsuit, we reengaged with our insurance carrier with the threat of a lawsuit, and they finally paid. I believe they initially denied our claim because they expected us to go out of business. Now that we had found ways to pay for our defense and to win, they were forced to pay for most of our defense. We were now cash-rich and enjoying the fruits of our labor.

CHAPTER TWENTY-THREE

Overdrive

I worked from when I woke up in the morning to when I went to bed. I used to say, "The writing on my grave is . . . 'She really tried.'"

THE COMPANY WAS GROWING FAST, which meant many new positions and hires. To maintain the momentum we had built with franchise licensing, we hired a new department manager. Things were going well.

I developed a proposed compensation plan for the director of franchise licensing and several positions within the company that were heavily bonus-driven. The idea was to encourage collaboration and support among team members. The success of one individual would be linked to the success of others in a positive way. If a person's peers and department performed well, they would be rewarded with a bonus. This approach allowed everyone to share in the joy and benefits of collective success.

New franchisees started coming in fast. We had to build infrastructure to support and train them quickly. I was concerned. "Do we have the right people in the right places to be able to manage this growth?" I asked in an executive meeting.

As is common in growing companies, especially entrepreneurial ones, we underestimated the challenges of steep growth. After a fast-paced year and a half, our franchise licensing director moved on.

By then, we had experienced back-to-back losses of franchise licensing leaders. I decided that the best course of action would not be to recruit once more. Instead, it made the best sense to learn more about our processes and plans with franchise licensing and better organize it. Our steep growth had introduced disruption in the organization and in the flow of the department.

It was time for me to take it on. I approached our CEO to partner with me in managing franchise licensing.

I wasn't in sales, and I had little experience in it. To be effective, I would have to learn about the systems, processes, and skills to sell franchises while managing the team and producing results. Of course, I still had my day job. But I knew I could do it. This was not a new skill for me. I had stepped into new roles and learned how to navigate them often. I also had our CEO to collaborate with me on this venture. We were off to the races.

For the following two years, I closely oversaw franchise licensing. I reviewed all our systems, processes, reports, and personnel in that department—much like I had done years ago at the mortgage bank. I held weekly meetings with the entire team, where we discussed challenges, opportunities, and the latest in the company and the department.

I believed that in the process of closely supervising the department, we would find someone who would be able to manage it. Plus, this time, the person would have been adequately observed and, therefore, vetted. We measured performance closely to determine if we were on the right track. We found many areas of improvement and weaknesses in our systems and processes. Methodically and gradually, we corrected and enhanced them. The result was fewer sales reps with better results, bringing in better-qualified candidates who loved our systems. We did identify a replacement and eventually handed the department over to someone in the ranks who we thought would be a good fit when given guidance and support.

The enhancements and changes in franchise licensing came at a hefty personal cost to me. I was already stretched thin with raising two children whose lives I was very involved in while managing a growing company's finances and related demands.

There was an enormous amount of stress on me with driving an hour each way to work—and at times driving back and forth to pick up my children, drive them home, and then return to work—as well as learning how to operate a company in a new space. Like many people in this country, especially women, I wanted to be an engaged mother, a terrific CFO, a successful entrepreneur, a good spouse and homemaker, a fit person, and a lovely individual and friend. This required a lot of effort and commitment. I worked from when I woke up in the morning to when I went to bed. I used to say, "The writing on my grave is . . . 'She really tried.'"

And try I did. I was exhausted often but kept my eyes on the prize of a meaningful life. Most of the time, I would use the little personal time I had to solve what we needed in order to grow the company. I would often think about how to grow the business while doing daily routines like showering and driving. I saw that the investments of time and energy I'd made were paying off by unlocking many new ideas and plans. We were growing fast and well. The personal, physical, and emotional tolls, however, were accumulating too. How much longer before the bill would come due?

CHAPTER TWENTY-FOUR
New Franchise System

. . . if one is building a new idea or enhancing an existing one, at some point, one would have to accept the risk of the unknown and move forward.

IT HAD BEEN A COUPLE OF GOOD YEARS. We had won the lawsuit and were selling franchises well. It felt like we had achieved success.

"We should have an off-site strategy meeting," I suggested to the executive team. "We need to figure out where we're going."

So, off we went for a multi-day strategy meeting, with spouses joining us at the tail end of the trip. This was a very successful trip that allowed us to step away from the trees and see the forest. It gave us a chance to create a destination for where we wanted to go.

We reviewed results and significant stats and asked ourselves, *What are we good at? Is it window coverings or is it franchising?*

After much soul-searching, we decided that we were good at franchising—not just window coverings franchising, but franchising in the home improvement space. We believed we understood designing for the entire home. With this new hypothesis, we had a renewed and exciting plan. We were going to test out how good we were in franchising in the home improvement space by establishing a new franchise system.

Wait! I thought. *We're barely scratching the surface with the window covering franchises, and now we're expanding it?* Though I genuinely believed this was the best next step for growth and though I had strongly promoted the idea, it still felt crazy and unsettling. My financial insecurities around any new venture grew significantly. I had to assess the risk and reward.

In growing a company, just as in building a life, you often have to press forward just as you start getting comfortable. I have come to understand through my experiences that looking ahead, staying focused, and putting in the effort to constantly challenge oneself are crucial for developing outstanding companies and individuals. It was undeniably challenging to push beyond our comfort zone, but we were convinced that the foundations of the systems we had developed were solid and that it made sense that our franchise system could be duplicated in other places in the home improvement space with a new product category. We knew how to create an effective system with all the related marketing, sales, and installation programs. It was time to test it out on another category of products.

Home organizational products were on the move, and we decided we could franchise a system that offered it.

It was time to create a new franchise system.

———

In 2006, US consumers were drawn to the idea of having an organized home. Reputable, well-established brands such as California Closets successfully raised awareness about the category. As often happens in the world of entrepreneurs, as we learned about the category and the industry, we believed that we could do things differently, perhaps better, and appeal to a new audience of customers. It was time for us to explore this opportunity as our new franchise system.

I had learned over the years, and as we worked hard to grow the company, that taking some time to study an idea was wise, but the research and exploration would have to then result in taking action. In other words, researching and studying a new space and idea are critical; however, if one is building a new idea or enhancing an existing one, at some point one has to accept the risk of the unknown and move forward. After a preliminary assessment of the potential in the home organization space, we consulted with someone who worked in the home organization industry. We were seriously considering expanding to this space, intending to learn about the home organization category to potentially create a new franchise system. We met with some founders and pioneers in the field to review the market size and potential, and see how we could fit in.

It's difficult to enter a new market that's dominated by well-known players, but we believed we had enough of a different approach and offerings to reach new customers. Unlike the established companies in this space, which were mostly focused on affluent consumers, we were interested in offering high-quality products at a much lower price.

Many great corporate strategies share the core view of earning market share: be first, offer a superior and never-before-known product, offer it at a reasonable price, and/or offer it to all new customers. Our plan was to offer our products to appeal to a larger population of customers. We knew these customers through our BB brand. We knew who they were and how to reach them.

We were confident that by offering this new category of products at a high quality with reasonable pricing, we could effectively cater to our familiar customer base. Moreover, we believed that this customer base was larger than most others catered to in this space, presenting an excellent opportunity for us.

We anticipated that we could franchise a system that sold reasonably priced, high-quality, custom products to the customer base that we were very familiar with because that was our core. But finding a manufacturer at our price point was a major challenge.

After networking, researching, and putting in a lot of work, we discovered a major manufacturer of home organizational products. We drafted a compelling business story for our new concept. Subsequently, three of us traveled to meet with the manufacturer.

This was a huge multinational company that produced a wide range of products. I've always had a hard time remembering names, but since this meeting was important to me, I decided to practice the methods taught by sales experts to remember them. I told the other two guys traveling with me about my plan, and they, too, decided to practice the same techniques.

"Remember, when you shake their hands, repeat their names in your head or say them out loud. Also, associate them with something so you can recall them later," I reminded my travel partners in the taxi on the way to the headquarters. I was confident that with this approach, I could remember people's names and connect with them even better.

The impressive main headquarters building sat on acres of well-manicured land covered with beautiful grass and gardens. As we drove up the winding driveway to the building, we saw the company's name on a large, well-positioned marquee. We looked at each other and smiled tensely. It seemed like we were going to meet the emperor at his grand palace.

When we finally arrived, we were greeted graciously by a wonderful administrative person who welcomed us and guided us to the conference room, where an army of men with great big smiles on their faces stood. They shook our hands one by one and introduced themselves. I was ready. I had prepared for this moment. After the introductions and handshaking, we proceeded to sit down. I performed a quick mental scan of their names using the methods I had learned, and . . . nothing! I couldn't remember a single one! I turned to the guys, wide-eyed, hoping they would remember. Neither of them did either.

The meeting could not have gone better, though. As it turned out, the manufacturer was looking for new avenues of expansion. Although franchising in the home improvement space was still not very well proven, we had made enough noise in the market to be intriguing to them. After months of continued conversations, proposals, and projections, we secured a supply chain with them.

Of course, to secure a supplier, we had to have a clear plan for establishing and growing the company. By then, BB was over ten years old, and suppliers were not interested in investing in creating new products for a company that would take another ten years to show reasonable growth.

We took the lessons we had learned over the years about growing a company and created a plan to grow this one more rapidly. I put together a model that incorporated what we had painstakingly learned during the years we had faced many challenges in establishing ourselves. This model showed a much faster path to achieving our goals. It was clear that experience helped.

We created a launch plan that started with offering the new franchise to our existing BB franchisees and friends and family of our system. The initial offering was at a discounted price. The plan was that once we had some franchises that operated the new system and showed success, we would then launch a broader marketing plan to bring in new franchises in stages.

A launch plan closely resembling our successful brand seemed logical and practical. It also convinced our manufacturers of the potential upside of partnering with us.

While continuing to grow BB with all the complexities of developing and operating that business, we also created marketing plans for our new system. Our marketing consultants offered many names for the new brand, but none of them seemed to resonate. We finally landed on Closet Tailors (CT), with a lot of mixed feelings about it. In 2006, we launched CT and expanded our BB offerings to Canada. It was a promising and exciting year.

Chapter Twenty-Five

Great Recession and Great Pain

By the close of 2007, we had successfully onboarded approximately one hundred new franchises for our innovative CT system. These franchises, primarily BB establishments, had willingly incorporated this new offering into their existing BB businesses. Alongside these, we maintained a robust network of hundreds of BB franchises, constantly pushing the boundaries of innovation with new products and marketing strategies for our BB system.

Like most other Americans, we didn't know that beneath the booming economy of 2007, debt, unsecured mortgages, and Wall Street speculation were already opening deadly new fault lines.

Then, the Great Recession erupted. The cracks in the financial system widened and yawned, and soon, it was clear that the housing sector would be the most severely hit. In fact, many considered the recession to be housing-led.

The recession landed at our doorstep. After a short time, the company began receiving calls from our franchisees reporting a significant and sudden decrease in consumer demand. To compound the issue, many of them were facing a situation like that of numerous homeowners across the country, with properties that were highly leveraged and underwater. Many homeowners in the United States had been given mortgages that exceeded their affordability. As property values had steadily increased in previous years, homeowners had relied on this value growth to refinance or sell. However, with the rapid decline in property values and tighter financial markets, many homeowners could no longer afford their mortgages and found themselves trapped.

Our franchises encountered similar challenges. Many of our franchise owners depended on a two-income household, as do many families. Large layoffs left many households with one income, which meant that many of our franchisees faced significant financial pressures beyond running their franchises.

In a world where home values were dropping rapidly, foreclosure rates were increasing, and the banking system was at the edge of collapse, few consumers were considering home improvement.

As the Great Recession reared its ugly head, we had only just started up our new sister franchise system, CT, most of whose owners were existing BB franchisees facing a major drop in business. We were losing franchises fast!

In the fall of 2007, my dad, who had bought a home near mine (though he only lived in it as a visitor a couple of times a year), went for what he called a routine checkup.

Since my departure from Iran many years before, my dad had reinvented his professional life. Amid the chaos of the revolution and the war, he had stepped down as CEO. He was a man in his early fifties with five children, most of whom were financially dependent on him. Much like many Iranians, his assets were taken or frozen. And he had a seventeen-year-old Shirin who was in dire circumstances. He, therefore, found ways to generate some income. An attorney by trade, he took on some cases. He also continued to pursue his passion for writing.

For over a decade, he read books in his native language, Azerbaijani. He kept cards next to him and wrote on them as he read. I watched him do this work for hours daily while I was still living at home, not quite sure what he was doing.

"I'm organizing the language and writing the first Azerbaijani-Farsi dictionary," he told me.

Millions of people in Iran speak the Azerbaijani language. However, to suppress them, the central government of Iran did not recognize Azerbaijani as a language. Instead, it was considered a dialect. This policy was in force for decades, well before the Islamic Republic took over. The net effect of the policy was that people who lived in those regions of Iran that spoke Azerbaijani were not allowed to teach it formally. They were also forbidden from naming their children names that were clearly Azerbaijani.

My dad decided to invent systems to write the language properly and create dictionaries to allow for proper communication between Farsi and Azerbaijani speakers. He spent at least ten years accumulating words on those cards and then organized them into a large multivolume dictionary translating from Azerbaijani to Farsi and Farsi to Azerbaijani. He was eventually recognized by scholars around the world, and specifically by Azerbaijani speakers in Iran, Azerbaijan (which used to be a state in the Soviet Union but became independent), and all throughout the globe. His books are now in the Library of Congress in the United States.

I did not see my dad for about ten years after I left Iran. And our time beyond that was limited to visits once or (rarely) twice a year. Over those years and until his fateful visit to the doctors in 2007, he had found ways to create even more meaning in life. He published his dictionaries, found ways to send all his children to the United States, and created retirement funds for retired attorneys in Iran. He was publishing periodicals in Azerbaijani, mostly focused on literature and culture. I know he loved his growing family, with in-laws and grandchildren entering his world. But he often spent most of his days alone in Iran. He made this sacrifice to ensure his family was well taken care of and that he and my mom wouldn't burden us. He brought meaning to his life and the lives of others both because that was how he was made and because he didn't want us to feel pressured to take care of his mental and emotional well-being.

So, when the doctor showed concerns about his blood-test results, we could not really process the gravity of what we might be facing.

"Mr. Behzadi, we need to do more testing. Your platelet count concerns me," the doctor said.

Only a week later, we were told the horrifying news.

"You have advanced-stage leukemia. There is not much we can do at this point. You have only a few weeks to live," he said grimly.

I didn't believe it. None of us did. It made no sense, and it was indeed not happening to Behzad. He was still lean with a straight stature (which he intentionally maintained). He was relevant, smart, witty, and looked great. He was the strongest man I had ever known.

Behzad Behzadi faced adversity head-on. He had built a life with dignity, courage, and determination after he had lost his father at a young age. He had leaned on those experiences to instill in me the qualities that had brought him lots of success. He had taught me to be self-reliant, confident, caring, honest, and genuine. He lived his life with principles that showed up in the way he touched others. His employees, children, and grandchildren learned from how he lived.

Surely this diagnosis was a mistake.

But he took his diagnosis the same way he accepted everything— with grace.

Because he wasn't feeling sick yet, he made it a point to get together with my two children and my sister's two children. He met up with them weekly and had us videotape him, telling us stories of his life—the dos and don'ts and what he had learned. It was very insightful. Although the kids weren't that old, they were old enough to understand.

Then, he got sicker and ended up in the hospital for six months. While he was there, my siblings and I were like soldiers going in and out, ensuring he was never alone. We didn't make a schedule or a calendar. There was always somebody who would step up. For the entire six months, someone was always by his side.

Because I had young children and a full-time job, and my sisters were working on their own and had more flexibility, I was the one who would take the night shift most often.

I would wake up with my children, give them their breakfast, and send them to school. Then, a few times a week, I would go straight to the hospital after work. I would change into my sweatpants and sleep on a cot in his room. It was a long goodbye.

He was a good-looking, sweet man with blue eyes, tall and handsome. Because of his pleasant demeanor, everybody in the hospital was in love with him.

He had an uncanny ability to connect with people authentically. He would see an individual and quickly zoom in on what was good and right about them, making sure to highlight their goodness. It was a positive way of making connections with people. He did that with all the hospital staff. Most importantly, he always found something positive to say to everybody.

"Thank you. You're so good at taking blood," he said after a lab technician stopped by.

"You had the fastest response I've seen!" he told the nurse when she rushed in after a bleeding episode.

It was hard for his caretakers to ignore his kind, deep blue eyes and sweet words. I'd had the privilege of knowing both as a child and had missed them as I grew up on my own. I cherished the moments we spent together during his stay in the hospital.

He never complained. I'm sure he had all kinds of pain because they kept telling him his platelets had dropped, and they would give him infusions. I know they're painful, but he never once said he had pain. Never once did he raise his voice to anybody, including us. He wasn't dismissive. If you walked into his hospital room, he would acknowledge you and ask about your day. He was just a great human being.

As his health worsened, he was moved into the ICU. One day, I was at work and decided to stop by, even though it wasn't my night to stay. When I saw him, he was breathing so hard that the hospital bed was shaking. I thought, *Oh, I've seen this before with Rozita. I know what this is.* My mom and middle sister were there, and I told them, "I want you to know this is it. It will not end well."

By then, my mom had been married to him for fifty-five years. She was a teenager when she married him, and she didn't know life without him. For most of her life, she had been a homemaker. They were a loving couple.

My sister took my mom home and told her I would let them know if things worsened. I stayed.

My oldest sister later came by, and the nurse pulled me over to speak with me. I asked what the protocol was, and she said they would give him morphine to ensure he wasn't in pain. She said they believed it would be just a little longer before he passed. So, I went back into the room and told my older sister.

I think the morphine got a little low at one point, and he woke up. He opened his eyes, and he looked panicked. I held his hand and told him it would be okay, and then he went under again.

My mom and middle sister returned at about 3 AM after I'd told them it was clear it was time. As they entered the room, with my dad's bed still shaking due to his labored breath, my mom and sisters stood at the foot of his bed. Then, my mother started singing to him in his native language, Azerbaijani. The sweet, familiar, ethnic songs sung in her beautiful voice, echoed by me and my sisters, filled the room. I didn't know how much he could hear or understand. But the love and culture came through with the sweet melody of the songs we had heard and grown up with.

I stayed with my father, holding his hand. I remembered how all those years ago, he would hold mine as I would step on his feet, and he would carry me to dance with him in the kitchen. It was now my turn. My turn to hold his hands and dance with him as he danced the last dance he would do on this earth. As I held him and sang in harmony with my mom and sisters, I whispered under my breath. I asked him if he could hear us and, if he could, to show us somehow.

He moved his toes! *Wow*, I thought. *He can hear us!*

So, I started talking to him softly. "I love you, Baba. You made me who I am. You gave us all a wonderful life through your sacrifices. You can go now. Do know that you've taken care of everyone so well. We're grateful for you. Don't worry. You can go now."

Somehow, I felt that his responsible, caretaking, fatherly instincts kept him from letting go. Somehow, I felt he needed to know that he had done a beautiful job.

"We release you. You can go in peace," I told him, holding back my tears. I felt like this wasn't about me and what I wanted. I wanted him to live forever. But I knew the state of his body's struggle would not allow him to stay with us much longer. I didn't want him to suffer. So, the only way to reduce his suffering was to let him know that he could go.

I threw in one last comment.

"But if there is a beyond, please come back and tell me. I need to know," I whispered in his ear as the melody of my mom and sisters' singing filled the room.

My sister echoed my mom's singing. The beautiful songs in his native language of Azerbaijani filled the room with love and kindness. His breathing started slowing down as if he were calming down to better hear the singing. I continued to hold his hand and caress his head. I whispered loving words that matched the melody of my mom and sister's singing in his ear.

His heart rate started dropping. It was so much like what I had seen with Rozita, so I knew the time was coming near. I whispered, "You can go. You can let go. We love you."

Then, he was gone. My mom and sisters walked up to him and said their goodbyes.

My father,

the person who loved me the most,

the man whose influence had created my optimism about life,

the model of integrity, authenticity, and love,

the parent whose belief in me was the foundation upon which I had learned to expand,

the loving father whose positive influence had reached beyond geography or time,

the giving soul who had touched so many with his dedicated work to help others and entire cultures—

was gone.

I went home that morning with sorrow that was hard to bear. I reflected on all the years I had missed being with and around him. I felt sorrow for not having lived close to him so that he could see me and my children growing up. I felt sorrow for never returning to sit under the walnut tree he had planted for me and my family. I felt sorrow for the unbelievable sacrifices he had made to send us out of Iran so that we could find a new home and build a new life. I felt sorrow for not having his loving presence to guide me. Above all, I felt grateful, touched, and humbled to have had his presence in my life as an example of grace and dignity that I could look up to. In my heart, mind, and psyche, I am and will always be sitting at the little desk next to his in the basement of our home as he worked and I doodled. My love of writing was born as I sat next to him while he read and I wrote. He was a gift, and so many were gifted with his gracious presence and love.

I was sad and very much overwhelmed. So, I did what I thought I could do. I ensured his memory was taken care of with dignity.

My pain over the loss of my father was deepened by the sorrow of losing his continued presence in my life. I had lost him many years ago, not by either of our choices. This final loss amplified so many other losses. There would be no beautifully written story of regaining his company for years to come. I had the opportunity to grow with him again, but now I will carry his spirit and voice with me.

His presence, his love, his support, and his influence carry me through life to this day.

Memorial services were held for him in a few cities worldwide. We had a memorial service for him in Orange County, where we lived. I had taken the role of planner and, as such, had asked if all the children and grandchildren wanted to speak. By then, there were eleven grandchildren in the family. My daughter, Sara, was the youngest of the eleven. She was nine years old. Many of the grandchildren opted to say a few words.

The memorial service was well attended, and the speeches were touching and beautiful. It was a fitting goodbye for such an amazing man.

Chapter Twenty-Six

Feel the Fear but Don't Be Afraid

Surviving so many existential challenges in my life had helped me develop the tolerance and skills I needed at this pivotal moment. I had learned to stay focused and calmly address problems . . . With the vast economy of the United States, there have always been consumers who weather the storm of market downturns. Based on this understanding, I believed it was our job to find out how to reach out to those customers.

As I struggled with processing my dad's passing, I was aware of the challenges across the country and the world with the worst financial crisis since the Great Depression. The pressure was on.

I was enduring this long and sad goodbye while dealing with the most significant existential challenge the company—and the entire economy—had ever faced: the Great Recession. I was committed to ensuring we did all we could to help our franchisees survive. Of course I was concerned about the company, but I was mostly concerned about the people and how their lives were being affected. I felt a sense of obligation to our franchisees. We had to find solutions and do so quickly.

The country was inundated with news of foreclosures and haunting images of deserted streets and abandoned homes. This recession struck with unprecedented severity, drawing comparisons to the Great Depression of the 1920s and '30s. Daily reminders of the fragile financial system and substantial layoffs underscored the urgent need for assistance. Our support staff was overwhelmed by frantic calls from endangered franchisees on the brink of losing their businesses and homes. We had a proven track record of successfully bringing new franchises on board and providing them with training and support to help them succeed. Before the Great Recession, our franchise renewal rates were very high, and we had very few terminations. However, 2008 was a very different year.

For the first time in our history, we were going backward. Franchisees were going out of business fast! Many of the reasons they were failing were not related to our system. They were external, such as people losing their second incomes or being overly burdened by mortgages with sharply spiking interest rates or the severe decline in consumer demand, the likes of which we had not seen. People were losing their homes and were not interested in improving them. They also had little, if any, disposable income to spend on our products.

There was sheer fear around the office. We had grown the company and invested a lot of our lives in it, and it seemed like we might lose it all overnight.

Don't panic, Shirin! I told myself. I was afraid and anxious and knew that this was appropriate. I recognized my responsibility to our employees and franchisees. It was essential for me to remain calm and thoughtful as I worked to address our challenges. Understanding my role as the financial manager and operations executive of the company, I needed to concentrate on finding the best ways to navigate this unprecedented time. Surviving so many existential challenges in my life helped me develop the tolerance and skills I needed at this pivotal moment. I had learned to stay focused and calmly address problems. I had learned that by consistently applying sound principles and staying close to "doing the right thing," adversities could be overcome. It was time to put all those lessons and skills to work to help our franchisees and company survive.

I love spreadsheets. Love them. Ever since I was a young staffer at EY, I have worked on projections for my future on my spreadsheets. They're just a great way to create a road map. As CFO, I used them all the time to measure, manage, and forecast. It's no wonder, therefore, that at this time of high stress, I used the same tool.

"How bad can it get before we are out of business?" was the question I posed. After doing all the math and related projections, I realized that the good news was that the bar was pretty low, and we had some time to react. Fortunately, and in part because it had taken us too many years to find ways to grow, our infrastructure was not too large, and our foundation was solid. We had a runway to solve this very difficult challenge.

We took a short time to absorb the shock and lick our wounds. Then, it was time to plan and act.

In every economic situation, there are some people who do fine. In fact, there are some who prosper. Even during the Great Depression, some people thrived or at least lived their lives normally. With the vast economy of the United States, there have always been consumers who weather the storm of market downturns. Based on this understanding, I believed it was our job to find out how to reach out to those customers. I set the expectation to survive and thrive through this. I believe my life experiences were instrumental in this way of thinking and mobilizing.

"Are we going to die? Is anyone arresting us? Putting us in jail? Executing us? Is anyone alone in a foreign country with little resources? If the answer is no, we can survive all of this." That was my attitude, one that I freely shared with our teams in many forms. I knew we could get through this. We just had to believe.

For me, I knew that the calamity that was going to defeat me hadn't been invented yet.

"Bring it!" I said out loud at an executive meeting. "We got this!"

After all, I had reached this point in my life by doing just that: surviving and thriving because I had expected to.

Over the years, as we had focused on growing the company, we intrinsically knew what made us and our franchisees' offerings to consumers special. But like many companies in growth and prosperity mode, we had not taken the time to define ourselves clearly. The challenge before us required us to be much more aware of who we were and why our customers bought our products. Although, in hindsight, we didn't define ourselves and our brands far enough—something we did much more effectively years later. Even so, we still ended up with enough insight to move forward.

We spent countless hours reviewing, testing, and analyzing what could work. We also had to do it all relatively fast.

What we learned was that, rather than brand marketing, it was time to focus on direct response. We had to find ways to generate leads from customers interested in exploring home improvement and then send them to our franchisees. We also had to clearly explain why our processes and products were better than any other solutions those same customers could find.

This process taught me the company's essence better than ever before. Testing and pushing our messaging while measuring and adjusting it made us better direct-response marketers. It also highlighted that perhaps some product enhancements were necessary.

Over the years, as we had grown rapidly, we had enjoyed success without having to push our product offering or innovate. Our soul-searching exercises as we attempted to solve the reduction in consumer demand highlighted that we had indeed stepped away from our core offerings. It also highlighted that we were missing innovative products our consumers wanted. So, we went to work.

Our manufacturing partners were feeling the pain of the drop in consumer demand even more significantly than we were. They had equipment, staff, and fixed overhead to worry about. The bottom had fallen out for them even more rapidly than it had for us.

We may be able to write our own ticket. Manufacturers are looking for ways to sell their products, and there aren't many stores still standing. We could very well be one of their most reliable sales channels, we thought. *So, why not capitalize?*

"Let's renegotiate with our suppliers," we concluded in collaboration with our vendor alliance team. "Let's return to them and lay the foundation for new agreements. We can explain that we now use our collective marketing dollars between the corporate office and franchisees to recruit consumers through well-tested and documented direct marketing efforts. Our marketing dollars combined with our franchisees' ability to visit with our customers in their homes create a compelling marketing narrative. What we need to be able to sell our products—and therefore our manufacturers' products—is our supply partners' commitment to innovative products priced appropriately for our franchisees and customers." This became our action plan.

We held meetings with our major manufacturers to be able to educate them about the potential for our collaboration. They were a success!

We now had committed manufacturers with products that suited our customers at prices that they could afford and that our franchisees could benefit from. It was a win-win-win situation.

Our marketing efforts proved fruitful. Most suppliers of home improvement products were independent. Our franchisees competed in that same space. The advantage of our franchises over any others was that they operated effectively like an independent dealer. Still, they had the backing, sophistication, and pooling of the resources that we could bring. As a result, although many independents unfortunately left the business during this time, our franchisees fared much better. In fact, some picked up the business left by those who could no longer service their clients. The pie of consumers looking for our offerings had shrunk, but now, we were the largest slice.

During the Great Recession, we made many more enhancements to our company. We improved our franchise support—because we had to. We became better marketers—because we had to. We ended up with better products and even better terms with our manufacturers—because we had to. We improved our marketing messaging for franchise licensing to "If you are at risk of losing or have already lost your job, isn't it better to own your business and therefore your destiny?"—because we had to. I had been here before. I had been left to fend for myself as a teenager in Turkey years before. I had learned Turkish, and I had learned the way things were done. Not because I wanted to but because I had to. And it had paid off. Those experiences prepared me for this challenge. I knew I could do what was needed because I had to.

The net result of these changes was that we understood our core offerings better. We also understood and connected with our customers more effectively. We created a better, more responsive infrastructure. We designed and implemented better relationships, terms, and products with our manufacturers. It didn't seem like it as we were suffering through navigating the Great Recession, but applying what I had learned to help overcome this adversity actually created more opportunities for us as a business and for me as a person.

As the fog of the Great Recession gradually lifted, our pie of consumers got bigger. Having earned the title of the most dominant player in our space, we experienced a fantastic growth trajectory like nothing we had experienced before.

The Great Recession was a terrible period. At the same time, it was a fantastic learning experience. Our growth and success beyond the Great Recession was unprecedented. I'm sad that our country and so many good people had to deal with the setbacks of this dark chapter in our history. I'm also grateful for the lessons I learned through it. Perseverance, tenacity, and commitment to building the company were the main reasons we survived these trying times. Much like in my personal life, the challenges in my professional life were uninvited but absolutely necessary to create a better company. Our growth trajectory from 2008 onward was like nothing I would have expected. I had learned how to deal with and navigate severe economic headwinds, a lesson that would prove useful for many years to come.

CHAPTER TWENTY-SEVEN
Bobby

Bobby (Babak) was a very big baby. When he was born to my middle sister, Shirana, he was the biggest of the grandchildren. He had blond hair, a light complexion, light eyes, and a small mouth. From early on, he had the uncanny ability to be a comedian. Even before he started talking, I would crack up and laugh wholeheartedly as he made faces to entertain me. He was an entertainer.

One day at my sister Sherry's house, all the grandchildren were playing. Someone gave them candies. Bobby, at two years old and by far the youngest, took his candy and inspected it. He loved to eat, so this candy was definitely up his alley. Then, he noticed that I was watching him, and instead of eating the candy, he stretched his fist up and offered it to me! I was amazed to see a two-year-old, who clearly adored his candy, saving it and then offering it to someone else. That was my beloved Bobby.

After his sister, Neda, was born, Bobby would enjoy letting her do her thing. Neda was loud, active, bossy, and cute as can be. Bobby enjoyed sitting back and letting her operate as aggressively as she wanted. There were many birthdays of Bobby's where he didn't even open his gifts because he let Neda do it. He was just less than eighteen months older than her.

We lived only minutes apart from Shirana and her family. My children were about ten years younger than hers. They all went to the same elementary school, though many years apart. Bobby and Neda would spend many days every week at our house, and we loved it. They were like my children, like Sam and Sara's older brother and sister.

When Shirana announced that they were going to move to Texas, I was devastated. In fact, we were all devastated. We loved those kids, and we had just settled into an area where our children could grow up together. Yet, it was not meant to be. When Bobby and Neda were preteens, Shirana and her family moved to Dallas.

Shirana made sure the kids came back to visit and stay as often as their schools would allow. I would happily host them every Christmas break and if they came back during the summer. In fact, my children, Sam and Sara, and Shirana's children, Bobby and Neda, and my other sister Shani's children, Idean and Rameen (close to my children's ages), would all sleep in the same room while they were visiting and for weeks at a time.

So, when Bobby offered to take care of the four younger kids while we were all on a family cruise, it made sense. Or, when he would visit and would take them for rides, it would make sense. Or, when they would all come over and jump into our pool, and Bobby would use a surfboard to create fake waves for the kids, it would make sense. And therefore, when he took them to rent their tuxedos for my dad's funeral, that also made sense.

My dad passed away in February 2008. In April of that same year, Sam, Sara, and I visited Shirana and Bobby. We also drove up to Oklahoma to visit Neda, who was attending college there. Shirana and her family had bought a ranch in Dallas and had all kinds of animals. Bobby took my kids for rides on their farm equipment and showed them around. We had a wonderful time.

On a warm summer day in August of 2008, I got ready to go to work as usual. Because it was summer break for the kids, they would stay home with Gosia. I put on my suit and came down to say goodbye to them when Gosia asked me to take the phone. She was pale and seemed confused. "It's your sister-in-law. You should take the call before you leave," she said.

"Bobby is gone. He was killed in a car accident," my brother's wife told me abruptly. I guess there was no good way of breaking the news.

I was stunned. Absolutely speechless. "What do you mean? What happened?"

I learned that he had worked long hours, dropped off his friends as their designated driver, and then fallen asleep behind the wheel. As I hung up, Sam and Sara had gathered at the table. They knew something had happened. And I told them. I don't think any of us, including me, who was supposed to be the adult in the room, could process this. Looking back, I was so shocked that I didn't know how to handle the moment—something I'm very sorry about today. I was frozen, confused, and numb. There was no room for emotions yet. The only thing I could think of was my sister. I had to go support her. We had to all go to support her.

I called my sisters one by one. "We have to go to Dallas. If you want to go with me, I'll buy the tickets." Of course, they wanted to go. I sprang into action as per my tried-and-true tool to deal with trauma. I knew that my sister, Bobby's mom, needed us the most. And that I was going to take care of her.

I called the airline and explained the situation to beg for seats. "What morgue is he in?" the customer service rep asked.

What do you mean, "What morgue?" What? How is this even possible? Are we talking about my Bobby? The loving, funny, beautiful Bobby? How is this possible? Then, she proceeded to ask me to spell his name. Every letter brought more tears to my eyes until I started sobbing. I just couldn't understand what was going on.

That afternoon, my sisters and I were on our way to Dallas. We had the last row on the plane, but the kind flight attendants knew what we were traveling for and took great care of us.

When I saw Shirana and Neda, I just sobbed. There was nothing I could do. Or was there? As usual, I found what I needed to do. I found ways to take care of them.

"This is my baby. I'll see to it that he's well taken care of," I declared. After much sobbing and agony, I asked, "Where is he? And how can I see him?"

My sweet Bobby had started work at 5 AM that morning. He then agreed to go out with his friends that night after an exhausting day. But he was not going to drink. After dropping them off, he sped back home very tired. On a stretch of the flat Texas highway, in the early-morning hours, he had fallen asleep and driven into the guardrails. There were no brake marks. Bobby was twenty-one years old.

I did my best to take care of Bobby and Shirana, her husband, Kami, and Neda. My goal was to make sure his loving family saw him peaceful and at rest. I believe we accomplished that.

A family that had just lost its father, my dad, Behzad Behzadi, six months prior, now faced the heart-wrenching tragedy of losing Bobby. Having organized the funeral, I was the last person to kiss him on his forehead. I'll forever cherish that kiss. Our goodbyes to him were emotional and agonizing. His family, his mom, his dad, and Neda loved him beyond words. And his cousins, including my children, who adored him, talked about him at the service in tears.

I've never gotten over his loss. He is forever in my heart and my life. I've learned to live with this reality but have never embraced it. I love Babak and will forever. He taught me to have a zest for life and to be kind and loving. His loving influence has shaped me and taught me to embrace those I love. And he also reminded me of the fragility of life, so that I know to cherish it.

CHAPTER TWENTY-EIGHT

Through Death and Back Again

I didn't know that the largest challenges, challenges larger than pain, were yet to come. Each would teach me, in its own way, to discover my true self and vision.

By THE END OF 2008, I had faced the most devastating recession that had caused a significant existential challenge to the company. I had also suffered the loss of my father, and I dealt with, agonized through, and emotionally processed the most heartbreaking loss of my nephew, Babak, at twenty-one years of age. It was hard to imagine how much harder and more severe life could be.

Somehow, however, I had found ways to stay focused on the company and lead through this Great Recession. I had somehow found the strength to be there nightly for my father and help ease his transition while processing his passing. There was just so much loss and confusion. I'm not sure how I found my way through it all. I believe a lot of it was based on doing my best to do good for others. Staying focused on that principle helped me navigate those choppy waters and keep my head on straight. I also believe that building resilience through the adversities I experienced throughout my life gave me the tools to find my way through these tragedies.

So, when 2009 came around, I welcomed it. I hoped and prayed that it would not be as hard a year as 2008.

For many reasons, including the significant drop in home values, it was the right time for us to find a new, larger home in a better neighborhood. I set out to shop for a new home and found one in October. We had just moved in when my headaches started getting worse. I had always had headaches and thought that was just how I was built, but the speed and severity of these headaches became much more intense.

One day, I woke up very sick. I felt like I was out of my mind. I sent my children to school, as Sam had just started high school, and Sara had just started middle school. I then called and asked a neighbor to pick them up when it was time for them to come home. I called in sick to work and went to bed. And that's when it all started—vomiting violently, nonstop.

As sick as I was, it didn't even occur to me to call for help. This is where years of training to be self-reliant, a quality that had saved my life before, became a detriment. It's interesting how this works. Often, we adopt strategies in life that help us get through tough times.

And yet, those same strategies can become a pattern, a compulsion, if repeated frequently. They can then become potentially harmful. Throughout my life and until that point, I had learned to only rely on myself. I had focused on doing well by others. But on that day, considering the health challenge I was facing, I needed help. I should have called 911 but didn't. Not until Sam came home.

When Sam returned from school that afternoon and found me in that condition, he sprang into action. He observed how I looked and behaved and made a wise, quick decision to dial 911. That's how bad it was. I looked like I was dying. Looking back, I'm still in awe of his maturity and ability to think quickly at such a young age. He was only fourteen years old.

"How did you think and act so quickly?" I asked him years later.

"I learned that from you," he said with a smile on his face.

I'm grateful for his swift and caring action.

The paramedics moved quickly. I reached the hospital shortly after, and the doctors immediately went in search of any medical condition that would make me so sick. Abdominal conditions, such as vomiting, can have many causes. They just couldn't get it to stop.

Because I had a history of endometriosis and had had surgery a couple of times, their first guess was that the headaches and vomiting had to do with female issues. I thought so, too, because it made the most sense. Hormonal changes can make you throw up.

They released me from the ER, and yet the headaches and nausea wouldn't go away. I went in and out of hospitals, still vomiting. The doctors had no idea why. I did my best to endure the pain as much as I could, and I went back to work.

Finally, through a cousin who was a nurse, I was introduced to a local cardiologist. It made little sense to have a cardiologist deal with my abdominal issues, but at least he took my case seriously. After he examined me, he said it was not normal for someone to have problems with their abdomen for so long. He then admitted me to the hospital to figure out the real reason I was suffering.

I was in the hospital for seven days and had all sorts of tests— endoscopy, colonoscopy, you name it. They were looking at potential rare viral or bacterial infections. Nothing showed up except for a minor issue they thought was a female issue. In the meantime, I continued to throw up regularly. I despaired of ever getting an accurate diagnosis.

Then, my doctor, who had expected to land on a diagnosis within the week, came into my room looking puzzled and said, "Tell me the story again." I repeated a step-by-step account of the day when I was rushed to the ER. In retelling the story, I mentioned the headaches again. He said, "Well, you had a headache. Let's explore that. Let's take a look at your head now."

I was sent for a CT scan of my head. After the image was taken, the kind technician looked at me with care. He had seen something and knew I would have to learn it from my doctor. Within a short amount of time, I was back in my room.

I had been in the same hospital room for seven days by then. The room was stark, with beige walls and cold hospital lights. It was a private room because doctors weren't sure that what I had wasn't contagious. There was one bed that was situated by the window. There wasn't much to see out of that window, but I was grateful to see natural light through it. I was tired and sick and had been through lots of tests. I was on a cocktail of sedatives, which made me confused and slow, to manage my symptoms.

The room had a distinct hospital smell. It felt cold, uninviting, and lonely. I had visitors only occasionally. Since I didn't have a diagnosis and the stay was exploratory, my family and I thought it would be short and not require many visits.

"No, really. You don't need to come," was my response when my sisters or my husband offered to visit. Looking back, I realized that I did want company, but at the time, I was more focused on not inconveniencing them. I didn't want them to take time off from work and make the journey to the hospital. Yet another example of self-reliance run amuck! We also intentionally kept my children away from the hospital because as far as I was concerned, they didn't need to be exposed to the sadness. I was trying to shield them.

As I settled into my bed after my CT scan, my doctor entered the room. He had a concerned look and wanted to quickly share the news.

"Shirin, there is a growth in your head. It's a brain tumor that we believe is on your pituitary gland," he said somberly.

I was alone in my room when I was given the news.

Having been heavily medicated for pain and vomiting, I had a hard time processing the information he was giving me. What I did know was that it was not good. But I also believed that it was nothing. My natural reaction—much like the one I had when my dad was diagnosed—was to assume that it was all a mistake.

"You need to see a specialist immediately. I'll give you the name of a specialist at the University of Southern California. Be sure to get in touch with them as soon as possible and go see him," he urged me.

Now that I had a diagnosis, I was released from the hospital. It was near Christmas, and the doctor at USC gave me an appointment on January 2.

I was working to help my company recover from the Great Recession while Sam and Sara started new phases of school. Despite my physical struggles, I was trying to stay positive and engaged, but time was not on my side—I needed to figure out my next steps. Since I'd been told at the hospital that there was perhaps a female issue as well, I pursued that angle with an OB-GYN. To his credit, he kept saying, "This is not a female issue. These are not the right symptoms." I had an ultrasound done with his nurse practitioner, and she saw some hemorrhaging. I now believe I was hemorrhaging because my entire system was in distress. Looking back, he was right. It was not a female issue, but it presented itself as such.

The nurse said, "There's some hemorrhaging. Should we just take some things out and leave others?"

I said, "Just take it all out. Nobody knows what this is. Let's do it all." And just like that, we scheduled a hysterectomy in January. I had not yet seen anyone about the brain tumor.

We drove to the surgeon at USC in early January. USC is a teaching hospital, so several student doctors were in the room with us. The surgeon had an image of my head pulled up on a big screen and pointed to the growth in my image.

"You have a tumor that's lodged between your optic nerves. Can you see well?" he asked.

Still stunned, I saw how the tumor was bending the optic nerves, a whitish-gray invader growing over them like the cocoon of a poisonous moth.

I said, "I think so. Sometimes I have a hard time keeping track of fast-moving images, especially on a computer monitor."

It was so overwhelming. I don't remember much of what the surgeon said, but the primary takeaway was that this wasn't a pituitary tumor. It was a tumor lodged between my optic nerves. He showed me how the tumor had bent the nerves and was pushing on them. It is expected that one would lose part or all of their peripheral vision due to such pressure. In the long run, if that kind of tumor continues to grow, one's entire vision—and, eventually, life—is put at risk. You simply can't have something continuing to grow in your brain.

The doctor sent me for a vision test to determine whether any damage had already been done to my vision. I passed it with flying colors, and the doctor was surprised that my peripheral vision was intact.

"Well, this is good news. Although your nerves are under substantial pressure, your vision hasn't been impacted yet. This means we have to act quickly so that things don't get any worse," he explained after he reviewed the results of my vision test.

He then explained that the tumor would not respond to chemo, and radiation wouldn't work either because of its location. If I did radiation between my optic nerves, I would go blind. My only option was surgery, in which there was no guarantee I'd live or that I would maintain my sight if I survived the surgery. At that time, though, it was my best option.

"Go home and get your affairs in order, and do not postpone the surgery," he suggested. He also explained that, from the look of it, the tumor was not likely to be cancer, but because of its location and my age, it would grow if left untreated.

This was a lot of information to process. I never expected this to happen to me, but again, no one ever does.

Other than my sisters and eventually the executive team at work, I did not let anybody else at work or other friends or my children know how sick I was. I told my sisters they had to keep it hush-hush because I didn't want to create a lot of anxiety in my kids.

I didn't lie to them. I just downplayed everything. That's why I didn't tell anybody else either. I was so busy taking care of everyone else's feelings and needs that I didn't take care of my own. I didn't have a strong support system for myself, and that would later become part of what I examined as I recovered from the surgeries. I've since learned that this behavior is not unusual for a trauma survivor. At the time, this approach made perfect sense to me.

I'm a very emotionally connected and extroverted person. If I must, I can be on my own, but I prefer being around people. I care for people. I like engaging with people. And yet, through this life-threatening ordeal, I had little support. What I did have was necessary and helped save my life. I've learned since to support others through their health challenges. Healing requires connection and affection. I'm lucky to have had some, and I'm confident I could have used more. My life and the relationships that I've built since then are so much richer because I've learned firsthand what good support systems look like.

I am grateful for my resilience. I believe it may have been passed down from my parents and ancestors, but it was developed through the hardships I've faced and worked through. I've learned to tackle adversity, which has taught me resilience. Adversity and trauma can be valuable teachers, as long as they don't overwhelm us. Dealing with challenges is like exercising a muscle—the more we face and overcome, the stronger we become. Avoiding hardships and challenges is impossible, but we can choose to learn and grow from them.

To be clear, not all adversities and traumas can be faced. If they're too severe for the level of resilience we've built, they could destroy us. To have resilience in facing a challenge, two conditions need to be met. First, you must have embraced challenges in the past and in your life with the belief that you can grow through them. You should not avoid challenges but face them to develop the ability to overcome them. Second, the adversity should not be so severe that it would be above your abilities. The saying "What doesn't kill you makes you stronger" is true, but you must have built the strength to manage what could be fatal. I had to tap into my resilience to deal with my life-threatening illness. I believed I had it in me.

———————

Once I accepted the diagnosis, I decided to do some research and find the right surgeon. I was still sick and had all my leadership responsibilities. And now, I had to learn how to deal with my condition. I had to learn fast and make the right decisions to save my vision and my life. I contacted another physician and saw two or three other specialists. I learned that the first doctor's opinion was unanimous. There was no alternative to brain surgery, and delaying it would not bring any benefits. It was inevitable, and the sooner it happened, the better.

During my research phase—I'm still puzzled how I managed to research, as sick as I was—I read a short book that a renowned surgeon had written about brain tumors.

One of his opinions was that surgeons, especially brain surgeons, connect with their patients during surgery. With no intended insult to other surgeons, he believed that there is a special, almost spiritual, connection once a surgeon opens up a patient's skull and touches their brain. He advised that it's best to work with a brain surgeon whom you connect with as a patient.

As I continued my search, my cousin, who had initially introduced me to the cardiologist, called me out of the blue. "Shirin," she said, "one of our physicians came and whispered in my ear and said, 'Tell your cousin to go see Dr. Daniel Kelly at St. John's.'"

I immediately called Dr. Kelly, and because it was an urgent brain tumor, his office gave me an appointment within a couple of days. When he walked in, I knew. I thought, *Oh! This is my doctor. This is who I want doing my brain surgery.* I just bonded with him. What a miracle!

Dr. Kelly specialized in primary brain tumors that originate in your brain. A subset of rare primary brain tumors are ones around the optic nerves. Dr. Kelly was at the forefront of surgeons who successfully removed these skull-based tumors, like mine, endonasally (through the nose). Dr. Kelly and a small group of surgeons would go in through the nose with instruments, drill a hole in my skull to reach the tumor from below, and then remove the tumor. They would then use the septum (which they would cut as they went up through the nose), turn it around, and use it to close the hole in the skull.

Before this method was invented, surgeons used to take bones from other parts of the body to cover the hole in the skull. The risk with this method was that the new tissue could die, which would then potentially reopen the hole. By going through the septum, the surgeons could leave the top of the septum still connected to the skull. This meant that the septum would continue to live and therefore offered a much better option for closing the hole for the long term.

I trusted him. He suggested we wait because he had a new partner, Dr. Amin Kassam, who was coming on board. He wanted to wait so they could do the surgery together. I was to be Dr. Kassam's first patient at St. John's. Dr. Kassam had been one of the pioneers of this particular surgery, and he was just then joining the team.

They also had a new ear, nose, and throat (ENT) specialist, Dr. Carrau, joining them shortly. Dr. Carrau had partially created the methods used for this surgery, and I was going to be one of his first patients at this hospital.

Unbelievable! I thought as I heard the news of Dr. Carrau coming on board. *As unlucky as I am to be sick, I'm exceptionally lucky to have the three world-renowned surgeons in this very limited number of surgery cases operate on me!* I reminded myself with a smile on my tired face.

I was optimistic. Perhaps the same optimism had shown up all those years ago as I sat at the gas station booth reflecting on my seemingly dire situation. The same hopeful thinking that energized me then to dream of someday running a big company. The same hopeful voice that had guided me through numerous obstacles in life was back, this time aiming to literally save my life. There was serendipity at work.

Yet, I was still trying to decide if I should do the surgery. I called their office once, and I was so nervous.

Dr. Kassam said, "Listen. You just have to get it done."

I scheduled my operation for March 15. I told my sisters, and it was a cry fest. I did my best to make them believe what I believed. I never doubted that I was going to be okay. I would lie in bed and tell the tumor, "You're going to go, and I'm going to stay. You're going to go, and I'm going to stay."

Facing crises of great magnitude taught me to lean on that same ability to expect what I want. I found positive and hopeful attitudes and visualizations that helped carry me through to the resolution.

I'm so thankful that I trusted my instincts. They led me to the best surgeon for me. I was grateful for the serendipities of my diagnosis, my choice of doctors, and all that was happening. Each new twist and ray of hope fed and strengthened my tenacity and courage. I held the resilience I knew I was capable of in my heart and used my past lessons and awareness regularly.

In the days leading up to the surgery, I prepared myself for what could happen. I asked my surgeons dozens of questions. I asked them about the risks. I got the standard reply that there are risks with every surgery, but there were a couple of big ones to keep in mind.

The biggest risk was complete blindness. They weren't sure if the tumor was feeding from the same blood supply as the optic nerves, and if it was, there was a possibility of an optic nerve stroke. I started researching how to manage my life without vision while continuing to earn a living for myself and my family. The second-highest risk was that, because they were going through my nose, bacteria could be introduced into the brain.

Ultimately, there was too much to worry about, and I turned my trust over to the surgeons and assured myself that whatever happened, I could handle it.

I didn't know that the largest challenges, challenges larger than pain, were yet to come. Each would teach me, in its own way, to discover my true self and vision.

———————

The surgery was scheduled for a Monday morning. By now, my kids had seen me extremely sick, first with a hysterectomy and now six weeks post-hysterectomy, still suffering from debilitating headaches and vomiting.

What seemed to concern them most was the fact that I'd barely recovered from a hysterectomy, and suddenly, now I was about to undergo brain surgery. I had been sick for months, and my children were as distressed as I was over this new event, if not more so. My doctors wanted to wait six weeks (and no more) between the hysterectomy and the brain surgery to ensure I could handle the anesthesia again, because we were all aware there needed to be a gap between surgeries for the body and brain to recover. March 15 would be the right time.

My second sister, Shirana, quit her job to stay with my kids. At the time, she was still living in Texas and had lost her beautiful son, Babak, less than two years before. Shirana has always had the biggest heart. She was the same sister who took the fall for me all those years ago in Iran when the Guards found a book in my luggage. And she was arrested as a result because she was protecting me. This was the same sister who selflessly worked to pay rent when we lived together so that I wouldn't have to work as hard while I went to college. This was the loving sister who set aside her pain and lovingly gave up her job to stay with my children. Shirana made Sam and Sara feel loved and cared for. She picked them up from school and bought them fun snacks. She let them watch funny movies. She stepped into the role of a loving mother while I was in the hospital and recovering. I will be indebted to her forever for all the kindness she has shown me. Shirana is a gem.

At 5 AM, my husband drove me to Santa Monica and checked me into the hospital. My oldest sister, Sherry, showed up, which made me emotional. The medical staff prepped me, and she said goodbye and kissed me on the forehead.

I had focused clarity as I was being prepped for the surgery. I kept thinking and knew, *This is going to be okay.* I expected to survive this.

The staff asked me to walk into the surgery room rather than be wheeled in on a gurney. The operating room was huge, but the bed was narrow, white, and very cold. Giant cameras and television screens were around the room, along with several nurses. A few people in surgical scrubs were sitting at a computer, and I was told they were computer specialists.

Dr. Kelly and Dr. Kassam would be operating together. They would go through my nose with two devices. They were not yet in the surgery room.

The anesthesiologist was standing at the head of the surgery table. After I settled onto the cold, narrow bed, he introduced himself and then explained, "I will be giving you small doses of anesthesia in ten-minute increments. The idea is that I can bring you out quickly if needed. We may need to bring you out since we will be operating on your brain. You're in good hands. I'll be monitoring you the whole time." He comforted me.

With that, I closed my eyes. As I did, I saw a huge, brightly colored field of flowers and heard a voice say, "You're going to be okay." And that was the last I remember of the surgery.

"Shirin, open your eyes. Can you see? Can you see?" I opened my eyes to the smiling face of Dr. Kassam, who was leaning over me.

"I can see! I can see!" I started rolling my eyes, checking out every corner of the room. I was groggy and relieved to know my vision was saved.

"We did it! We took it out!" Dr. Kassam said with a smile.

When you're first born, you don't remember the face of the doctor who birthed you. But when your life is saved and you're born once more, you do remember. I'll forever remember that kind face and that smile.

"That was the good news. I also have some bad news," he said hurriedly. "We got it. We think we got the whole tumor out! But you were in surgery for over ten hours, twice as long as we expected. Once we reached the tumor and got a clearer picture of it, we discovered it had grown tentacles around a bunch of arteries. We had to unwind the tumor's tentacles, which were the thickness of a strand of hair— and if that wasn't enough, the texture of the tumor itself was also unusual." He kept explaining the surgery as I kept trying to figure out if it was bad news or just his explanation of what happened.

"Typically, these kinds of tumors have the texture of the inside of a grape, so surgeons can simply suck the tumor out," he said. "In your case, we had to chip away at the tumor, like getting gum off the bottom of a shoe." Apparently, all this was going on through a tight passage and a hole the size of a dime, crammed full of cameras and cutting instruments.

"It was amazing," he said, concluding his post-surgery explanations. "And that's why it took us ten hours."

I nodded as he explained. I would need to think about things later when I wasn't in a brain fog of recovery and in so much pain.

All I needed was the good news—that in spite of the unexpected challenges, I could see! But as excited as I was that the surgery was a success, the reality was that I was still in extreme pain. Why wouldn't I be? My face was literally broken during the process. My septum, the part of the nose that separates the left and right airways of the nasal cavity, and divides the two nostrils, had been cut and turned around to cover my skull. My system was in a state of shock.

"I'm in pain," I told Dr. Kassam.

"Here's the bad news. We can't give you pain meds, Shirin. I'm sorry. Not for a while," he said.

This was one fact they had not told me before. They couldn't give me pain meds because the tumor and the surgery were neurological, and they had to keep giving me tests every hour on the hour to make sure I hadn't lost anything or had a stroke. If they gave me pain meds, they wouldn't be able to tell if the pain meds were making me act funny or if I was in severe neurological trouble. Pain medication would interfere with the tests.

My head was pounding. Every bone in my face, especially my cheekbones, was on fire. Burning, throbbing pain that brings tears to your eyes. My nose was broken, and the septum was cut into pieces to be used to cover the hole in my skull. It felt like someone had punched me in the nose. I was shocked to hear that I wasn't going to be given any pain assistance.

Perhaps it was my years of enduring pain that helped me through. In the fogginess of post-surgery, I pulled all my strength together. I was resolved.

Shirin, this is physical pain. You can do it. You can get through this. Relax and focus. The pain will pass, I repeated to myself as I bore soul-crushing pain.

Maybe it was the loss of my entire way of life as I left Iran, the loss of my best and only close friend, the loss of my beloved father, the loss of Babak, or all the challenges and setbacks I had as a poor Iranian immigrant woman trying to build a life that had prepared me for this fight. I was prepared. I was determined. I was bringing all my being into this fight. This was the fight for my life—literally.

I knew that what was going to break me hadn't been born yet. I was going to give it my all, and I expected, believed, and worked toward beating this setback too.

I have since met many survivors of all kinds of life-threatening conditions. I'm well aware that the Divine ultimately makes the decision as to who lives or not. I've known many brave souls who fought valiantly and courageously to survive. Not all of them did. However, I do believe that surviving is certainly assisted by our committed belief and good work to achieve it. Trying our best may not guarantee survival, but without it, our demise may be guaranteed.

I was in intensive care with a balloon inside my skull, under the hole they'd drilled. They placed it there during the surgery and filled it with saline to keep the septum in place. There was a tube coming out of my nose from the balloon that was attached to my cheek.

My entire system had gone awry. Removing the tumor had apparently unleashed a cascade of side effects and destabilized several body systems. Everything was wildly out of control. I was in the ICU for days.

When I started feeling better, Dr. Kelly said they would take the balloon out if I could bend my head and I didn't have a leak—clear fluid that would indicate my spinal fluid was leaking through the hole in my skull. The moment came to remove the balloon, so they drained the saline out and pulled it out of my nose. Then, they had me bend my head. No leak. I had passed the test.

I was finally sent home. I had gone a long time without washing my hair. I still couldn't wash it myself at all, even after being discharged. After my husband and Sam left for a school event, I had an idea. "Would you wash my hair?" I asked my daughter, Sara, who was twelve at the time. She bravely agreed. And didn't wash it just once, but ten times because there was so much blood crusted throughout it. Sara was already showing signs of resilience. Perhaps witnessing how I had made it through this ordeal with determination and perseverance reminded her of how very strong she was.

Sam took it upon himself to bring me my medicines when they were due. There were other adults like my husband and Gosia and, from time to time, other family members who took care of me. But Sam took charge of the timing of my medications.

On my first day home, Sam brought me a memory stick with my favorite songs. "Here, you can listen to your songs while you're resting," he said with his always infectious smile. I was excited to have music to listen to.

I was such a fan of rap—2Pac, Eminem, Dr. Dre, Missy Elliott, and 50 Cent were all on this memory stick. The upbeat music that Sam and I had bonded over reminded me of better days, like when I'd pick him up from the beach in my SUV, blasting our favorite tracks. He'd loved that time, and his friends had thought it was cool to see a mom playing their music. I'd been a fan since long before they were born! This playlist filled my days with joy and gave me energy during my darkest times.

The doctor had told me I could take pain meds at home but to watch for my pain getting worse. Sure enough, I began to deteriorate badly. I kept asking for pain meds more frequently. I didn't fully real-ize how bad things were getting until one day when I was walking with my husband into a lab near our home to take my weekly blood test. As I was tenderly making my way, a woman approached me and asked, "I'm sorry if I'm intruding. But can I say a prayer for you?" She had tears in her eyes.

"Yes. Please." I knew she thought I was dying. Little did I know, she was right. She put her hand on my shoulder and whispered her prayers. I couldn't even keep my eyes open. The pain in my head and face was too severe.

When I got home, I decided that it was time to finally call the doctor's office. They said to drive back to Santa Monica, an hour's drive away, to the hospital immediately. Dr. Carrau was there and checked me out. The pain of the tests he put me through was excruci-ating, as he had to go up through my nose to vacuum fluids and blood out of the nostrils.

The doctors were worried about meningitis, so they sent me for a spinal tap. The doctor performing the spinal tap asked me to roll over on my stomach, and I told him I wasn't allowed to because of the potential risk of the hole in my skull opening up again. I still had another four months to go before I was allowed to roll over on my stomach or bend my neck because the hole needed to heal and seal itself.

"The risk of meningitis is your biggest risk right now, so roll over," he urged as he worried about me dying.

As soon as I rolled over, I felt a lot of what felt like water gushing out of my nose. But I knew what it was. I said, "This is my spinal fluid! This is my spinal fluid!" I don't think he understood what I was trying to say; I'm sure he had never dealt with anything like that before. Eventually, I was admitted to the hospital as a routine next step of the procedure.

The headache pain became so intense that I still can't describe it. For the next few hours, I heard bubbles in my cheeks. I was in such severe pain that I couldn't move my head. Inside my head, there was a rush of pressure. It was as if my brain was hitting a wall over and over again. Every move created a feeling of death. So much pain beyond description.

If I moved my head, even by inches, pain searingly flared, licks of flame from a fire. I was covered in sweat from the severity of the pain in my head. I didn't know then that my brain didn't have that all too critical fluid cushion. No one knew this at the time. All they figured was that I was recovering from the spinal tap. All I knew was to be strong and deal with the pain.

Nurses kept doing clinical tests and asking me question after question. Thankfully, I was awake and aware. Finally, eight hours into the incredible pain, I pushed the button, and a nurse came in.

"This is it," I told her. "You will not leave here until you get me my doctor. I had brain surgery ten days ago. I shouldn't have this pain. Something is wrong. I know I sound right and remember facts you ask me, but I know something is really wrong." I took charge with my last bit of strength, a move that ended up saving my life.

Thankfully, the nurse found Dr. Kassam, who had just walked out of surgery. As soon as he saw me, he said, "Let's take you for a CT scan."

When they pulled me out of the CT scan machine, the technician asked, "What are you here for?"

I replied, "I had brain surgery ten days ago." He sent me back to my room, where the head of the ICU and many nurses were waiting for me.

The head of the ICU introduced himself and said, "Shirin, you've lost all your spinal fluid. Your surgery has failed."

What he didn't tell me was that I was about to die.

I didn't realize at the time that losing any of your spinal fluid was risky. Losing all your spinal fluid in the skull was impossible to survive. That would typically mean your heart stops and you stop breathing. But I had lost more than they had ever seen anyone lose. My skull was empty, without any spinal fluid. In other words, they assumed I was about to die.

Even though it was ten at night, they opened the surgery room. Nurses started swarming me, searching for a single vein to put anesthesia in me. My veins had collapsed, and there were no good veins to use for an IV.

The anesthesiologist ran out of the room, telling the nurses not to touch me. But they did anyway.

One nurse found a vein, and then they were yelling at each other. The vein collapsed. They had now lost the one vein they thought they had. Every minute counted because with the brain exposed to an environment of no spinal fluid, surely I couldn't live much longer.

When the anesthesiologist ran back into the room and realized what had happened, she screamed furiously, "What are you doing?" Then she looked at me and said, "I'm going to give you something to help calm you down."

I said, "You guys need to calm down. I'm calm. It's you guys who need to calm down." She gave me something that not only calmed me down but also put me under. I found out later that they got into my system through a vein in my foot.

My nightmare wasn't over. After being given enough medicine to paralyze me but not enough to keep me knocked out, I came to in the middle of the surgery. I knew that they didn't yet know that I was aware and awake and that I could hear them drilling. I couldn't move to let them know I was awake—my body was paralyzed. Finally, I don't know how, but I coughed a couple of times. One of the nurses said, "She's awake!" They put me under again. This time, I stayed asleep.

They went in and found the hole where the fluid was leaking. They took some fat from my abdomen, glued it back, and watched to ensure it wasn't leaking. This took five hours.

But I had a new problem: How would I get more spinal fluid? It wouldn't be as simple as a blood transfusion. The body must make more fluid to replace what has been lost. The risk was that if I couldn't make more fluid and make it quickly, I wouldn't survive. There was no guarantee I would be able to produce more.

The immediate crisis was over, but I was still not allowed to move because they wanted to ensure that my body started making the spinal fluid. It was critical that I did not put any weight on my brain stem. Then, my liver started failing because of all the medications I was on. In addition, I was running a fever they couldn't bring down.

Throughout my recovery, Dr. Kassam would ask me, "What do you want to eat?"

"Pancakes," I would say, and he would buy me pancakes from the cafeteria himself.

Dr. Kassam told me that he was devastated when he found me back in the ICU and had to do my second surgery. He thought that he had lost me . . . he thought he had killed me, a pain he couldn't bear.

That time was filled with lucky coincidences. For instance, I didn't know that coffee, which I love, helps you make spinal fluid. Guess who was drinking coffee all day long? They would do a CT scan in the morning and another at night to see if my spinal fluid levels were building up. I don't know how much the coffee contributed.

Sometimes, therapy dogs were brought into the hospital to cheer patients up, and those helped too. The white standard poodle that came over occasionally and sat patiently on my bed was the highlight of my day, especially since not too many visitors could stay in the room. I needed a loving touch, and those beautiful pets offered me lots of it.

There I was, trying to recover—a lonely, difficult place to be, and I was demoralized, needing family and support. Family and friends did their best to keep me company, but the hospital was far away, and I had been there for too many days.

A female rabbi was at the hospital. I am not Jewish, but she would stop by my room when she knew I was alone and would hold my hand and pray. I had kept it together and was doing my best to be strong. But on those occasions, as we would pray together, I would let go. I would cry and feel my pent-up emotions. I am indebted to her for her kindness. I was so fortunate to have superb caregivers like her during this time that was fraught with danger and near death.

When it became evident that most of my skull was again filled with spinal fluid, I was released. Although it wasn't completely full, the danger was averted. I was instructed not to bend my neck. If I needed to pick anything up, I had to bend my knees or approach it sideways. I wasn't allowed to lean forward at any point for at least four months, and only after my doctor approved it. Days after my surgery, my doctor ordered physical therapy to make me sit and take a few steps.

"You heal by moving," he told me. That was exceptionally hard. The physical therapist would put a belt around my waist and himself, and then help guide me to take a few steps at a time. Those steps were harder than any workout I'd had before or have had since.

When I was released, I had to retrain myself to walk. I had a bed in the family room, and it became my mission to train myself to walk. I would wake up, get up from my bed, take one step, and then return to the bed, with hope and a plan to take one more step the next day.

In the first few weeks after I came home, I made a little progress during the day while managing my extreme anemia and continued fevers. I slept a lot, but anytime I woke up, I mustered up all my strength to take those steps. One step at a time was truly how I lived those days.

I used the timing of my children coming home from school as my cue to encourage myself to participate in life. I would brush my hair, put a little makeup on my very pale, tired, sick face, and greet them with a smile.

I was involved with work soon after I got home. Although I didn't have the stamina to spend much time doing so, I contributed. My company was still dealing with the aftermath of the Great Recession. I would use my cell phone and my laptop and participate in meetings in any way I could. My team would check in with their projects every day. And as I continued to make progress in my physical recovery, I engaged more and more with work.

My commitment to the organization and our stakeholders mobilized me to heal. My desire to participate in the survival of the company paralleled my desire to survive.

My daily routine of one step at a time worked. I wasn't improving on a straight line, however, as there were setbacks from time to time. What I learned about growing a company was helpful to me during my recovery. Keeping in line with my vision of full recovery while taking action was exactly what I needed to heal. Healing came slowly and gradually. My one step at a time finally resulted in successfully climbing the stairs to my home's second floor. Then, four months after my second surgery, after a visit with my team of doctors, I was given the green light to bend my neck again. That felt like victory!

The recovery was a jagged, unpredictable process, often taking two steps back for each step forward. Every setback was demoralizing, and yet, using my life experiences, I did not let them dictate my life. I would acknowledge a given setback and mourn it. Then, I would remind myself of my vision of a healthy life and keep applying myself, showing the courage and determination to face each setback head-on.

I had survived so much already. I had done most of it with little or no support, and sometimes with people rooting against me. Despite these terrible odds, I survived and started building a meaningful life. Surely, I was able to weather this storm. I was determined to continue to build the life I desired, and I knew I could do it. It hurt, and it was hard, but I was certain I had it in me.

As the fog of illness gradually lifted, I found myself with a heightened sense of awareness. I felt like I had awakened. I could see and feel things more clearly than ever before, and I experienced a profound sense of enlightenment and inspiration.

Gratitude for life had always been a part of my being. A new level of appreciation and gratitude became even more present. I remember the first time I could go grocery shopping; I looked around at the shoppers and wondered why so many were walking around like zombies. Did they not realize what a fantastic gift they had? This newfound appreciation for life made me feel deeply grateful and reflective.

It was genuinely surprising that I had survived, and I cherished this knowledge. But I also had a strong sense of responsibility. Why had I been saved? What was I supposed to do with my new gift of life? What was the message in all of this? Little did I know I would spend the rest of my days answering those questions.

After the initial and severe risks were averted, I found myself waking up in the middle of the night in a sweat. I was reliving my ordeal and reexperiencing so much of it, including the fear of death. One night, I came to terms with the fact that I was indeed experiencing post-traumatic stress disorder. I worked on processing it with the hope of someday finding help with it.

I went back to work physically within two months, even though I wasn't allowed to bend my neck and I had an hour's drive each way. I returned to work not because I'm some kind of a workaholic or was hell-bent on my career. It was because I was responsible for so many employees, franchisees, and my family. I wanted to do good in the world, especially now that I had been saved.

After my doctors finally gave me the green light to bend my neck, I started moving faster and better. Recovery would take many more months, but I was going to live and live fully. I was grateful, joyous, and somewhat scared—but optimistic as a new woman who had a much keener sense of her surroundings and deep empathy for others. I became a new, more aware person. Everything was better and clearer.

My sense of vision became sharper. I felt like I could see the richness of life and all its shapes better.

My sense of touch became stronger. I could feel more subtle sensations than ever before.

My sense of hearing became more focused. Whispers of nature became music to my ears.

While my sense of smell remained stunted for the next decade, my sense of taste became more acute. I became more sensitive to and grateful for the slightest bursts of flavor I managed to encounter.

I experienced a sharpening of my perceptions about people, a shedding of the little anxieties and distractions. I felt like I could see through people. There was life before the brain tumor and life after it. Life after has been much richer and more authentic. Indeed, facing death brought me greater life.

CHAPTER TWENTY-NINE

Cracks Starting to Show

THE GREAT RECESSION WAS a highly challenging period for us at the company. We had never seen circumstances like this—a shared experience with the rest of the country and the world. Having to respond well and quickly to a very unusual situation with fast-paced changes tested our ability to solve problems. It also tested our relationships.

We had been working together for many years. Before I joined, the guys had been working together for a few years more. We had essentially grown up together as our lives had changed and evolved. This meant we had gone through life stages and their related challenges together. Having not had any training or awareness of how life stages and new relationships affect existing ones—and having had no training or awareness of childhood trauma and its lasting effect on life—we reacted poorly. Everyone brought their own life stories, challenges, and traumas with them to highly evolved, complex relationships as roles and circumstances changed. We were not making money, and then we were. We were a small company, and then we became large. We had a steady growth plan, but then we didn't. These were many changes for six people who each had their own stories and little guidance on how to incorporate them into their work.

The Great Recession posed an existential threat to the company. The stress of potentially losing everything was very high. Like any high-stress situation, it resulted in misunderstandings, a rehashing of past experiences, and a general fracture in our bonds.

We survived the recession and, in time, grew through it, but the damage to our relationships was great.

As the company recovered and started growing again, the scars and fractures of past internal misunderstandings, coupled with individual life challenges and changes, resulted in many employees not being eager to continue working together. Passive-aggressive bursts in meetings escalated to passive-aggressive behaviors all day. Some guys would simply not show up to work. Others would refuse to take on any new projects. Others had moved on to new lives. It was a disaster waiting to happen.

"I've come up with all the ideas around here. I built this company," one of the six of us would say.

"Are you kidding? All the best and only significant ideas have come from me. You just ride my coattails," someone else would respond.

"I should have been paid more than you guys. I took on more responsibility and worked more hours, and you took me for granted," said another.

"You only understand what *you* do. You have no idea how to deal with and grow the rest of the company."

"I'm tired of cleaning up your mess. You have problems and have to be handled."

What made it all worse was that a few of the team members had intertwined family relationships. Over the years, divorces, remarriages, and some bad blood had occurred. Families and children who had grown up together were now moving in different directions.

Lives had changed, and much of it was because of success, power, and money. And we didn't have the tools or the insight to deal with these changes. The net result was a large fracture in executive management—unfortunately, not an unfamiliar scene in entrepreneurial companies that grow to success.

I was the only woman in the mix and the only person with significant experience outside of the company. I also had a strong ability to be diplomatic—a skill I had learned through life. I would find myself running between different stakeholders to simply keep the peace and to keep the company going.

As the energy, desire, ability, and know-how of our leaders were reduced compared to our company's size, concerns grew. Cracks of personal challenges showed up in company operations. Some of our training, manuals, operations, and support weren't updated regularly. We were making money, but our continued leadership in our space was at risk.

Many days, as the only executive in our executive wing, I sat in my office, juggling many parts of the company. I knew that the road we were traveling on would not end well. We were going to lose it all. Our good work, creativity, hard work, and collaboration would go to waste.

There is no such thing as staying the same. We either make ourselves better or allow ourselves to get worse. No matter how hard I tried, the complexities of personal relationships coupled with the legacies of prior work experiences, impacted by everyone's childhoods and past lives, resulted in an unsolvable situation. We couldn't work together—and most people didn't want to anyway.

I believed the company was on solid ground and poised to improve. However, the existing management infrastructure would not allow that to happen.

Great success, dreams realized, financial windfalls—these are seductive experiences. However, success is not a booster or guarantee of managerial cohesion. As we've seen in so many instances, achieving corporate success requires leaders to redefine expectations, goals, and responsibilities.

When we met in 1999, the guys had one dream: to sell the company for $50 million. By 2012, we were substantially larger than that. I knew it was time to bring in partners to help us all exit. I just had to figure out how.

Serendipity.

In August 2012, I received an email inviting me to an event. I received many emails with invitations and generally deleted them because I just didn't have time, but, for some reason, I read this one.

The email said, "We would like to invite you to an event. One of our partners, Mike, suggested we contact you."

I remembered Mike. I had worked with him briefly at EY before I left and had liked him, so I decided to learn more.

EY held an event in November in Palm Springs that was designed to celebrate entrepreneurs. Although I would generally pass, I decided to attend this one. It changed the course of my life.

In the same year, 2012, cracks started to show in my personal life as well. I had married my husband when I was twenty-two to create a home for myself. We were both immigrants looking to establish a life. That was how we bonded, and we had married after only briefly knowing each other. We were both lovely people but had a lot of immigrant baggage that we brought to the relationship. The relationship itself was founded on convenience and a desire for safety. It worked well toward its purpose.

Over the years, I had taken career steps that supported my core principle of wanting to be a mother who happened to work. After I had my children, I stepped back even more to allow flexibility in my life to be an engaged mother. Yet, even with all the strikes against me, I had managed to build a strong career. Unfortunately, the emotional gap already present between my husband and me was only exaggerated by all our challenges in building a life and then by my life-threatening ordeal. As I slowed down in my recovery, I became well aware of our emotional distance.

I had chosen to build a home. I loved the idea of having a home and building a life around my family. Being a mother was the essence of my life. I had left my family, my home, and my life suddenly many years before. I certainly appreciated and cherished my new home and life. I had no desire to leave or change my nest, but I also had to face reality.

I had made choices to the best of my ability as a young woman dealing with so much change and challenge. I now knew, however, that staying in my marriage was not sustainable.

As hard as it was, and with a heavy heart, we decided to separate at the end of 2012, and our divorce was finalized the following year. This process and its eventual outcome were some of the hardest times in my life. I reached deep within to find the courage to move forward and to find the most peaceful way to part ways. I stayed anchored in my core principle of being an engaged mother as I navigated this complex, heartbreaking, and exceptionally difficult process. I was, however, able to use the skills I had learned throughout my life to create a new, joyful, and meaningful life for me and my children. Eventually, we each found our footing in life afterward. I'm grateful for that.

The cracks in my work and personal lives happened close to the same time. Looking back, this all makes sense. It was time for change.

I had to raise my teenagers and save our company and career, using all I had.

CHAPTER THIRTY

Time to Sell

My attendance at EY's Strategic Growth Forum was life-changing. By 2012, I had been to many events. But this one was a multi-day event designed for people like me. An ocean of two thousand professionals was there by invitation only. These were entrepreneurs. They understood my plight, my journey, and the many challenges to come. It was a supportive network of nice people whom I very much needed and appreciated—especially at that phase in my life. I knew I would learn about the potential next steps for the company through this network.

I came back to work energized and shared my findings with the guys.

"What if we were to find the right partners who would buy the company and allow us to move on with our lives?" I asked everyone during one of our semi-forced meetings.

I firmly believed that the company we had built with two brands under the same umbrella had potential. But I knew that unlocking this potential would be very hard, given our existing dysfunction. I was also aware that all six of us had dedicated much of our lives to growing the company. We would lose it all if we let things proceed as they were going. If we were to reap the benefits of our many years of sacrifice, we would have to change some things. Perhaps it was time to sell.

It was our responsibility to our franchisees to keep the company intact and growing. With this as my most important goal, I asked the question, "Does everyone want to sell?"

"Yes, yes, yes, yes, yes," was the consensus across the board. "As long as the price is right and I don't have to work anymore," was the sentiment that echoed.

"Well, we would have to determine the price range and how things would work. But I'll take the lead to find out," I promised.

Starting in 2013, I set out to network and educate myself about the landscape of private equity (PE) and its appetite for a company like ours. I connected with folks I had met along the way, starting with those I met at the EY event, to learn more about our perceived value in the marketplace and the process of recruiting and securing the right capital partners.

It was time for a new phase for the company and my life.

CHAPTER THIRTY-ONE

Love

It was much like my conversation with my dad many years ago about quitting that special school. He calmly pointed out that I had the talent and capability to shine. Perzan had the same effect on me. I am keenly aware of how fortunate I am to feel the love I feel for him and to be loved by him . . . He's literally been the man of my dreams. I'm so grateful.

YEARS AGO, I HAD A VIVID DREAM—one I never forgot and would never forget. It was one of those dreams that felt real. But what was exceptionally unique about it was that I felt the emotions. I woke up disoriented and shocked about how real it had seemed.

I dreamed I was walking out as a bride holding a bouquet of flowers. I saw myself walking down a beautiful aisle toward an altar where a man with black hair was standing. I couldn't see his face but felt his presence. I also sensed the most amazing emotion I had ever felt. I was holding my pretty bouquet in an outdoor venue, walking up to a man I absolutely, wholeheartedly loved.

I jumped out of bed. *What was that? Was that a hope? A dream?* I had no feelings toward the idea of past lives . . . but was this a past-life experience? It was all so puzzling because it was so very real. I really felt it and enjoyed it. But ultimately, I considered it a beautiful dream and moved on with my life.

"In my next life," I chuckled with unease and sadness.

After overcoming a life-threatening illness, I made a solemn vow to live authentically, honoring the gift of life that had been graciously granted to me. It was a pivotal moment, a time to wholeheartedly embrace authenticity in all my relationships. The scary, uncomfortable process of divorce in my forties was one of the darkest times in my life. I had been displaced since I was seventeen, and here I was voluntarily displacing myself. It took courage and a belief in a better life.

"Hey, what are your plans for this Friday?" a friend of mine, Emily, asked one day.

"I don't know," I replied.

"Well, now you do. You're coming with me to a birthday party," she declared.

I gave her a noncommittal yes. I wasn't sure if I wanted to go.

She explained that the birthday party was for a world-famous female bodybuilder. I found this intriguing because it was not the social circle I was used to. "Maybe I'll go," I told her.

"Well, I'm counting on you going. The theme is bling, so wear something blingy. And it's in Newport Beach. See you Friday," Emily said.

I came home from work on Friday pretty tired. I didn't think I wanted to face a bunch of bodybuilders that night, but Gosia insisted I go.

Begrudgingly, I dressed up. I wore a black dress with shoes that would be considered blingy to Emily's standard. I dreaded my decision to attend the event all the way there. I felt like I could have stayed home and relaxed.

It was December 13, 2013. I love the number thirteen—I'm not sure why—so I took that as a good sign at least. Emily was waiting for me in the parking lot of a lovely restaurant. A lot was going on at this party. There were various interesting people, many of them bodybuilders. And there were cameras to capture the event.

As soon as I walked in, two tall men approached me and asked me for my driver's license. They seemed like security. I showed them my license, and we started talking. As it turned out, they were not professional security. They were simply assisting the birthday girl, who was trying to be a reality star. They had both recently moved here from another state and were renting from her. She had asked them to help out.

One of the guys was a little shorter—about six feet, with brown eyes and hair. The other was taller—about 6'3" with green eyes and black hair.

"What's your name?" the green-eyed man asked.

"You already know from my driver's license. It's Shirin," I replied, smiling. "What's your name?"

"Perzan."

"Perzan? I've never heard that name. Is it Persian?"

"Yes," he said.

Perzan and I talked, danced, and connected for the rest of the evening. He was born and raised in Albany, New York, by his wonderful parents, who were both doctors and Zoroastrians. When I was kicked out of my high school in Iran after I had complained about how girls were treated, I still had one more year of high school to complete. I ended up going to a school for Zoroastrians. What a full circle this was! I was very familiar with the religion and the belief system. I loved it.

Good thoughts, good words, and good deeds are the tenets of the Zoroastrian religion, which was born in Iran as the first monotheistic religion in the world. I loved the tenets and had always held a special place in my heart for Zoroastrians.

To say that we bonded from the moment we met is an understatement. Our connection was out of this world. We understood each other on a deep, almost spiritual level. Perzan and I became best friends, confidants, teammates, and a bonded couple.

Early into our relationship, we were talking about some profound, personal experiences when Perzan suddenly held me, looked me straight in the eyes, and said, "Someday, we'll retire in Mera Flores." I burst into tears. *Who is this wonderful, loving man? Where did he come from? How is he so clear as to what he wants? And that it's me? And where in the world is Mera Flores?*

I've been in love with Perzan since we met. Sometimes, I feel like I have always been in love with him—I just didn't know him yet. He has taught me what true, pure love is. I've learned that genuine love allows you to be you. True love accepts you for who you are . . . both good and bad.

Real love connects two people while allowing them to be the individuals that they are. I've learned that deep love may get messy, but it's always present even in the worst of times. I've learned that genuine love has resilience; it has patience. It forgives. It is always there. My genuine, true, real, and deep love with Perzan has been my guiding light since I met him. We've had many adventures, lots of growth, many obstacles, numerous challenges, thousands of laughs, and hundreds of tears. We've fought, made up, loved, and created a beautiful life together over these years.

We got married almost three years after we met. Just as I had seen in my dream many years ago, he waited at the altar with his black hair in my view. I walked down the aisle with my beautiful bouquet of flowers as I felt emotions I had never had the pleasure of knowing before.

Our vows and the overall feel of our wedding reflected our deep love and admiration for each other. My children are Perzan's biggest fans. And my family—especially all the kids—love him dearly. I've been embraced and loved by his large, close-knit extended family. And I feel blessed.

Early in our friendship, Perzan had a simple but insightful observation.

"Shirin, you are the golden goose," he said to me one day.

I didn't understand what he meant. But as he explained, it expanded my perspective and belief in myself. He generously told me how he believed in me and my intelligence and competence. He made it clear via examples of what I had accomplished and was capable of. It was like holding a mirror in front of me to show me who I was. It was much like my conversation with my dad many years ago about quitting that special school. He calmly pointed out that I had the talent and capability to shine. Perzan had the same effect on me. A light bulb went on! I had been operating in the shadows of others at the company. I had played a key role in almost every aspect of its growth, yet had not found the courage to take credit for my work.

I had allowed others to imagine that they were the sole reason for the company's success. Of course, no single person was solely responsible for our success. However, I had played a critical role. Unfortunately, those outside our core executive team did not adequately recognize this. Internally, my contribution was well acknowledged and evident within our core executive team. I have learned since that my experience was not that unique. I've learned that many people, especially women and people of diverse backgrounds, often experience the same thing. It's more comfortable and acceptable to take the back seat to one's success even when it's glaringly deserved. I've had many conversations with highly accomplished people who felt like an impostor and believed owning their contribution and worth was somehow unacceptable.

Looking back, I suffered from some of the same misunderstandings and uncomfortableness. Perzan opened my eyes to this weakness. I became aware and conscious of it. However, although this was frustrating and often counterproductive, it didn't pose an existential crisis for me or the company. What posed the crisis was something that had to be addressed quickly.

My life with Perzan has been rewarding, loving, touching, and fun. He's my best friend and my biggest fan, as I am his. I am keenly aware of how fortunate I am to feel the love I feel for him and to be loved by him. These feelings were the ones I had in my dream so many years ago. He's literally been the man of my dreams. I'm so grateful.

Chapter Thirty-Two

Steering to a Sale

I soon learned firsthand how change, as planned and as desired as it may be, can create significant anxiety in people.

Building a company while attending to children and life leaves you little room to create and maintain professional connections. When I set out to find a solution for the company and its stakeholders' best interests, I knew I had to find the right kinds of experts. So, I started casting a wide net to connect with equity finance, banking, and PE experts. Luckily, I had a good running start with peers and the like whom I had stayed in touch with—as lightly as I had. To make the right connections and make them promptly, however, I had to make it a priority. In 2013, I worked a full-time job helping run and grow a sizable company, navigated a new relationship, and researched colleges for my children. Finding the right connections at that time became a new and active job for me. As I spread my wings, I joined professional organizations and attended meetings by myself. I would walk up to groups of folks and introduce myself and the company. All those years of finding new connections when I was on my own in Turkey and then as an immigrant in my new home had prepared me with the skills to find common ground to connect with others. With repetition, my network grew. It took a couple of years and lots and lots of hours of networking to build a solid and reliable professional network. From there, I explored options.

I was introduced to EY's investment banking arm in 2014. By then, I had sat through numerous meetings with potential investors and partners and had yet to find a group that I found trustworthy and aligned with how we operated. Our fateful meeting in 2014 was memorable. The approach, style, and step-by-step guidance the EY team offered resonated with us. No wonder I had found myself at home at EY all those years ago. I had a connection with the culture and style.

I reflected on the many years before when I was working and going to college full-time to earn my accounting degree. It was then that I had thought of applying for an internship. This was seemingly an impossible feat since I went to a state school that was not well known for its business program. But I'd had the audacity to apply for an internship with EY. And although many told me that it would be nearly impossible, I pursued it with my usual nonconformist approach. Having earned the coveted spot granted to only a few in the greater Los Angeles area, I became an EY intern, and after graduation, an EY employee. I enjoyed and celebrated my experiences there and grew a lot.

It was time to bring EY to the rest of the team.

Communication within the executive team was critical from the first visit and throughout the process. Not everyone was well versed in finance, and the transaction was going to be complex. Therefore, I had to ensure I kept everyone up to speed. Frequent group and one-on-one meetings with the team did the trick. The power of effective and frequent communication had already shaped much of my life and career. Working with others from varied backgrounds had taught me that to ensure voices were heard and people felt included so that they worked toward the same common goals, there needed to be clear communication. Therefore, much of my time was invested in discussing our status and action steps with each of the members of the executive team. My goal was to distill information to the level of experience each person had regarding these types of transactions. These efforts were in addition to providing EY with the information they needed to lay the groundwork for our potential transaction.

In one of our internal planning meetings, the stakeholders all agreed that if our bankers were able to bring in a buyer who would be willing to buy the company for a particular amount (and we wrote this amount on the board) and be willing to allow everyone to leave the company, the team would be excited to do the transaction. The number we discussed was multiple times more than the $50 million we had talked about all those years ago.

Without disclosing our desired price, I provided our bankers with all the information needed to arrive at a proposed value for the company. It was both surprising and touching to see the *exact* same number we'd written on the board—this time as the value of the company arrived at by the team of bankers! We were on our way.

The idea of all of us leaving after a transaction was complete was one our bankers thought would be difficult but possible to do. They promised that they would do their best to accomplish this. Our team had worked at the same business for decades, and almost everyone was exhausted. It was time to leave.

With an agreement on the proposed value and positioning, we shifted into overdrive. The plan was to create a Confidential Information Memorandum (CIM), customary in these transactions, and then set out to generate interest from investors, mostly PE. There were many complicated steps along the way, including performing internal examinations of our financial and other records before opening them up for review by outsiders.

I now had a third job: providing the banking team with information, discussion, analysis, data, records, and financial information. The bankers' requests were enormous, and many real-time responses were required. My only collaborator and partner on this long project was our internal general counsel, Jennie. Everyone else took a back seat.

After months of hard work, we were ready to showcase the company to outsiders and in the CIM. We went through a monthslong process of meeting with and providing information to parties that were prescreened by our bankers as viable potential investors.

It was time to review our management presentations to the finalists on the list of investors. Our bankers selected these finalists through a well-thought-out and rigorous process.

Management presentations were well rehearsed walkthroughs of the company, its operations, and growth plans. They were multi-hour and sometimes multi-day reviews of all aspects of the company that would help potential investors understand the company and its potential—only a few members of the management team presented at these meetings.

Bankers moved interested parties along a very strict timeline through which potential investors would submit their interests, bids, and requests.

Once we received all the proposals (bids), we reviewed them with the bankers. Amazingly, most of them were close to our chosen number, but one stood out. Culturally, personally, financially, and strategically, they were a great match, and we wanted to proceed with them.

Due diligence is a difficult but necessary step for the type of transaction we were organizing with this PE firm. We had clearly shown documents, data, and explanations about the company, but they would have to verify them to be accurate. This process took some time and added even more work to those of us who were involved with it—an exhausting ending to a winding and exhausting road.

When it looked like we had almost finalized due diligence, the PE firm invited us to fly to New York to meet their partners. Only our lead investment banker, myself, and the CEO flew out to attend.

The firm's office in Manhattan was on a high floor. The welcoming and gracious receptionist showed us to a big conference room with large glass walls that had breathtaking views of Manhattan. I sat near the end of the table facing the view, by my name tag, which was clearly placed there by the meeting organizers. The two others sat next to me. Within a few minutes, the fantastic partners I had previously met and worked with entered with broad smiles and warmly shook our hands, welcoming us. After that, several men with big grins, wearing blue button-up shirts and dark pants, entered one after another. Each of them had a welcoming look on their face. The main partners sat next to me and made all of us feel valued, respected, and welcomed.

The large conference room was now full of people sitting and standing. I looked around and found only one woman sitting by the window. After a moment of catching my breath, I uttered, "I've never been in a room with so many men with such great hair!" They burst out laughing.

For the next thirty minutes, we fielded questions. Attendees were well versed about the company and the deal. They wanted to learn about what we believed, thought, and saw as potential. It was a grueling experience, but I wasn't worried. I was confident that we knew this company very well; and that all the months of preparing the material for the CIM and explaining the company, its operations, and future growth opportunities to the team at EY had also prepared us.

All those years of trials and tribulations, as we were trying to find ways to grow the company, and all the setbacks, challenges, and disappointments, had taught us the foundations of what made the company what it was. I did my best to explain them transparently to the group that was asking those questions. It felt as if they liked the answers and liked the company. We had done all we could. The ball was in their court to decide if we would be moving forward with finalizing our deal.

Days passed and we didn't hear back from the PE firm. The excitement and elation we had felt were gradually being replaced by dread. If we didn't close this deal, we weren't sure what to do next. Now that we had emotionally and mentally decided to move on and away from the company, finding the energy and strength to go back to it and build it once more would be very hard.

"Do you have a minute to talk?" Steve, our partner at EY, asked.

"Sure. I hope it's good news," I said.

"It is. The PE firm wants to move forward with the deal. After our meeting with them in New York, they would like to make a couple of changes. They want to have you, Shirin, stay and run the company as CEO. With it, they want you to roll over more of your equity until the next exit," Steve explained.

I believed I could run the company according to the expectations outlined in our CIM. But like everyone else on our stakeholders' team, I had planned on cashing out and leaving. The prospects of staying, keeping a larger portion of my equity, and performing to the rigorous expectations of PE were a lot to digest.

Leading up to finalizing the transaction, the executive team was very tense. Although the outcome of selling the company, taking our payments, and walking away was attractive to us, it was also all a big step and nerve-racking. Those fractions and frictions that already existed in our entrepreneurial company became even more prominent.

Over the years, all of us had grown close. Our families knew each other and had bonded. I babysat their children, and our kids played with each other. We used to go to lunch almost daily and discuss our personal lives. We talked about our daily challenges, our hopes, and our dreams. I was there when a couple of the guys got divorced and literally consulted with them as they went through their settlements. We had become a close-knit family.

Unfortunately, much like when I left my family in Iran to move to Turkey to save my life, I was forced to leave *this* family. It was time to sell to save the results of our hard-earned work. And it was time to part ways because we could only finalize this transaction if I agreed to stay.

I'd had my heart set on leaving like the rest of them, hoping to take some time off to figure out what I wanted to do next. But it was now clear that the deal would not go through if I didn't accept the proposal. So, I did. In time, I found myself excited and looking forward to the new challenge.

I soon learned firsthand how change, as planned and as desired as it may be, can create significant anxiety in people. I naively expected celebration and excitement from my teammates, who were finally reaching their dreams. Though I am sure that, with time, everyone ended up happy about the freedom they had earned, the prospect of leaving what they had built and had been used to initially created a lot of angst. I have now learned that this reaction is common after a transaction like this—especially for entrepreneurs. But at the time, the level of anxiety and resulting adversarial reactions were shocking to me. I was doing my best to manage the volatility in the group while negotiating contracts with investors and getting the company ready for its next phase of growth. I was aware that the real work would start after the transaction was completed because the new owners had high expectations of our performance. I would have to deliver on lofty performance goals.

Personally, and emotionally, the burden I was carrying was very heavy. I had to be smart and agile in responding to continued investor requests and helping close a complicated deal with all its twists and turns, including long contracts and tax considerations. We had to make sure any infighting or misunderstandings would not destroy our deal. I had to prepare for a big job while processing all the changes that were happening at the same time. Luckily, all the years of hardship while relying on myself had created the strength in my core to be able to weather this severe storm.

We finally hashed out all the points of our internal and external issues. We all had to compromise on some points, but we finally arrived at an agreement. The company was sold in November 2015.

I'm sad and heartbroken that we couldn't find a joyful way to go our separate ways. We eventually found amicable agreements and a more civil parting of ways. But emotionally, personally, and relationally, we didn't fare well in our goodbyes. Perhaps many years of hoping and dreaming had created expectations that could not be realistically met. I missed my friends and wished them well—and promised myself to do good work and create more value for our franchisees, for our company, for our investors, and for them. My hope was that everyone would, in time, reap the benefits of our success and learn to enjoy their new lives. It was also my hope that as they earned their financial freedom, their remaining equity in the company would continue to grow through our continued good work. My dream was that the increased value of the company and their related equity would be one more reward for them. I'm happy that it eventually was.

PART FOUR

Becoming a CEO and Making Empathic Change a Reality

Chapter Thirty-Three

CEO Years

"Shirin, this is no time to panic. You know this company like you know yourself. Everything that's been built here, you've been involved with. This is not the end. It's an exciting new beginning. You've been through dire life situations. You've faced death. This is not death. Use your best efforts; expect the best outcome. Utilize all the lessons learned; lean on the good people around you. And deliver on what you promised to franchisees, employees, and investors. You can do it." It was the self-talk that mobilized me.

IN OCTOBER 2015, I was invited to participate in our PE partners' yearly meeting with its investors. Theirs was a reputable and large fund that had brought in notable investors. As a part of their annual meeting, as is common practice, the PE firm would invite a few of their portfolio CEOs to present their companies. We had yet to close our deal, but I was invited to present at their annual meeting in November 2015. When I was flying out to this meeting, we had not yet signed our agreement. I was prepared but not sure if I would be able to present. I checked in to the hotel, settled in, and reviewed my presentation again. Exhausted from the travel and the tough months leading up to this trip, I went to bed early. I woke up in the morning to frantic calls from our lawyers.

I received texts and messages such as, "Where are you? Please respond. We need to contact you ASAP."

I immediately called the lawyers. To my relief, it turned out that all parties had finalized and signed the agreement the night before, except for me. I quickly powered up my laptop and signed our contract. As I made my way to the annual meeting, a smile of relief and joy spread across my face. The deal was finally done, and I was ready to share this news with the world!

When I took the stage, I said, "We just signed our deal with this firm this morning. The ink isn't dry yet!"

The presentation to a room filled with business professionals, all diligently taking notes, went exceptionally well. When I revealed that our franchisees were installing a staggering 40,000 units a week, I noticed a wave of surprise and admiration sweep across the audience. This was a testament to the success and potential of our business, and it was a moment I would always cherish.

The PE firm's team congratulated and welcomed me. As I returned to Southern California, I remembered the words someone told me at dinner after the annual meeting: "I'm one of the investors in this fund that invested in your company. I know that we're in good hands with you." I took that trust and our franchisees' trust seriously. I had committed to doing good work and was going to deliver on that promise.

Before the press release was issued, I wanted to break the news to our franchisees. By then, we had been in business for over twenty years. For most of those years, we had one brand. For all those years, we were a closely held entrepreneurial company. Franchisees were used to seeing the same few faces representing leadership within the company. We had intentionally built our presence and marketing image around a few people. All that was about to change.

I would soon announce to everyone that we were now owned by PE and that we would be building a professionally run organization while maintaining our entrepreneurial spirit. I realized that all these changes were significant to employees and franchisees alike. Another significant development was that many of the C-level executives who owned the company had been bought out and planned to exit from their roles.

As I sat back in my office in California after my whirlwind visit to New York while we closed our deal, I took a deep breath and looked around. We had most of our executive offices on the side of the building where I had mine. Some executives had already moved out of their offices, and some were slowly clearing them out. It was the American dream: build a company beyond your wildest expectations and sell. The life they had been seeking to create had taken shape. And now they had the chance to experience the freedom to build whatever they wished. It was the end of an era for all and the start of a new one for many—including the company.

As I scanned the building from my seat, I counted the executives we had left. A chill went down my spine. I now had to be the CEO, CFO, COO, chief information officer (CIO), and chief marketing officer (CMO) for the company. Those roles would have to be filled in time. But at that moment and until we could find the right people to replace them, all those functions were vacant. They were *all* my responsibility.

I also had the fate of our franchisees tied to my decisions and actions. And I had all those investors who had trusted me with hundreds of millions of dollars of investment in the company.

Cold sweat covered my body, but just for a moment.

Shirin, this is no time to panic. You know this company like you know yourself. Everything that's been built here, you've been involved with. This is not the end. It's an exciting new beginning. You've been through dire life situations. You've faced death. This is not death. Use your best efforts; expect the best outcome. Utilize all the lessons learned; lean on the good people around you. And deliver on what you promised to franchisees, employees, and investors. You can do it. It was the self-talk that mobilized me.

With clarity and resolve, I called our vice president of marketing. "Let's work on our communication with our franchisees first, and then talk to our suppliers and partners. Let's ensure we are transparent and optimistic," I confirmed with her. "Franchisees need to be informed and understand that they are significant partners in our new chapter."

We made announcements via calls and webinars as well as in writing. I have learned over the years from providing information to franchises across the country and from various backgrounds that presenting information in different ways helps ensure that it is understood and retained. Every person learns slightly differently depending on their learning style. This is especially important for busy people like franchise owners.

We trained our support staff on the phones to be able to answer franchisee questions, and I made myself available as well via our webinars and any other means. The key to effective leadership and business communication lies in consistency and message discipline at every level. In our information-saturated society, the human brain disengages when confronted with too many inconsistencies. Luckily, our national convention in January 2016 allowed us to discuss our plans in person with franchisees and address their queries. Although many of the previous executives were no longer employed at the company at the end of November 2015, I felt like they would appreciate participating in the upcoming convention to say their goodbyes and to be celebrated. I invited them to provide updates about the work that had been done in the previous year. Although it was a few months past the close of the transaction, and I knew inviting prior executives was not necessary, I believed that providing a respectable farewell was the right thing to do. So, I extended an invitation, and they accepted.

As we attended the convention, our brand and marks were everywhere. With over 2,000 participants and 100,000 square feet of vendor showcase spread over a span of days, this was a substantial conference. I was about to lay out an ambitious plan to build on what we had created and move it forward to its next phase of growth. The time had come to move from an entrepreneurial organization to a professionally run one that maintained the same entrepreneurial spirit. I wanted our franchisees to dream about the ability to create well-known brands in the home space that could work together. My hope was that they would believe in a vision that we could create a platform of brands that would provide customers with the best products sold and designed in a consultative manner. We were uniquely positioned to deliver on this platform that would then give franchisees the best chance of succeeding. I needed their trust, cooperation, and belief. A lofty ask for a lofty task . . . but it was time.

In the days leading up to this convention, my schedule was jam-packed from morning till night. Our transaction had closed in November. I had to immediately move forward with working on keynotes, messaging, and the overall plan for the upcoming convention in less than two months.

We had three consumer-facing brands. One was mature and large. One was in its growth phase and still being built. The last one was at a very early stage with a handful of franchises. The requirements of running each brand and seeing to their health were many. Marketing, support, training, licensing, technology, and all facets of franchise operations would have to continue to run well while we had to fill many of the roles. This was an enormous, high-pressure environment. Of course, PE requires rigorous reporting and performance measures.

"How about I bring in an off-site CFO for now? I used to play that role years ago, and I know there are competent people who do the same. In fact, I have a friend who used to be a partner in a large accounting firm that may have someone for us," I explained to our partner at the firm. He agreed. Fortunately, my friend introduced me to a competent temporary CFO to take some of the load off me and organize the elevated reporting requirements from our PE partners.

Though the large conference and its planning loomed around us, we had to maintain success in every aspect of business.

"We have a good team that was right below the C-executives who know a lot about their departments. I'm going to engage everyone. Let's start with a weekly cadence of meetings," I told Jennie, a trusted advisor.

We started building a team. We also continued to work on our delivery and messaging at the convention, focusing on energizing and informing our franchisees.

"I'm going to share my commitment to franchisees," I told Jennie.

"What do you mean?" Jennie asked.

"I want to be personal and transparent. I want franchisees to know that my commitment to them is personal."

"I don't know if this is a good idea. You would have to make sure it's crafted right or else it may not be received well. It sounds like a lot for them to digest."

The morning of the conference's opening, I woke up early and realized I had a headache. In the dark, I reached for where I thought I had my headache medicine. Perzan was arriving later, but my daughter and son had come over to stay and keep me company. So that I wouldn't wake them up, I didn't turn on the light. As I reached over, I tripped and hit my head with a big bang on the table! *Did I break it?* I was so worried because the sound was awful. After I caught my breath, I went into the bathroom. Miraculously, I hadn't broken or bruised anything. *Phew.* This was a good sign, and I took it as such.

I got dressed and walked to the convention area. It was a long walkway with signage and lights along the way, all highlighting our company. The air buzzed with a mood of anticipation as I received an occasional wave or "Hi!" from a franchisee who had arrived early. I found my way to the greenroom, where we were preparing. The audio guys checked my mic and put it on me. People were taking their seats in this large capacity room. Lights were bright, and upbeat music was playing.

As people took their seats, our two MCs welcomed everyone and explained the logistics. Just then, one of our marketing consultants, a nice woman who tended to get nervous, said, "I'm worried that they may hate what you have to say, and because of that, they may hate you!"

That wasn't what I needed to hear. Luckily, over the years I had learned to tune out discouraging and negative voices that came from others' limitations and fears.

Then, the voice of God announced my name: "Ladies and gentlemen, your CEO, Shirin Behzadi!" I walked out into the blinding lights. As I took the stage, I took a deep breath. I was ready, and delivered our message for the next two hours. When I present, I don't use notes. I prepare for what I want to say and then deliver it naturally. But during this long two-hour presentation, I did have some slides of numbers that showed results over the previous year.

I talked about how we were all committed to the growth and prosperity of our entire system. I discussed the foundations we would build to create a trustworthy platform that would benefit all our franchisees. When it was time to close, I paused and wondered if I should make it personal. The hesitation only lasted a minute. I was going to take the risk. I shared part of my journey with the company and what had brought me there.

"A few years ago, I was diagnosed with a brain tumor. I had two young children, and my responsibilities here at this company. I couldn't believe it. This was the kind of thing you always believe happens to other people. Soon, I learned that I had only one option, and that was to remove my tumor surgically. This was a risky surgery.

"I know many of you have experienced health or life challenges with your loved ones. What many of us learn from these experiences is life-changing. It's a gift you never ask for, but when you receive it, you value it.

"What I learned from my surgeries and the very difficult and life-threatening recovery was a confirmation of what's most important to me: that I have to live an authentic life with honesty and integrity. That the person I look at in the mirror every morning would have to be proud of her treatment of others.

"It is with this conviction that I make a promise to all of you. I promise I will always genuinely have your best interests in mind. We will make lots of decisions. Some may be bad, but most will be good. But no matter what, they will always be made with the best interests of you and your families in mind. That is my promise."

A humbling standing ovation marked the beginning of the company's next chapter.

Would I be able to write a great ending?

CHAPTER THIRTY-FOUR

Brand Vision

I also knew there was a lot of energy and knowledge in the teams that did the work. So, I embarked on what I called a listening tour . . . It was to promote discussions and open communication. It was to encourage innovation and innovative solutions. We needed to allow people to express themselves and partner with us to help improve the company.

AFTER THE CONVENTION'S CHEERS FADED, it was time to execute a vision for growth and excellence. We had a high demand for our products and delayed projects from previous years. We had an executive team to build. We also had to adhere to the commitments we had made to our PE partners.

Rather than move to execution immediately, I decided we had to learn where we were and where areas of opportunity existed. Having been at the company for so many years and having run many functional areas, I believed I knew where low-hanging fruits of improvement and opportunity existed. But I also knew there was a lot of energy and knowledge in the teams that did the work. So, I embarked on what I called a listening tour. The idea was to engage teams throughout the company and to hear them out—to open the floor to hear from people about where they believed gaps and opportunities existed. It was to promote discussion and open communication. It was to encourage innovation and innovative solutions.

I met with teams in various areas of the company, ensuring we weren't only meeting with teams that were usually included in discussions. Rather, we took time and care to make sure we covered all areas and functions within the organization. I had learned over the years—having been that person within the organization who had seen opportunities and mistakes firsthand but didn't know how to let management know how to tackle them best—that peers and team members could shed light on the blind spots in the organization. So, it was clear to me that an organization that had been around for over twenty years with the same leadership probably had those same blind spots, gaps, and areas of opportunity that others in the organization could help us discover. We needed to allow people to express themselves and partner with us to help improve the company. This is why it was important to engage teams from all areas and in many tiers of employment. It was critical to have a short agenda and long opportunities for discussions. The approach was to be open and collaborative, not prescriptive.

What we learned from those conversations was invaluable. There were clearly areas that required immediate improvement, such as training and support. It became clear to me that we had two overarching challenges.

First, who we were and what we offered to our customers weren't clear to everyone. As it happens, as companies grow, especially entrepreneurial ones, that essence gets lost. If we didn't know who we were and what problem we were solving for customers, how would customers ever know that? This lack of clarity was a pressing issue that needed immediate attention. We had to do an in-depth review of our brand presence and bio to establish a clear and compelling brand identity.

Second, as the company grew over time, its structures were built loosely. Loose and poorly thought-out structures create power grabs, which in turn creates chaos and stagnation. We had to create a new culture, new habits, and a new, firm foundation. This was not going to be an easy task, especially for a company that had been around for a couple of decades.

I met with my direct reports to improve the operational issues the listening tour identified. I would take a direct leadership role in developing and executing a brand identity initiative. To achieve our growth metrics, I knew we had to reposition ourselves in customers' minds and the minds of our partners, suppliers, and employees. I told the board in an early meeting, backed by a solid business case, "We need to take the time to understand who we are and where we're headed as a company before we can define it well to our customers and franchisees. Sure, we have some images and words about the company and our products, but we haven't done any work around this with good methodology and research." The board agreed, and we started using those same listening tours and expanding them to surveys of customers and partners. We wanted to understand how we were seen and how we could be seen. This process taught us a lot.

―――――――

Knowing that it was critical to have a good methodology around this exercise, we took the time to thoughtfully plan out questions to ask of our various groups of stakeholders: franchisees, employees (including management), partners, and eventually, our customers. The customer surveys were to be deployed after the first groups so that we would have more clarity as to which questions to ask. The questions were designed to explore what the participants' thoughts and perceptions were with regard to:

- Who we are
- What we offer
- Where we are headed/who we want to become

These broad categories were carefully organized and questioned to encourage the clearest responses and outcomes.

What we learned from this process was profound. First, we found gaps of perception and inconsistencies between our internal groups. We had three brands at various stages of evolution. We had also been around for over twenty years. As folks had joined the company and as we had grown and expanded, we had lost consistency in our messaging and approach. The result was a perception gap among our employees and teams as to who we were, what we were solving for our customers, and where we were headed.

There was also good news in all of this. The essence of who we were and what we offered showed up in consistent ways across the various groups. Though not clear and concise yet, many of the elements were common in the responses. This gave us a common ground on which to build.

We accumulated all that information and, through methodical discussions and collaborations, created brand bios, first for the parent company and then for each of our consumer-facing brands. This exercise took a few months as we efficiently worked through it. We communicated our progress to our franchisees and shared our findings with them while doing our best to hear feedback from all stakeholders.

The project proved to be one of the most significant steps we took as a company. The brand bios created the foundation for clear messaging and a voice for each brand. With it, we knew we could communicate better and more effectively to our consumers and our franchisees. From there, and over the next year, we overhauled each of our brands' look, feel, and messaging.

Having identified who we were and what we offered allowed us to focus on where we wanted to go. In collaboration with our franchisee representatives, we created our vision. This vision and our new brand bios provided us with our essence and our north star. It allowed us to organize everyone in the same direction.

Before embarking on this journey, I understood we had just brought in new investors who had found value in each of our brands. I was also aware that change was hard, especially for franchisees who ran their own businesses. But I knew that I had built my life, and I had helped build this company, believing in and expecting an aspirational goal. That goal had mobilized me over the years and mobilized us as small-company entrepreneurs to our success. We had to take ambitious but thoughtful steps to create that north star for everyone in the organization. We had to make sure that everyone understood who we were and where we would go. That was the only way we could bring substantial growth and opportunity to a company that had been around for so many years, and that operated in an industry known for modest growth. I believed we could do it. I believed we had something special to share with our customers. We had to define it well and align all our energy to accomplish it. Our new brand bios and our vision created that exact positive momentum for the company.

Of course, while we were building the brand bios, we had to operate and produce the high results we had set as our goals.

I asked our PE partners for assistance in recruiting a CFO and CIO. I wanted to hold off recruiting a CMO until we finalized our brand bios. And my timeline was even longer for a COO. Because of the rigorous reporting requirements (made by any PE partner), we had to fill the CFO position rather quickly. I appreciated our partners' generous assistance from recruitment to the interview process, leaving me to talk to the last few finalists. Once I could rely on reporting being done, I could move forward with building the infrastructure that we were missing. We had to move from a chaotic decision-making process to an organized one. And the best way to accomplish that would be to create clear, functionally sound areas and departments with well-defined expectations that could be measured. This was a lofty goal, as we were also expected to show continued growth.

Chapter Thirty-Five

Inside Out: The Strategic Path from Vision to Execution

Some of the best ideas come from some of the most unlikely people. It's just wise to hear people out. It's even wiser to make them know they matter. I've learned that when people believe what they do and say matters, the best comes out of them.

I HAD DEVELOPED A DAILY ROUTINE. After exercising, eating break-fast, and getting ready, I would pour myself a coffee to go, and start driving for my almost-hourlong commute to the office. I had done this routine for years with not much change except for one. My relatively new addition was that once I exited the freeway, I would park my car for a few minutes in a small strip mall parking lot, take a deep breath, and allow thoughts or themes to come to my mind for the day. I would write them down and then drive to work. I started doing this to put myself in the right mindset for the day.

Being a CEO is a pretty lonely place. Being a CEO with most of the C-bench vacant is especially lonely. Being a CEO with expectations of substantial results while caring for thousands of business owners is another level of lonely. I had to use all my experiences, expertise, resources, and focus to deliver on my responsibilities. This moment of daily pause was a necessary step to zoom in all my focus and energy.

I vividly remember one particular day. I had an excellent workout in the morning and felt refreshed. My drive was relatively smooth, with less traffic than usual. So, when I pulled over to my spot to park, I had a sense of clarity. I took out my phone, went to the notes section, and wrote:

It's about honesty. To be honest with yourself, to be honest with others, to be honest when it's uncomfortable, to be honest when it's hard. It's through honesty that you can truly engage and grow . . .

This note turned out to be longer than usual. After I wrote it, I had an idea.

What have I written about thus far? I scrolled through my notes and realized that a pattern had emerged. In a short while, these daily notes had developed some themes.

I was looking for clarity. In order to be effective in my role, I would have to have personal clarity. I needed to understand. I needed to take my advice. I needed to explore these questions in my role as CEO:

- Who am I?
- What are my core values?

- How do I bring value?
- Where am I headed?
- What is my vision?

This was my epiphany.

There was so much change happening at the company and so much more we wanted to excitedly implement that it required a steady, well-defined presence from me. I had to have clarity and a vision.

"I believe a big part of my job is to be like an orchestra conductor," I told Kelly, who was sitting across from me, as we reviewed our upcoming marketing plans. "I need to make sure each person is seated in the right seat in the company. A seat that reflects their talent. I mean, in an orchestra you wouldn't have a violinist assigned to play the flute!

"But it's also my job to make sure each person has their sheet music for what is expected of them to do," I continued. "And then to put it all together, bringing harmony together requires my attention as to how various teams and departments function together."

Kelly raised her eyebrows. "That's very good. Wow. I love it. How did you come up with it?"

I laughed. "Maybe years of attending my daughter's orchestra performances. But really . . . throughout my life, I've had to work extra hard to showcase what I knew or to share my ideas. I mean, I've worked my way up in a male-dominated field. Also, I was a poor immigrant with a strange name. I wasn't the most likely candidate to turn to for the best opinions. And yet, I often had good points and contributions to make. Because of that, I've been tuned into people from all walks of life. And it's served me well. I've paid attention to employees and peers alike throughout my career. You know what— some of the best ideas come from some of the most unlikely people. It's just wise to hear people out. It's even wiser to make them know they matter. I've learned that when people believe what they do and say matters, the best comes out of them. If we're going to be successful here, we will help our employees, franchisees, and partners blossom."

Kelly agreed, but we both knew this wouldn't be easy. Our fairly large company required a major overhaul to help it grow into its next phase.

I had arrived at answers as to who I was in the context of the CEO of this company. I was going to be authentic and honest. I was going to care about our franchisees and employees as well as our partners, with an emphasis on helping them blossom.

Reflecting upon my own life, I realized that success had followed doing the right things. I realized I had never set out to make a specific amount. Instead, I had set out to be a mother who was engaged, a CFO who did her very best every day, and an entrepreneur who focused on the best interests of the company—and the result was that I had been richly rewarded.

"You keep repeating your motto," Carmen, our marketing consultant, told me.

"What do you mean? What motto?" I asked with curiosity and some excitement. While exploring my answers to my own questions, it would be nice to know if I had a motto.

"You keep saying 'doing well by doing good.' You say it in meetings, and you even said it at the convention a few times. That's your motto—doing well by doing good." She was a brand builder and an observant marketer. She had paid attention, and she was right.

"It's so perfect and so what I believe. I love it. Chasing success for the sake of success doesn't work, in my mind. At least it's not a sustainable and rewarding path to success. Doing good work, good by others, and working on bringing good to people's lives does work. They bring success. Doing well by doing good. That's it."

And with this, I had much more clarity.

To answer the question of why I could effectively perform my job well, I observed and pondered. I could only explore this question when I had a bit of downtime in a given day or week—and there weren't many of those opportunities. This is when I started meditating. Knowing that I had limited time, I made it simple for myself. I would take a few minutes each morning to spend with myself. This practice proved exceptionally powerful. It was because of those few minutes every day that I learned to pause and reflect when making decisions at work. I've maintained this practice since.

So, in time, the conclusions popped up in my mind as I was going through my day. My mind was working overtime in the background to help me find the clarity I was searching for.

As for why I would be effective in my role, I realized I had a good mix of experiences. I had financial management knowledge, having been CFO of various organizations for years. I also had a lot of experience in operations, having overseen most areas of this company and others in my prior experiences. I had been with the company for many years and had either personally organized or helped organize the most significant parts of our operations. These experiences and skills made me uniquely qualified to know this company and its operations and setup very well.

I learned to become a good problem-solver through my life experiences and adversities. As a teenager, I found my way in and out of Turkey. I learned how to stay focused and find solutions in those dire circumstances. Those lessons taught me that I had the ability to solve problems and to find solutions creatively. Building on that confidence, I found my way to become the CFO of a good-sized bank in my twenties, where I consistently learned how to solve problems across the organization and as market circumstances changed. Learning to step away and go out on my own was a great lesson learned as to how to become self-reliant. All those adversities sharpened my skills to become a problem-solver and a creative thinker who believed in the ability to find successful outcomes out of many difficult situations. Those skills are critical to being a good CEO.

For years up to the point of taking on the role of CEO, I had been on an entrepreneurial journey. Many of the systems and ways of operating the company were built due to a lot of trial and error, and lots of tenacity; those years filled with challenges and setbacks taught me to understand the plight of entrepreneurs. The company I was leading was a franchise system, and therefore, at its core, it was about supporting franchisees. Those franchisees were business owners, much like we were. Not only had I been a part of their journey bringing them on board, but I could also relate to them. The ability to connect to franchisees was another quality I brought to this position.

I realized I had both the financial and operational skills to be an effective CEO, and I also realized that years of problem-solving and creative thinking would be useful for my job. Being an entrepreneur and having been with the company for many years made me especially qualified for this particular position with this particular company.

But after all that analysis, I realized there was something else— something above all else.

I genuinely cared.

Adversities in life had taught me empathy. I had witnessed suffering as mothers sent their children to war when I was a child in Iran. As a child, I had felt the sheer terror on my cousins' faces as we hid in the basement of our home while bombs exploded. The sorrow that filled the air at my aunt's home when her son was executed by the Islamic Republic of Iran had been palpable.

Empathy had become my savior. It was my signaling beacon that helped me find my way to Rozita's bedside before she passed. It was the reason I had stayed in touch with her as she struggled with domestic abuse.

Understanding people has helped me navigate through my career and work with people from vastly different backgrounds than mine. I had learned to connect with others through caring.

Empathy has proven to be robust, useful, and reliable. I was rewarded for caring, and it felt good to care—even when it was hard.

I cared deeply for our franchisees who had put their trust and their investments into our hands. I cared for our employees who spent a large part of their days with us. I cared for our investors and stakeholders who had put their trust in me and my team's performance. I also cared for the communities and the world we live in. I believed that it was that care that made me qualified and ultimately, effective. I was not going to betray people's trust or let them down.

Caring was one of my most precious core values and one that I promoted effectively to the company.

Having explored my core values and what qualified me for my role, my vision came clearly into focus. I wanted to create and build. I wanted to build a special company. I wanted to show that we could build a true platform that included a number of companies and could grow to include even more. I wanted our franchisees to prosper. I wanted our employees to grow and blossom. I wanted our partners, including the founders who had left some of their investments in the company, to see substantial returns. And I wanted to do all of this with care and authenticity. It was my true desire to build a foundationally solid company that embodied "doing well by doing good." *That* was my vision.

Although like most people, I, too, enjoy accolades, receiving them wasn't my goal. I liked being a CEO, but that title didn't define me. To me, accolades and titles are the results and rewards of creating a well-run organization. Little did I know at the time that this lack of attachment to titles would help me transition out of my position when I was ready.

The clarity around my core values and vision equipped me to pursue the challenging next steps in growing the company: changing *everything*.

CHAPTER THIRTY-SIX

How We Changed Everything

WE HAD STRENGTHENED OUR FRANCHISE BRANDS and revitalized operations. We involved our team members firm-wide by committing ourselves to engaging our partners and fearlessly seeking input and ideas from various perspectives.

We were prepared to execute our vision of creating a platform of brands that collaborated to offer tailored solutions for homeowners while also providing franchisees with the opportunity to own their businesses and lives. It was go-time. This process involved every functional area in the organization: new marketing, new operations, new culture, new space, and new company.

Here is an overview of our playbook for the change and growth initiative. Thanks to an extraordinary team effort by exceptional leaders, it offers many effective practices for everyone.

One of a franchisor's main areas of focus and substantial value creation is its marketing. When you buy a franchise (or license one), you're buying into its systems. Good, successful franchise systems have good marketing programs.

At our company, we believed we were good at marketing—and for many years, we were. Over the years, we had implemented a national marketing plan. Franchisees would pay into a national advertising fund monthly. We would then use those dollars diligently to advertise and support franchisee marketing efforts.

National advertising funds were small in our early years and naturally grew as the number of franchises grew. Regardless of the fund size, we took our responsibility to use those dollars wisely and efficiently very seriously and, with extra care, made sure we generated interest and leads for our franchisees.

We allocated those funds to develop and support websites for the company's franchisees, helping them establish a local online presence. We also created marketing materials for both national and local campaigns and executed marketing and advertising programs on radio and television. Additionally, we implemented marketing and advertising in print and other formats.

Our efforts included developing, managing, and executing digital marketing strategies, as well as providing support to franchisees in their local marketing initiatives. We actively monitored results to ensure optimal outcomes for the brand and worked diligently to generate the highest number of leads possible for our franchisees.

We had internal and external teams focused on marketing. Over the years, the landscape for marketing and advertising had changed significantly, with social media and digital marketing taking center stage. We knew quite well that we had used our marketing partners to the extent of their talents in delivering programs suited to the digital trend.

However, as we pursued discovering the status of our marketing efforts, especially in light of the brand bios, it became apparent to me that we were missing out on something big.

"How can we generate more leads for our franchisees? How can we accelerate our marketing efforts in their effectiveness?" These were questions and a problem I was keen on solving. I would ask these questions as I drove to work and as I attended to my daily responsibilities at my job. I knew we had performed well, but I believed there was room for significant improvement, especially after redefining our brands. Before long, I had an epiphany. It was a simple fact hiding in plain sight, but because we had always done things one way, it had not yet occurred to me. We were experts in and custodians of dollars we collected from our franchisees every month to use in advertising. Those national advertising numbers were great, but they paled in comparison to what our franchises were spending collectively on their local advertising.

We must find ways to make local marketing dollars more efficient and manage them better, I realized. Sure, in the past, we had talked about how they weren't as efficient as they could be. But we had not yet taken the steps to ensure they were. It was time to solve this problem.

As I arrived at this epiphany, I realized I needed to bounce it off someone with great marketing expertise. We didn't have a CMO then, so I contacted many people, including our board, to ask for referrals for a seasoned marketing consultant. I hoped we could use this person until we were ready to bring on a CMO.

That's how I met Mandi. She was an experienced marketer who had sold her agency a short while back and was ready to consult. I enjoyed her clear, no-nonsense style. She became my great partner and sounding board for all things marketing.

During our first lunch, and before I knew I would be working with her, I talked about my epiphany. "Historically, we've been focused on making sure that the dollars we collect from our franchisees toward national advertising are spent wisely. But I think we should add to this focus. I believe national advertising is the tip of the iceberg. The rest of the iceberg is all the local advertising dollars added together. It's by an order of magnitude larger. Let's find a way to help our franchises with their local presence," I told Mandi as she enjoyed her salad while we sat outside on a sunny day.

"Can you explain what you mean?" she asked as I sipped my iced tea.

"So, we collect millions of dollars annually and do our best to ensure we have a website, good advertising, good material, and so on, so franchisees can be successful. In doing that, we also insist on generating leads for our franchisees, and we do a good job with that. However, franchisees spend a few thousand dollars a month to advertise locally. Unfortunately, some don't advertise enough. If everyone were to spend what we recommend them to spend on their own, the total amount of marketing spend of our franchisees would be in the tens of millions of dollars, substantially bigger than the national fund. Yet, we have little visibility as to how they spend those funds," I said excitedly, knowing this was a lot of information I was trying to unpack during our first meeting.

"That makes sense. But how are you proposing to do it?" she asked as she kept up with my thought process.

"I think we should take the time to arrive at the best ways for franchisees to market. For instance, social media presence is significant. Taking that as an example, we would then vet and find the best partners to help our franchisees boost their social media presence. I'm sure there are companies out there that are large enough to take this on. We would then negotiate the best possible pricing and fees for our franchisees with a company because we can showcase the magnitude of spend we're talking about, which is much bigger than a single franchisee's spend. Once we do that, we can ensure the company's performance stays at the top, maximizing value for our franchises. This would also encourage franchisees to spend the right amount of money. Imagine how this could help lift every franchisee!" I was talking so fast that I needed to take a breath.

In typical Mandi fashion, she bluntly said, "It's a big job. But I can help you do it."

And so, we started our project. Firmly believing that my mission was to help our franchisees prosper, I knew that providing them with a well-thought-out platform to make their local marketing efforts more effective was necessary. It was time to create this platform.

We named our new marketing platform and began creating the programs critical to our franchisees' local presence.

Collaborating with Mandi and our teams, we identified key services for franchise success and sought partners to deliver effective local marketing programs for our franchisees. By then, we had grown large enough that our website was 110,000 pages deep.

To accomplish this seemingly daunting task, I had to be thoughtful.

Remember that your job is like an orchestra conductor's. Ensure everyone is in the right seat and has appropriate sheet music, I reminded myself.

It would take some time working with Mandi to make sure our internal team was in the right position. Measuring the performance and competency of outside agencies was easier. I asked Mandi to monitor and manage this aspect. We exited some agencies based on their lackluster performance and started working on bringing on new ones.

To make sure everyone was using the appropriate playbook, I had to engage every marketing team member. First, we had to confirm our alignment with the vision. We methodically crystallized the vision through consistent and clear communication and discussions with our teams. We did some very heavy lifting, mobilizing our teams around our overall vision and engaging the marketing groups with our strategy in a collaborative and agile fashion.

By the end of the following year, we had rolled out our new local marketing platform. Our franchisees could use this platform for their local marketing efforts. The services and fees were vetted and negotiated to be the best for our franchisees. Our internal marketing team managed the overall performance of our partners on the platform to ensure our franchisees received the best and most consistent service and results. This was a big hit at our second national convention.

While we were working diligently on creating our marketing platform, we worked on delivering leads to our franchisees. Business had to continue to go on as we updated and upgraded our marketing.

It seemed that everywhere I looked, I saw our much smaller competitor appear ahead of us in the digital world.

"We have so much more presence and sell so much more. How is it that they're able to get more attention online?" I asked Mandi at one of our strategy meetings.

"I think they're very good at digital marketing," she said.

"Darn. We need to get better at this," I said, frustrated.

As we revisited our internal marketing setup, we knew that we had to add to our bench and become much better at digital marketing. We had made a promise to our franchisees. Their success was our north star at the company, so this meant we had to be better in this space.

On a Tuesday, Mandi walked into my office with a grin on her face.

"I have a viable candidate to spearhead our digital marketing department," she said.

"Okay. Who is it, and why are you smiling?" I asked.

"Remember the competitor who keeps beating us online? This woman is the head of their digital marketing department and created it for them!"

We had found our person. When I met Adele and explained how our mission was to serve our franchises and that their prosperity was extremely important to us, she got emotional. She cared, and we bonded. Adele decided to join us because she believed in our vision and values. She was as passionate about doing good as we were, which made her very effective in her job.

After she joined, Adele created a digital marketing playbook, plans, and department, which she executed.

Our digital marketing efforts substantially lifted our presence and, therefore, leads to our franchisees. We generated more leads for them, which resulted in a double-digit increase in franchisee sales in the first year and kept growing. Traditionally, the home improvement space grows in single digits. With our new marketing efforts and all the other ways we enhanced our systems, we grew by over 70 percent over the next four years.

Part and parcel of our brand overhaul was a review of our look and feel. Although we had updated our marketing messaging and image over the years, we had not made substantial changes. Once we had clarified our brand bio, it became clear that we had to address our voice, look, and feel to the consumer. As franchisors, we had the right to change our look, feel, and marks. But to foster cooperation and excitement among franchisees, we wisely took our time. Through a series of webinars followed by open discussions—a formidable task considering the thousands of owners—we moved the project forward and came up with a new look and feel for our brands. We were making changes.

Chapter Thirty-Seven

New Operations

THERE WERE NO SACRED COWS. Since we were going to deliver on our vision, we had to ensure that all company operations, including training, support, legal, franchise licensing, finance, accounting, and operations, were well designed.

The listening tours helped me better understand gaps and opportunities within the organization. In the meetings we held early on as part of this listening tour project, I encouraged people to share ideas and to speak up about challenges and weaknesses. As people felt comfortable sharing their ideas and as they realized they were safe pointing out weaknesses, I learned so much. I learned that parts of our operations were in dire need of updates.

Training and support required lots of attention very quickly. The consensus was that although some updates had been done in the previous years, there was little clear methodology behind them. Changes and edits to training were, therefore, haphazard. Many of the manuals and support mechanisms had been held up by the good work and dedication of our staff. But well-thought-out systematic upgrades and updates were desperately needed.

"I can take on the training and operations manual," Jennie graciously offered.

This was soon after we completed our 2015 transaction with our PE partner. A lot was happening at the company, including ensuring franchisees and employees were settled in and adjusted to the new ownership and management. But change was needed.

I decided to stay on board and took on the challenge of bringing this company to its next phase of development. I must live up to those expectations because people rely on me. And I have to stay true to my vision. We can and will build this, I reminded myself.

"Thank you, Jennie," I said. "Let's please update our training and operations manual. I will provide you with the support and resources you need. I have all the confidence in you." And I did. I had a lot of respect and regard for Jennie and still do.

She took on this project, and we stayed close to our goal. It took a lot of hard work and effort, but in a few short months, she had overseen a major overhaul and upgrade to our training systems, including our operations manual.

Identifying our vision and core values highlighted discrepancies, weaknesses, and strengths in many areas of the company. There was a lot of enthusiasm around the chance to make improvements. Employees had renewed excitement about the future of the company. It's no wonder that, therefore, we energetically overhauled all operations. We created new departments that resembled more closely the infrastructure of our existing franchise systems and what we expected the new ones would require. With these updates, we were able to create opportunities for upward mobility.

I was keen on ensuring that everyone knew about and believed in our vision. We identified and communicated a north star to help orient the entire organization. Our north star was always "to make sure franchisees are as successful as they want to be."

The path to cultivating my abilities was created through understanding and having regard for people. Connecting with others, understanding them, and collaborating with them all brought me to this point. It made sense to me, therefore, to allow employees, franchisees, or others to be able to grow in their abilities as well. I believed everyone had something to contribute and that it was through emphasizing that they were important and that they mattered that we could see everyone live up to their full potential. This, to me, was the key to helping our organization and people thrive.

Much of human evolution has been built on collaboration and cooperation. We've built civilizations, tools, technologies, and lives through the intelligence, innovation, and cooperation of people. I believed the best way to accomplish our collective vision was to have everyone excited and on board. I believed that it was my job to promote cooperation by sharing a vision and a north star that resonated with the core of the company and that promoted the best in all players.

Therefore, communicating clearly and effectively was at the heart of this people-oriented approach. Good communication, done with honesty and authenticity, meant that it was also significant to have feedback if things were not going well. Therefore, we created a new robust communication department with plans to reach out to thousands of franchise owners all over North America.

Cooperation and collaboration required that we partner with our franchisees. For the first time in the company's history, we created Franchise Advisory Councils for each of our brands. It took some time for processes and people to find their footing. The net result, however, was better communication across the entire system that included the franchisees' points of view. We wanted to be able to talk across the organization and hear each other out.

My epiphany about my role as CEO being much like an orchestra conductor provided me with a visual that helped me stay focused on providing the opportunity for people across the organization to grow. It became apparent that it was important to acknowledge extra efforts and commitment by employees. If someone were to step up, learn, work hard, and take on responsibilities, the right thing to do would be to both acknowledge their accomplishments and declare them. That meant that we had to make room for new titles, raises, and responsibilities.

To model this approach, I implemented new titles for my direct reports, moving some management to C-level and some to executive titles. Coaching others to do the same, the organization started adopting this new approach. Upward mobility created a positive environment for many.

New roles meant new responsibilities. So that people had clarity about what was expected of them, we implemented a new and detailed financial matrix. I had learned over the years that what's measured is managed. We created budgets and key performance indicators in collaboration with the people responsible for delivering on them.

Early on, I negotiated with the board to implement the sharing of a success bonus with all employees. The idea was that if we surpassed some performance measures for the entire company, everyone would receive an equal bonus at the close of the year. This was in addition to any bonus and compensation program we already had in place for any individual. The success bonus, as it was shared equally, ensured that we always rowed in the same direction and knew what the direction was. It was wonderful to see that we were able to pay this bonus every year while we were operating the company.

All aspects of operations received lots of attention. Since our most important north star was to make sure every franchisee was as successful as they wanted to be, franchise support received a significant amount of acclaim. Based on our reviews of franchise support, we concluded that there was room for coaching. We hired and promoted coaches and traveling support staff. We expanded training to many times more than we had previously, both in-house and across the country.

We left no stone unturned. We successfully created a new company on the chassis of the old one.

Chapter Thirty-Eight

New Culture

Good leadership engages, informs, communicates, collaborates, and moves the organization forward. It requires helping systems overcome the discomfort required to build new and exciting opportunities. To move fluidly from inefficiently structured systems to well-designed, rewarding, and well-functioning ones, a good leader must shoulder and hold the system's anxiety. This is the sort of leadership that makes people confident that the words "Trust me. We got this. We can do it. I'll lead us through it" are true.

SINCE OUR PARTNERSHIP WITH OUR PE PARTNER, we had been on a fast-paced, energized, and effective sprint. To make improvements, we needed to ensure that we had the right structure in place. However, we didn't. We had been a company run with an entrepreneurial spirit and had grown organically with minimal external influence. Though we had grown, we had done so with a fluid structure. Roles and responsibilities were not clear. Deals were made individually based on relationships rather than established processes—as they often are in those types of setups. If people's agendas did not match the company objectives, they might superficially agree but wouldn't fully embrace and execute plans. It was increasingly difficult to run the company and run it well at its size in 2015 with that kind of structure in place.

It was abundantly clear to me that unless we made some fundamental shifts in culture, we would not be able to grow to the expectations we had set forth—for ourselves and our PE partners.

I was a C-level executive at a growing entrepreneurial company for years. Although I was intimately involved with all the aspects of operating the company, I had a limited inside view of the interactions among people at various tiers. I was aware that we had some structural and cultural challenges, but the magnitude and complexity of those challenges were yet to be discovered. I believed that to be effective as CEO and to help people grow in their roles, I would have to better understand what we needed to address as far as the company's culture was concerned.

We had created a cadence for meeting with and catching up with executives and teams within the company. This cadence was designed to help keep everyone on track toward our vision and to hear feedback from them. In these conversations, I started noticing a pattern—one that drew a picture of what we would have to address. This issue became very clear one day.

As part of our plan to communicate with our stakeholders, we designed and launched our very first vendor summit. For the first time in our history, we brought all our supply partners together for a two-day meeting to update them on our vision and progress and encourage them to think innovatively to help us all thrive.

It was after one of these summits that a few people from our marketing team pulled me aside and shared a specific interaction. They pointed out the example of someone in another part of the company going around the newly established processes to fulfill their personal preferences. They wanted to do things "as they had always been done."

We had been in our new phase with our new partners for just a few months. I had suspected and was concerned that we might have cultural or structural issues. But now, I had evidence. I would have to dig deeper to learn.

My inquiry highlighted that a few managers who had been with the company for many years had been toxic to others. When some managers had the opportunity to talk to me openly after I invited a conversation, it became apparent that some folks were pulling others back. These folks were used to making agreements and changes based on what they saw fit, and forcing their way because of *who* they knew. They were used to overreaching across functions and lines of responsibility.

I shared this challenge at our next executive meeting and asked for people's thoughts. What I learned that day and in the following months of exploring the same topic was that we needed to make a major cultural shift in the company. I also learned that there was a shared sentiment that I had to make some tough decisions about moving some people around and out—a decision I resisted wholeheartedly. I postponed the inevitable. This proved to be a mistake. A mistake that cost us a loss of confidence in some of our teams. Letting employees who clearly created toxic environments for others stand in the way of progress discouraged others. It was demoralizing to many. Luckily, because of the persistence and honesty of some of my management team, I finally agreed to the changes. In time, these changes reenergize and reengaged our teams. It was a tough lesson for me to learn.

Our company had existed for over two decades. We had started from the ground up and had created functions and systems as we had grown. We had brought on new employees as needed.

Over the years, relationships and circles of influence had been developed. People "got things done" through who they knew and how they would be able to influence them. This wasn't malicious. It was just the way things were done. And it worked until it didn't. It had worked for years as we were growing organically and gradually. Our new energized vision, however, tested this old paradigm. The way the organization was running was based on power, influence, and relationships. We needed to create an organization whose foundation was built on clear, well-defined roles and responsibilities with accountability for each. That would provide us with the ability to grow toward our vision.

Moving an organization, especially one of our size, through cultural and organizational overhaul is a challenging task. People used to accomplishing their goals through relationships would feel displaced or ineffective in a more organized structure. They could and would resist change.

Resistance could prove detrimental to the continued growth of the company. This was risky, especially as we had such lofty goals. I researched this topic and consulted experts about the change. Through all this work and research, I learned that making the necessary cultural moves would be an uphill process that would leave some folks out. The process would also require going through an uncomfortable phase of creating structure. The first phase of creating structure involved leadership being tight and solid.

My leadership style and way of operating are collaborative. Yet I understood that I would have to be more hands-on until the first layer of formal structure was in place.

Evolution and change often create anxiety in a system. The old ways of doing things may be ineffective and a barrier to progress, but they're familiar. Moving people and organizations from familiar to unfamiliar, as good as the new system may eventually be, is uncomfortable—sometimes painful.

Good leadership engages, informs, communicates, collaborates, and moves the organization forward. It requires helping systems get through the uncomfortable to build new and exciting opportunities. To move from fluid, inefficiently structured systems to well-designed, rewarding, and well-functioning ones, a good leader will have to shoulder and hold the system's anxiety. This is the sort of leadership that makes people confident that the words "Trust me. We got this. We can do it. I'll lead us through it" are true.

Our company was made up of three consumer-facing brands, each with business-to-business brands, and one umbrella company. We had been around for over two decades, and we had thousands of business owners in the system. The only way to help the organization, and therefore its franchisees, continue to thrive was to improve our infrastructure and culture. We had to grow up from loosely designed to professionally run yet collaborative. These softer skills required more art than science. It also required lots of empathy and the ability to hold anxiety for the entire system. I consciously took on the role.

After sharing my plan with the executive team and the board, I embarked on the journey. It was one of the hardest, most stressful, and most exhausting years of my working life.

Some of our executives were challenged with the new expectations as well. To help them through the transition, I offered myself as an anchor. I would allow team members to share their confusion and anxiety, and I would use those lessons I had learned over the years to meet them where they were. From there, I would consistently remind them of our shared core values and mission.

I shared one core message in various meetings and informal chats with the executives and their teams: "Jeff Bezos has been quoted to say, 'Disagree, but commit.' We will consider various points of view as a team. We will have debates and discussions, but we have to finalize our strategies at some point. Once we do, you will have to execute even if you don't agree with the direction. Otherwise, nothing gets done, or it won't get done right. I promise you we'll hear people out, but in the end, we need to move forward."

The rewards weren't immediate or readily measurable. But by the time we were ready to sell the company again in 2019, I knew we had almost completed the project. We had successfully overhauled many aspects of the company's operations with lots of success. We had embarked upon creating a marketing and technology platform and finished both. We had been preparing to acquire another franchise system, which we did at the end of 2018. We also successfully went through a rigorous sale process and sold the company in 2019. By the time we sold, all our brands were number one in their category. Our franchisees were operating out of 12,000 cities and selling nearly $850 million worth of products. We had delivered a true platform in our space that could house multiple brands. I am confident that our accomplishments would not have been possible without the cultural and structural enhancements we implemented.

Chapter Thirty-Nine

New Company

When the second half of 2018 arrived, I sighed in relief. Most of the big goals and projects we had initiated were either completed or well on their way. It wasn't always smooth sailing, as business never is, but we had made major progress. Our successes showed up in continued prosperity for our franchisees and top- and bottom-line growth for the company. By 2018, we had our name on top of a beautiful white office building with views of the airport. It was all built to our specifications and liking. It was our new space suited for the new, exciting company we had become. Our brands' updated look and feel were showcased throughout our space. Our vision and core values were displayed in every possible place. We had updated, changed, enhanced, and improved everything.

I knew it was time to seriously consider selling the company so our partners could reap the benefits of their investment. The time frame seemed appropriate, and the timing felt right. With that, we engaged bankers once more. Because of our substantial growth and the sheer size of the company, the process would have to be more rigorous and much longer. We knew we had a tough road ahead of us.

Luckily, having been through the process, we understood the expectations and due diligence requirements. We were a very well-run company and ready for scrutiny.

When 2019 came around, we were genuinely a new company. We had successfully transformed ourselves and built a platform. There was still much to do to integrate the newly acquired franchise company. But the decision was made to move forward with a transaction.

In February 2019, *Forbes* approached me for an interview. I assumed they would write about the company and thought the timing would be helpful for our sale. The magazine graciously sent out videographers and spent some time interviewing me. Within three weeks, on March 8, my son called me from New York: "Did you see yourself on the cover?"

I had no idea what he was talking about.

"You're on the cover of Forbes.com on International Women's Day! I can't believe you haven't checked it out yet."

And I didn't for many hours. I was overwhelmed and worried. I had lived a busy life building a family and a company. I couldn't bear to see myself anywhere in the public eye. And here I was!

The editor who worked on the piece told me, "Shirin, when I first heard of your story, I thought it was a story of a few people. I find your life unbelievable. There is a book and a movie in it!" I didn't know this, but this was the reason they highlighted the company while telling parts of my story. I was honored and surprised, but I also felt exposed and uncomfortable.

I was uncomfortable because this article and video covered my story and also highlighted the company. I had never talked about myself publicly. I am confident that no one who had worked with me throughout my career knew I had been without my parents since I was seventeen years old. I had never told anyone I had worked at a gas station. I had never talked about my arrests in Iran or the war I had witnessed. Because of my (almost) American accent and my career trajectory, almost no one suspected I had grown up elsewhere. I hadn't shared these facts not because I was ashamed of them. Rather, it was a combination of not feeling safe and not wanting pity.

I was a woman with an unfamiliar name working in a male-dominated field with not a lot of people who were like me. People are people. And I knew how to connect with them because we all have shared human experiences over which we can bond. I had no problem connecting with others and cooperating with them. My gut told me, however, that making those connections would be significantly harder if I were to highlight and call attention to our differences. Talking about my very different background would do just that. It just wasn't necessary or safe, I thought, to talk about my past.

I also didn't want to attract unwanted attention to myself. I believed that I had earned my positions in my life and career through hard work, tenacity, and genuine empathy. I didn't want to engender what I considered pity. I think that resistance was a mask for the pain I felt. I had yet to take the time to process my past trauma and found myself vulnerable.

I was quite comfortable giving presentations and speeches to large groups with a lot of care and connection. But those presentations and speeches were to highlight the merits of the company and our people. They weren't about me. They were about others. And I could do that with lots of passion.

The *Forbes* video and article discussed me and my past for the first time, which made me quite uncomfortable. The video highlighted and exposed so much that I had not talked about for many years, which was a tough but necessary step in my growth. It opened me up to so much more for years to come.

Chapter Forty

Exit

We had indeed done it. We had surpassed all the performance expectations set before us. We had more than doubled the value of the company.

WE HAD INDEED DONE IT. We had surpassed all the performance expectations set before us. We had more than doubled the value of the company. A company that had been around for over twenty years had doubled its size in four short years. We did it by relentlessly pursuing our vision and staying true to our core values. We had increased our franchisees' sales by hundreds of millions of dollars per year for four years. Our system-wide sales had grown by over 70 percent over these years in an industry that historically grew 24 to 30 percent in the same time frame. We had created a true platform where marketing, technology, and many services would be offered to franchisees of multiple brands. We had already grown three consumer-facing franchise systems and effectively six systems, including both consumer and business-facing. We had elevated our communication with our franchisees by bringing their voices into our decisions. We had included and mobilized our vendors to help us pursue our vision. We had improved our culture from fluid to collaborative and structured. We had updated the messaging, look, feel, and essence of each of our brands. We had clearly defined ourselves so that customers would know us better. We had done all of this in four years. We had indeed changed the engine to drive eighty miles an hour, and we had done it with care as we stayed close to our core values.

All this good work required a lot of my personal attention and energy. I had taken on many roles and continued to operate the two C-level roles of CEO and COO until the end. The highest personal cost to me was taking on the necessary cultural changes of the company. The anxiety of the system going through so much evolution was absorbed by me. The cost ended up being high, as I learned later.

We had built the platform with the expectation to be able to bring new franchise brands on board. To test the hypothesis that we could add new brands, in late 2018, we had to make a decision about acquiring a new franchise system that our PE partners had vetted. The challenge was that we had also started our own sales process a few months prior.

"I'm concerned about our bandwidth. I know I had been promoting acquiring another system, but frankly, the timing was pushed back to a tough time. We just started our own sales process, and I know how complicated and time-consuming that will be. I don't know if we can acquire another system so late in our own sales process. I know I personally don't have the bandwidth." I discussed this with our management team during a meeting prior to acquiring the new system.

After some discussion and debates, some of the executives offered their assistance and assurance that they would make contributions as needed. Although I had my reservations, our internal discussions arrived at a consensus that this acquisition would be good for the company. In the spirit of "disagree but commit," I did the same. We then decided to proceed.

Events moved swiftly with the advent of 2019. We had just acquired the new company at the end of 2018. As we onboarded the new franchise system, we focused on continuing to deliver results for our existing brands. We certainly didn't want to see our performance drop, especially as we were well on our way to selling the company.

Our own sales process heated up. We had started the project in the last quarter of the year before by attending meetings and creating materials for our bankers. We then commissioned a very well-known consulting firm to help us analyze our market opportunities and competitive industry landscape. We believed it was best to be well prepared. The report from the consulting company would prepare us for potential questions and any scrutiny headed our way as we embarked upon the sale process.

Working with consultants to prepare the study about the company required a lot of work on our end. I didn't have one job—I had three, being CEO and COO and now processing this sale! And it was about to get harder.

Once we were ready and had discussed and addressed potential challenges and questions from our potential buyers, we started selling the company.

Our bankers and internal team spent many hours preparing the materials and preparations needed for a robust selling process. It was a hectic few months until we were ready to invite interested parties to meet with us.

My experiences with our previous process were still fresh in my mind since it had been less than four years. The difference was that this time around, everything was deeper, more complicated, and bigger because the company was substantially larger and therefore, the buyers required more information and confidence. The stakes were much higher. However, having had the experience and the resulting success in the previous round, I had a lot of confidence this time. I also knew we had cleaned up, updated, and built a solid and well-run company.

"The company is doing very well. But we'll have to see whether the offers we receive will be what we expect. I know the thresholds for the management team require the company to be valued at a specific number. I hope we can get above that," one of our board members expressed with concern to me one morning. He had flown in for another meeting and had decided to stop by and see me for coffee and breakfast to catch up.

"I *know* we're going to meet and exceed our value threshold. One, we are worth that much and more. And two, exceeding that threshold is meaningful to our team. The bonuses they would be entitled to once we exceed that threshold are life-changing," I told him as I finished my second cup of coffee. I was in a rush. I had to get back to work since we had lots to do. Though I said it firmly, I had a tinge of uncertainty about our ability to sell the company at the valuation that would allow management to receive their full bonus.

Driving back to the office, I used my time in traffic to ponder. I had been moving fast, focused on building and producing results. But was all of that enough? Would potential buyers understand the value and be willing to pay the price that we wanted?

Why did you take this on, Shirin? I asked myself.

The answer, though clear and familiar to me, had a new punch to it.

I took on the role of CEO and worked to deliver above and beyond expectations because . . .

I knew I could.

I wanted to prove I could.

I knew the company needed an overhaul.

I wanted the franchisees to do well.

I wanted people in the company to do well and feel good about being a part of this journey.

I wanted all the stakeholders to feel like it was the best investment they've made.

I really wanted to do good work.

I really wanted to do good for others.

I wanted that little girl working at the gas station to know that her vision became reality.

I wanted the world to know that those dismissed little girls and boys have value . . . that they matter . . . that they can contribute positively to the world.

My purpose was bigger than me. It was bigger than the situation I was dealing with.

I found myself sitting a little more upright. I felt a rush of new energy going through me. Yes, I was exhausted from juggling so many responsibilities and projects. But I had just found a new source of energy.

I was going to finish this project and finish it well. I would use the tools that had served me well since I had sat at that gas station booth. I would envision success. I would feel, sense, and believe in a successful sale process at the end of which we would have exceeded our goals for the company's value. I would not only envision it; I would *expect* it!

With that, I pressed a little harder on the gas to get to work faster. I had results to deliver!

We had lots of interest and lots of good presentations to potential buyers. During these meetings, I used all my passion and conviction to showcase the company's potential. I fielded questions and laid out the growth opportunities for the company in actionable steps. I firmly believed that as they understood the company's makeup and vision, they would be excited to acquire it.

After a long and complicated negotiation process led by our bankers, we were extended many offers, some above our value threshold. It was a great development, but the process was far from over. We had months of due diligence and continued negotiations ahead of us.

We finally agreed to sell the company to one of the bidders—a larger privately held company. But before the final agreement, as is often customary, they asked me to spend some time with their team to talk about the growth prospects of our company.

"We built this platform with the expectation that we can add new franchise brands to it. Your biggest opportunity resides in acquiring and inviting new brands to be added to this platform," I explained in one of our meetings. "There isn't anything like this in the marketplace. There is no platform that allows home improvement brands to work synergistically together. We've done the hard work of creating this platform. You can now add many brands to it. We currently have four consumer-facing brands. With this platform, you can have more than ten or twenty. There is a lot of room for growth!" I explained excitedly.

They loved the idea and have executed it since.

Unfortunately, the extensive travel added to my many roles, as well as the absolute sprint in steep growth while elevating the company's culture and infrastructure, had exhausted me. I had been running on fumes for a while.

I noticed that I was physically moving slower than usual. My back-to-back meetings left little breathing room during the day, and my energy tanked by mid-afternoon.

"No one can keep up this schedule, Shirin," my doctor reminded me with concern in her eyes. "You've now been sick with various illnesses back-to-back. You're pretty depleted. I don't want to see anything really bad happen to you."

She didn't know that I had waited for and worked toward this outcome for most of my life. I was almost at the finish line. It wasn't about making more money. It was about my legacy.

"I'm almost there, Doctor." I looked at her almost apologetically as I lay on the exam table.

I was at her office because I had indeed been getting sick with all kinds of strange and seemingly unknown conditions. This time around, I had major rashes that looked like boils all over my right arm and leg. She wasn't sure what they were. But she was certain I needed to rest.

"Okay. Just do your best to rest. I don't want you to die!" she said bluntly.

That shook me a little. But, unfortunately, not enough. Within a week, I was rushed to the emergency room. I had woken up exceptionally sick that morning, and my family had to call 911. After a few days of testing and infusions, I was sent home. The diagnosis was nothing but exhaustion.

I explained to my executive team that I would have to find ways to do some of my work from home to allow for some healing. We were deep into our sales process, and a lot of due diligence work had been successfully done. I could conduct some of my meetings and work from home while I healed.

By July, we had completed all the work and negotiations for the sale of the company. In mid-July, I had a repeat of the same episode and was rushed once more to the emergency room.

The morning of the signing of the final agreement, I was in a hospital bed with an IV in my arm when our partner and chairman of the board called me to share the good news. "I can't believe you're in the hospital on a day like this! Congratulations! We did it!"

We did it! We had made it to the valuation we had hoped for. I smiled and hung up. I had to heal and then celebrate.

After the sale was complete, our PE partner generously offered an additional bonus to be used to thank our employees. This was in addition to the ones earned by the executive team. They left it up to me to decide how to distribute that bonus.

I loved the idea. It was all about the people. It was always about the people. The people who had done such good work to bring the company to this phase all deserved to enjoy the success.

"I want to give a bonus to every single person in the company," I told them.

I suggested that we use those funds to pay bonuses to everyone and not just some of the employees. They graciously agreed. I had the pleasure of sharing these bonuses with every single person in the company. *That* was one of the best days of my life. To be able to share the rewards with the people who had worked in the company was a gift to me. I cared about them, and I now had a tangible gift to show I cared.

I stayed on for two more months after the transaction was complete. Although I had initially thought I would have to stay longer, I knew I was ready to move on to the next phase of my life. I had dedicated twenty years to building this company, and I had grown through it. But it was time to create a new chapter.

I had the romantic notion that I would have the chance to properly celebrate my transition and take my time to say goodbye to our employees, franchisees, and partners. In hindsight, I wish I had asked for and taken the time to say proper goodbyes. I had spent twenty years of my life doing good in this company and for its franchises. A couple of weeks to let everyone know how much they meant to me would have been not only appropriate but necessary.

I wanted to be able to let our employees, franchisees, and stakeholders all know how much they meant to me and how I had done my very best to see to their success.

Unfortunately, as it turned out, this goodbye was to be short.

My life's journey had brought me to this point.

I had wholeheartedly done my best to bring value and goodness to the lives of our franchisees and employees and the lives of the consumers, suppliers, and partners we touched. As I promised them that day on the stage, I may not have done everything right . . . but whatever I had done was with their best interests in mind and heart. I hope they know that. And I hope they carry the value of caring that we emphasized so much to their consumers, their employees, their suppliers, their families, and their communities.

I cherish those memories and those times. And I will take their lessons to help others grow and thrive.

I'm proud of this journey. I'm proud to have traveled it with my core principles intact. I'm proud to have done it with integrity. I'm proud to have had the best interests of all our stakeholders in mind. I'm proud to have accomplished such amazing heights with growth despite personal and economic setbacks. I'm proud to have built the most unique platform in the market. I'm proud to have been authentic and honest. I'm proud to have served others in their growth journeys.

The gas station attendant had seen her vision become a reality.

It was now time to help others achieve theirs.

CHAPTER FORTY-ONE

Yes, I Did

I WAS BACKSTAGE IN MY LONG BLACK GOWN. My fellow finalists were sitting and chatting. They were all dressed in their best suits and tuxedos.

I could see the ballroom through the openings in the curtains separating the finalists and the attendees. The ballroom was large and filled with guests in their formal attire. Beautifully decorated round tables dressed up the already lovely room.

The setup and decorations were perfect for this prestigious award night. Tonight, at this gala, we would find out who would win the coveted award. We had gone through a rigorous process, and a few of us had made it as finalists. We had been videotaped in advance of the gala with the expectation that each finalist would be honored.

We would be introduced after the customary presentations. The idea was that each person's name and company would be announced and we would take the stage as our video played. We would then walk down to our seats. It was so that the finalists could be individually honored and to build anticipation and excitement.

It was time for us to start our walk. I waited for my name and, as previously practiced, took the arm of the man assigned to me. Having presented to large rooms of thousands of people as CEO, I was used to walking on to a stage. The blinding light, upbeat music, and the applause of the audience were all familiar, except this one was an awards show. As I had been instructed by the stage managers who had prepared us all for this presentation, I paused onstage as my video was played, and I walked down to a round of applause.

My fellow finalists all performed as expected. Then, we were all seated at our tables. As awards shows go, there was more talking, videos, applause, and excitement. Finally, it was time to announce the winner.

The voice of God announced: "And the winner for 2018 is . . . Shirin Behzadi."

To the excitement of my guests at my table and the round of applause that thundered across the ballroom, I walked up to the stage. It felt much like the day I had walked up to my first stage as I prepared to start the play I had written with my friend in elementary school. It was exciting and sweet. It was familiar and comfortable. I had since been on many stages of many sizes, and it was time to walk up to one once more.

With passion and consideration, I talked about our company and our accomplishments. And with gratitude, I shared my commitment to doing good. I looked around the grand ballroom with a smile on my face as my speech received resounding applause and a standing ovation.

Holding the beautiful award in my hand, I walked off the stage and back to my table.

My son, Sam, excitedly asked, "Mom, when you were working at that gas station at seventeen, did you ever think you would be here?"

"Yes, I did."

Acknowledgments

As a child, I used to love writing. When my fourth-grade teacher asked us to share what we wanted to be when we grew up, I didn't hesitate: "An author," I said proudly. Though my love for the creative arts never faded, life—with all its twists and demands—took center stage. And before I knew it, years had passed since I had spent time writing.

Then, on Christmas Day 2021, my children, Sam and Sara, handed me a gift—a simple binder, lovingly filled with notes and research. But it was more than pages and paper. It was a call to action. A quiet push. A bold encouragement.

"Mom," they said, "you have to write your book."

I knew exactly what they meant. The weight and truth of it hit me all at once. I sobbed.

It has taken me all these years to arrive at this moment. I wrote this book to share the stories and lessons that have shaped me, in the hopes they might serve someone else. I spent countless hours soul-searching as I wrote relentlessly in the quiet corner of our family room. These became some of the most difficult—and most profound—hours of my life.

To Sam Madani and Sara Madani: You inspired me, encouraged me, challenged me, and walked beside me. Your thoughtful questions and soulful conversations opened my heart and helped me grow. Thank you for being my greatest sources of inspiration—not just in this book, but in everything I do.

To my husband, Perzan Irani: Your love has been the steady foundation I cherish. With you by my side, I've found strength, perspective, and companionship on this journey. Thank you for your generous spirit, your steadfast presence, and your faith in me—always.

Throughout my journey, I've been touched by many good people, each leaving a unique imprint on my heart. My parents, Behzad Behzadi and Heshmat Hafezi, gifted me both their love and their gift for words. My grandparents planted their dreams in the soil of my soul. My sisters, Sherry, Shirana, and Shani, have shown me the deep, enduring bond of sisterhood. My family and extended family have filled my life with richness and meaning.

My new daughter, Raina, has brought light and beauty into all our lives. Her family—especially her mother, my new sister, Meeta Singal—has been a true beacon of love and kindness. My adopted family, Gosia Jurczak, helped raise our children with unwavering care and devotion. And my extended Irani family has shown me the enduring power of love and support.

To each and every one of you: thank you, from the bottom of my heart.

I never had a single mentor. Instead, I've had many people who generously contributed to my growth. And I am grateful for each of them. Thank you to Tom Hammond, who took a chance on a young pregnant woman and promoted me to my first CFO role. And to Jean Vaziri, who saw in me what I hadn't yet seen in myself, and told me over a decade ago: "Shirin, you'll write and speak. You'll do great things." Jean, your belief in me, your friendship, and your guidance continue to mean the world to me.

To the friends who have walked beside me: Kath Carter, my constant—your presence is a daily reminder of all that is good. Thank you for nurturing our bond and bringing Misa Art into my life. To Misa: thank you for your beautiful spirit, your generous support, and your art, which now lives in the pages of this book. To

Pamela Sanchez, Fariba Beighlie, and Jasmine Irani—your support and encouragement helped me find the courage to write.

I owe my life to the extraordinary care of Dr. Daniel Kelly, Dr. Amin Kassam, and Dr. Carrau—and to the many doctors, nurses, technicians, and support staff at St. John's and affiliated institutions. Your work matters deeply. You saved my life—and the lives of many.

To the coaches and guides who have illuminated my path—there have been many. Thank you for your wisdom and light. Thank you especially to my brilliant friend Les Brown.

To the many colleagues and collaborators through the years: thank you for walking parts of this journey with me.

To the franchisees, teams, stakeholders, and friends at Home Franchise Concepts: your partnership shaped more than just a business; it shaped me.

To the generous audiences who've welcomed my voice into their hearts and halls—your listening has given my words their wings, and in return, you've given my life a richness beyond measure.

To those I've had the honor to serve alongside on boards and in advisory roles: your trust and wisdom have left lasting imprints.

And to the BOMANI family: you've added richness and meaning to my path in ways words can scarcely hold.

Each interaction was a lesson.

Each experience, a gift.

Writing a book is both daunting and divine. I'm thankful for the encouragement of friends and fellow philanthropists Lawrence Armstrong and Sue Parks. And to Herb Schaffner, Matt Holt, and the entire team at BenBella and Matt Holt Books—thank you for your talent, your care, and your belief in this work.

So many people have touched my life—some through grand gestures, others in quiet, fleeting moments. Many may never know the depth of their influence, and that, perhaps, is the beautiful mystery of being human: we are threads in each other's stories.

About the Author

Photo by Kristin Ellis-Karkoka

At seventeen, **Shirin Behzadi** fled her home country. A year later, she found herself working behind bulletproof glass as a gas station cashier. And three decades later, she was a billion-dollar CEO.

Shirin exemplifies resilience and self-reliance, and she believes that her successes come from turning adversity into opportunity. She has dedicated her time to inspire entrepreneurs and leaders by serving as a keynote speaker, investor, board member, and advisor. Her mission is bold and simple: to help others dream audaciously, lead courageously, and thrive through life's toughest moments.

Shirin is a recognized award-winning leading entrepreneur in North America who has garnered international coverage and visibility for her achievements, most notably featured on Forbes.com. Her story began with a courageous leap—leaving behind everything familiar, including her family, to build a meaningful life in the United States. Even when she was working as a gas station cashier, she believed her tenacity would empower her to become a success. She paved her way forward relentlessly, becoming a respected CFO and later a transformative entrepreneur and CEO. After a successful partnership with a private equity firm, Shirin led the creation of a one-of-a-kind platform in the home services and franchising space—scaling across 12,000 cities in North America. She continues to serve as an advisor and investor, using her hard-earned wisdom to support others in building bold, enduring businesses.

Shirin is a passionate philanthropist, serving on the boards of organizations driving change locally and globally. She lives by a simple and powerful motto: "Doing well by doing good."